SEEKING THE FACE OF GOD

Evangelical Worship Reconceived

⌐

J. Daniel Day

For Ann —
With good memories!
prayer for your ministry —
Dan Day

© 2013

Published in the United States by Nurturing Faith, Macon GA,
www.nurturingfaith.info

ISBN 978-1-938514-40-1

Unless otherwise noted, all scripture references are taken from the New
Revised Standard Version of the Bible.

"Cathedral Service" from Peter Kocan, *The Fable of All Our Lives.*
Copyright © 2010 by HarperCollins Publishers Australia. Reprinted by
permission of HarperCollins Publishers Australia.

As the Apostle Paul prayed, the church of our time must rediscover 'the power to comprehend, with all the saints, what is the breadth and length and height and depth' of the love of God in its worship. Dan Day gives us a "guidebook" for that journey. At the same time a deep exploration of the historical and biblical roots and intensely practical help to those who seek to connect depth and seriousness to the context they serve. Readable, thoughtful, helpful—this is a book the church needs.

Dr. Gary Furr, Pastor, Vestavia Hills Baptist Church
Co-Author, The Dialogue of Worship

As I read Day's manuscript, one image kept coming to mind. It was the image of a Wednesday night business meeting in a small Baptist church. Fifty minutes into an hour-long contentious debate among folks who really do love each other, the church, and God, one quiet person finally stands up and speaks calm wisdom into the room. His words summarize the argument and put it into a biblical and historical perspective that gently nudges the noise toward solution and progress. Dan Day is the person. This book may well be the speech.

Terry W. York, D.M.A., is Professor of Christian Ministry and Church Music at Baylor University's George W. Truett Theological Seminary in Waco, Texas.

Seeking the Face of God is an important book and one that deserves careful attention by leaders in worship in all churches. Rooted in a deep knowledge of church history and engagingly written, it offers rich insights not only in the understanding of worship but also in its practice.

Glenn Hinson is Senior Professor of Church History and Spirituality at the Baptist Theological Seminary of Kentucky in Georgetown, Kentucky

CONTENTS

≈

Seek the Lord,and his strength: seek his face evermore.
Psalm 105:4 (KJV)

❧

When thou saidst, Seek ye my face;
my heart said unto thee,
Thy face, Lord, will I seek.
Hide not thy face far from me . . .
Psalm 27:8-9a (KJV)

❧

But we all, with open face beholding
as in a glass the glory
of the Lord, are changed into the same
image from glory
to glory, even as by the Spirit of the Lord.
2 Corinthians 3:18 (KJV)

❧

. . .the throne of God and of the Lamb shall be in it
[the holy city, new Jerusalem];
and his servants shall serve him:
And they shall see his face . . .
Revelation 22:3-4a (KJV)

FOREWORD

∽

This book is written for church-going people, written to have a conversation about worship. It's written to remind us of just one thing: Worship is about God. It isn't about selling God. It isn't about being inspired by God-referencing programs. It's not even about "experiencing" God. Worship is about God. Period.

It takes only four words to state this. For many readers this assertion will be easy to affirm—it seems so obvious. But, as is frequently the case, the obvious isn't always clear. Specifically, just what does this statement of the obvious mean? If we say that worship is "about" God, in what way or ways is it "about" God? For that matter, what does the word "about" actually mean? And how might one tell if a worship service is really "about" God or "about" something else? If it is "about" God, does this mean that the worshipers themselves are irrelevant? That their needs, their culture, their longings don't matter? Indeed, what would a worship service that's truly "about" God look like? In the course of the book I hope to offer clarifying, credible, and hope-creating answers to questions like these. Arising from within that discussion will actually be a conception of worship that is different from many typical evangelical understandings. However, I'm not so foolish or vain as to imagine that mine is the final word on this subject—my desires are much more modest. What I hope is that these words will be persuasive enough that you'll understand why our evangelical worship must be reconceived and made less about us and more about God.

The metaphor of "seeking the face of God" is used here to characterize this kind of worship. It is, of course, a biblical phrase that's seen often in older translations of the Bible. Newer translations, attempting to convey the theological meaning of the facial reference, helpfully and accurately render it as seeking God's "presence." Nonetheless, there is a graphic and personal quality to the older, literal rendering. So for this and other reasons explained more fully within the book, "seeking God's face" is used here as an image of worship that is about God.

Fortunately, a glimpse into its meaning has been artistically provided in Michelangelo's famous Sistine Chapel painting of the Creation. The best-known portion of that painting is the cameo of the almost-touching fingers of the Creator and the newly-created Adam. The strength and power of God is so agonizingly close to the lifeless, drooping finger of Adam—an unforgettable depiction of the need of the human and of the life-giving power of God. But Michelangelo gave a parallel rendering of this same truth in his presentation of the eyes of these two. Each figure's eyes are locked upon the eyes of the other, especially Adam who seems to be seeking the face of God as though through a dreamlike state of innocence and confusion. It is particularly in this second cameo that the heart of worship is shown, for "Christian worship . . . represents the mutual gaze of the human and the divine eye."[1] In this open-hearted seeking of God's face (whose eye and face is clearly turned toward and seeking us), worship is given a vibrant, lustrous image. And that is what this book seeks to explore and encourage.

Much of what is said here comes from pondering what I find in the Bible—as well as in a score of thoughtful and scholarly books about worship and culture written by folks who also have meditated upon what they found in the Bible and in the Church and its history, and in their own spiritual history. Many of their books are mentioned or footnoted in this one. Certainly, the details and patterns of historical understandings of worship found in those books are one of the clarifying gifts this book tries to transmit.

But a larger bit of this book doesn't come from books; it comes from four decades of planning and leading worship in seven churches in five different states. Occasionally within these pages there are even digressions into reminiscences and "preacher stories"—although I hope not so many as to be off-putting. No apology is offered for this; it grounds these reflections in the real, practiced life of the local church and its clergy, not in the think-tanks of the academy. Though I hope academic readers will find these pages credible, they haven't been written for their attention.[2] Rather, think of these words as a pastoral conversation with worshipers and with those charged to lead next Sunday's worship. Think of this as one pastor/professor's attempt to meld the ideal and the actual into a form that is possible.

Another important source for what you'll find here is conversations with divinity school students. Following my years as a pastor, a professorial role was given to me—a role that thrust me into worship conversations with persons of all ages and evangelical orientations. Most of them bore evidence of some tint of Baptist coloration but, thankfully, they were complemented by many from other streams: United Methodist, African Methodist Episcopal, Lutheran, Church of God in Christ, Episcopal, Pentecostal Holiness, Disciples of Christ, a wandering Presbyterian now and then, and some who preferred no label other than Christian. They made for some lively class periods! If they happen to read these pages, I hope they will see that, on more than a few issues, their wisdom has been heard—sometimes agreed with and other times still being pondered or still being resisted. To all of these—the authors of the library books (and of the Book), the members and ministerial colleagues in the several churches I've been privileged to serve, and the patient students of "DIVI 4000: Christian Worship"—to all of them I express my sincere gratitude.

My thank-you list can't end there, though. It must include some faculty colleagues at Campbell University Divinity School: founding Dean Mike Cogdill, who originally trusted me with the assignment to teach worship, and to Derek Hogan, Barry Jones, and Cameron Jorgenson who

read and responded to various portions of the developing manuscript; and
to two pastor-friends (Don Gordon and Ed Beddingfield), three teacher-
friends (Adam English, Bill Leonard, and especially Paul Richardson)
who lent their critical eye at various times during its development—and
two former students, Jonathan Altman and Louisa Monroe, who gave
most useful feedback. A cluster of friends were also kind enough to read
and respond: John Killinger, Jim Rinker, Bob and Marilyn Russell, and
the "Band of Brothers" at First Baptist Church in Raleigh, NC, being
foremost among them. Most of all, I thank my patient and encouraging
wife, Mary Carol, who listened to most of the book's content far too
many times, and managed to sustain steadfast interest in and support of
the project (and me) throughout the writing—of such is the Kingdom of
God! Each of these has proved to be an invaluable conversation partner,
though I can't imagine that any one of them is eager to add an Amen to
everything I've finally written. My hope is that there is enough truth and
common sense loafing around within these pages that some discriminating readers will spy them and give them a Sunday job.

Notes

[1] Bernhard Lang, *Sacred Games: A History of Christian Worship* (New Haven:
Yale University Press, 1997), ix. Lang is to be credited also for the suggestion of the
Sistine Chapel painting as illustrative of "seeking the face of God."

[2] Academics will quickly note my omission of many subjects typically discussed
in worship textbooks: baptism, weddings, funerals, ordinations, art, architecture, symbol-
ism, aesthetics, etc. This work, however, focuses only on the typical evangelical Sunday
service, its purpose and activities, believing that this is foundational to all the rest. For
those interested in the wider issues of worship studies, recent textbooks that address
them well are Frank C. Senn, *Introduction to Christian Liturgy* (Minneapolis: Fortress
Press, 2012), Gail Ramshaw, *Christian Worship: 100,000 Sundays of Symbols and Rituals*
(Minneapolis: Fortress Press, 2009), and Ruth Duck, *Worship for the Whole People of God*
(Louisville: Westminster/John Knox Press, 2013).

Worship is the supreme and only indispensable activity of the Christian Church. It alone will endure, like the love for God which it expresses, into heaven, when all other activities of the Church will have passed away. It must, therefore, even more strictly than any of the less essential doings of the Church, come under the criticism and control of the revelation on which the Church is founded.

— William Nicholls, *Jacob's Ladder: The Meaning of Worship*, Ecumenical Studies in Worship No. 4 (London: Lutterworth, 1958), 9.

I

CONFRONTING WORSHIP CONFUSION

*"I hate, I despise your festivals,
and I take no delight in your solemn assemblies.*

Take away from me the noise of your songs, I will not listen . . ."

Amos 5:21, 23

❧

Worship isn't often thought of as being a game, but in 1937, a Roman Catholic writer did just that. Romano Guardini, a student of liturgy and spirituality, said that as we worship we are like children at play. Observe any child playing a game or busy with free play and you'll likely be impressed by how very earnest the child is, how important this is to them. They will work at it as intensely as Picasso ever labored over a canvas. But because this worker is only a child with limited abilities, the product is not likely to be a work of great artistic value—indeed, there often is nothing tangible to show for all the energy expended. In one sense, therefore, this work has no purpose, no real importance; it's just "child's play"—if we measure only by adult efficiency criteria. But using wiser criteria, this work is supremely important to both parent and child. Consider the child's devastation when the freshly-made mud pie isn't bragged upon or recall the happy pride when a parent witnesses the difficult somersault being accomplished for the very first time. As Guardini put it: "To be at play, or to fashion a work of art in God's sight—not to create, but to exist—such is the essence of the liturgy. From this is derived its sublime mingling of profound earnestness and divine joyfulness."[1]

Guardini's captivating analogy opens many avenues for reflection. A primary one is its challenge to the dreadful self-seriousness some of us bring to the time of worship. Reimagining worship as being the "play" of God's children before their Heavenly Father can grant us a refreshing lightness of being, a freedom not to take ourselves so seriously. But, another avenue for reflection is to wonder if this particular game has any rules. Here, of course, is where Guardini's analogy begins to be stretched beyond its intent and where the gravity of worship reappears. Nonetheless, for the sake of meeting a new thought, press his analogy this one step farther:

Rules reign . . . or do they?

Games are ultimately nonsensical if there are no rules. If you are not "It" when you are tagged or if three strikes doesn't mean you're "out," then the game is more frustrating than fun. Guardini, writing as a pre-Vatican II Roman Catholic, would certainly have insisted upon some rules for the playful game of worship. As the title of his book declares, he wrote only concerning *The Spirit of the Liturgy*, not about the substance or order of it. Even so it is a legitimate question whether the "game" of worship has any rules—especially today, among evangelicals.[2]

The question surfaces when one attempts to make sense of the stunning number of options and understandings of worship currently found within the evangelical family. The catatonic, dutiful dreariness that characterizes some of our worship services shouts that if the God being worshiped there isn't already dead, good Christians ought to pray for him, because he is surely in hospice care. But down the road there's another church where the decibel level and energy will rival the long-ago priests of Baal who "raved on" from morning until noon, crying aloud, limping about the altar they had made (1 Kings 18:20-29). And across town there's a place where you can feel the heat of an in-your-face revivalist's sermon and musically bathe in the healing waters of "Just as I Am." Worship leaders under still other roofs are attempting brave blendings of all the above—and possibly throwing in anything else that's reported to be working somewhere, be it skits or screens, solemn processions, real-time tweets, burning incense, hip-hop scripture readings, or meditation before icons—but the concoction, as often as not, gets served up without a discernible order or purpose greater than "everybody having a good time in God's house today"—if old-timey lingo like "God's house" is still spoken anywhere. Fortunately, there are also many places where the worship service, like Goldilocks' three bears, feels "just right"—at least for *some* of those in attendance.

But wait, there's (so much) more!

In addition there are mega-churches that manage to scratch several of these worship itches at one time, all on one campus (or several satellite campuses). According to researcher Scott Thumma, in the main worship center of such a church one might find a service using a praise band and contemporary praise music that follows a traditional order of worship. But in another location on campus (or in another city), at the same time, there would also be a service for those who prefer a much more expressive praise service with a healing time, led by a younger cohort of leaders. Meanwhile, over in the gymnasium "a group of teens might be drinking soda and eating doughnuts while rock or grunge music, lights, and video accompany free-form worship. When it is time for the sermon, however, people in each of the venues simultaneously see the senior minister deliver the sermon on a video screen."[3]

Youth ministry authority, Thomas Bergler, author of the disturbing work, *The Juvenilization of American Christianity*, describes another familiar worship scene:

The house lights go down. Spinning, multicolored
lights sweep the auditorium. A rock band launches into
a rousing opening song. "Ignore everyone else, this time
is just about you and Jesus," proclaims the lead singer.
The music changes to a slow dance tune, and the people
sing about falling in love with Jesus. A guitarist sporting
skinny jeans and a soul patch closes the worship set with
a prayer, beginning, "Hey, God . . ." The spotlight then
falls on the speaker, who tells entertaining stories, cracks
a few jokes, and assures everyone that, "God is not mad
at you. He loves you unconditionally."[4]

From a Canadian context, homiletician Paul Scott Wilson,
reports advertisements for an "Express Church, Out in 45 Minutes
Guaranteed," and drive-in churches with prepackaged Communion elements distributed as one drives in, presumably permitting those who
don't like people to communicate and leave without greeting one soul.[5]
One tech-savvy group, LifeChurch.tv, has taken this privatized worship
concept to the Web and made it possible for Internet users to worship by
watching their service online, respond to altar calls through a link appearing on the screen, make a financial contribution via a virtual collection
plate, and even chat online with other people watching the service.[6]

Constance Cherry, worship author and faculty member of the
Robert Webber Institute of Worship, reports that on just one page of her
local newspaper, she found advertisements for "'Western worship' with
free pony rides, a 'Biker's Service' featuring the Sons of God motorcycle
club, and a church with a 'new theater seating system complete with
drink holders for your lattes.'" The most curious of that day's ads stated:
"Sometimes the truth hurts. So you might as well be comfortable. Your
favorite jeans, our drums, guitars, and coffee should soften the blow."[7] In
another place Cherry provides a measured, benign assessment of all this,
saying that worship, like all facets of today's church, is in a "particularly
unsettled period."[8]

Lester Ruth, professor of worship at Duke Divinity School, verifies just how unsettled this period is by listing "a cacophony of terms [to] describe the wide range of worship services"[9] one can find today: linear, organic, multi-sensory, indigenous, innovative, authentic, praise, blended, transformation, seeker, spirited traditional, creative, classic, boomer, liturgical, buster, Gen-X, millennial, African-American, Hispanic, Euro-American, etc.

Were we not talking about something as significant as Christian worship—described by William Nichols as "the supreme and indispensable activity of the Christian Church"—one might giggle in amusement at this. However, Christian worship *is* our subject and, in light of this mind-boggling array of worship options, is it not understandable why one might wonder if our worship has become a game with no rules? Cherry's kind assessment that evangelical worship is in "a particularly unsettled period" is demonstrably true, and these examples show it's also a profoundly confused and confusing period.[10]

Responding to all manner of cultural and demographic changes and expectations, and attempting to share the gospel with every segment of a postmodern culture, evangelical worship has become astonishingly diverse.[11] One might also say it has become chaotic, possibly giving new meaning to the ancient phrase "all the people did what was right in their own eyes" (Judges 21:25).

"Different strokes for different folks"

It's legitimate to wonder, of course, if ultimately any of this matters. Some might say that the net effect is that God is being praised and that all kinds of people are getting in touch with God and that this is all that truly matters. To put it most colloquially, "Different strokes for different folks." This is a plausible response whose chief merit is that it has truth within it. Who is in an authorized position to speak infallibly for God, offering decrees about *right* worship and *wrong* worship? Presumably, God is great and gracious enough to be pleased by the honoring "play" of loving children, with or without "rules." So, there is surely some merit in the response that says "different strokes for different strokes."

Indeed, no less an authority than James F. White, a Methodist who taught worship for twenty years each at Notre Dame and Southern Methodist University's Perkins Seminary, commended this kind of "indigenization"[12] in his influential 1971 book, *New Forms of Worship*. White insisted it was arrogant and even suicidal for the Church to continue to offer only the form of worship that appealed to an over-forty, white, literate, middle-class male—which was the straitjacket in which White believed Protestant worship of the 1970s was bound. In this opinion he was not alone; many voices from within the church and academy agreed with him.[13]

However, White also devoted two early chapters of *New Forms of Worship* to explaining the nature of Christian worship through what he called theological and historical norms and to delineating what he termed worship's "hard core" components. Thus, even as he commended new forms of worship ("We can no longer afford to offer a menu with only one dinner on it."), he was careful to draw parameters and to identify some "rules" these new forms were obliged to honor ("We do not for an instant mean that anything goes as long as it is relevant and currently modish.").[14]

This present book is in essential agreement with White's position although I stress "rules" much more than I plead for new forms. The need for new forms is demonstrably no longer a concern, but the concern for parameters has become all the more urgent in the forty-plus years since White wrote. Hence, the position taken here is that the response of "different strokes for different folks" is now at best a half-truth—a half-truth in full need of White's historical and theological norms. The thinness of our latter-day creations begs for bolstering heft.

The burden of this book, therefore, is that worship is not simply a matter of personal taste or of meeting consumer demand. Worship is about God—and God is not for sale, not a commodity to be marketed like aspirin through either "high" or "low" church services. There is a definable "thing" called the Christian worship of God with characteristics that constitute its unique integrity and therefore what purports to be the worship of God cannot be determined solely by majority vote or audience ratings; it must incorporate enduring essentials or open itself to the charge of being something less than the worship of God.

Are there any losers in this game?

More than thirty years ago Virginia Stem Owens grumbled about the "diabolically clever" strategy she saw being enacted concerning the Church's worship. It began, she believed, with even Church leaders (she didn't name them, but perhaps White's name was on her list) supplanting "organized religion" in favor of the "supposedly spontaneous spirituality of our times." According to her

> [t]he plan unfolded something like this. 1) The Church's manner of worship is dull and outmoded. It no longer appeals to "modern man." 2) The Church must continue to grow and change (key words in contemporary value systems) in order to relate meaningfully to this modern man. 3) Our pattern of worship must therefore be refurbished and made more appealing. 4) The pattern for remodeling that we should follow is what is now most appealing to the majority of modern men.

Owens noted the first crest of worship innovations visible at that date, e.g. the skits, the clowns, the dialogues rather than sermons, and the balloons and puppet shows used in the service of "celebration," the updated word for worship. Her assessment of the gains in reaching modern man achieved through these novelties? "Nothing happened," she declared, and in fact, "in the competition for the titillation, stimulation, and entertainment of human sensibilities, the church came in somewhere behind the traveling carnival in the supermarket parking lot.

Somehow the promised patrons failed to materialize," she said. "Modern man was neither amused nor impressed."[15]

Yet, something had happened. American evangelicals as well as mainline denominations had broken free into a period of free-wheeling experimentation with worship forms—a liberation that we now can see was inevitable, given Vatican II's liturgical *aggiornamento* ("opening the windows" to allow fresh air to blow through the Church's life and four-hundred-year-old Tridentine Mass), the stagnate nature of much Protestant worship, and the extensive "freedom" revolution of the 1960s. As a result, evangelicals were swept up in the onslaught of huge winds of worship change without an anchoring knowledge of the history of Christian worship or a corresponding theology of worship.[16] Though many were unquestionably brought to Christ through these new worship forms, it is now becoming much clearer that there were also "losers" from this development.

In the opening decade of the twenty-first century, a cluster of well-researched books began to appear,[17] written in response to findings from the largest and most detailed study ever made of America's teen-spirituality, the National Study of Youth and Religion conducted from 2001-2005. Among its many intriguing findings, the NSYR revealed a dismaying amount of shallowness and theological ignorance among the nation's adolescents—even among those who are regular participants in church activities. One paragraph aptly expresses the core of the study's discoveries:

> . . . nobody expects teenagers to be sophisticated theologians. But very few of the descriptions of personal beliefs offered by the teenagers . . . , especially the Christian teenagers, come close to representing marginally coherent accounts of the basic, important religious beliefs of their own faith traditions. The majority of U.S. teens would badly fail a hypothetical short-answer or essay test of the basic beliefs of their religion. Higher

proportions of conservative Protestant teenagers than other Christian teens proved able to summarize the elementary beliefs of their tradition, though often in highly formulaic terms . . . [U]nderstanding and embracing the right religious faith and belief according to their religions does not appear to be a priority in the lives of most U.S. adolescents—and perhaps many of their parents . . . [R]eligion simply doesn't seem consequential enough to most teenagers to pay close attention to and get right.[18]

It is a truism that every generation seems to find alarming and lamentable evidence of the biblical and doctrinal ignorance of those in the pew. Previous jeremiads, however, have never had such meticulously-thorough research to support their moanings. The findings of the NSYR provide statistical ground for concern. The amount of variance from the theological norms espoused by the houses of worship frequented by these teens was so overwhelming that Christian Smith, the study's author and interpreter, was actually able to identify and describe an alternate theology at work. This was the practical, functioning faith of these teens, in effect a parasitic kind of faith hosted by and drawing its life from the older established religious traditions, "the new spirit living in the old body"[19] of those traditions. He termed this new faith *Moralistic Therapeutic Deism*, and codified its creed in the following statements:

1. A God exists who created and orders the world and watches over human life on earth.

2. God wants people to be good, nice, and fair to each other, as taught in the Bible and by most world religions.

3. The central goal of life is to be happy and to feel good about oneself.

4. God does not need to be particularly involved in one's life except when God is needed to resolve a problem.

5. Good people go to heaven when they die.[20]

Again, the NSYR is a composite of the belief-world of the nation's, not just evangelicalism's teens. Thankfully, it appears America's conservative Protestant teens fared better than many others, albeit using "highly formulaic terms" to express their faith. Still, this portrait doesn't create great confidence in the overall convictional base of these teens' faith, nor of that of their parents, since Smith believes these adolescents "seem to be merely absorbing and reflecting religiously what the adult world is routinely modeling for and inculcating in its youth."[21]

Searching for a culprit responsible for this situation, no one villain can legitimately be isolated and indicted. Even so, dare we exempt the public worship of the past fifty years from any responsibility for it? Demonstrably, this was the half century when our worship has been most experimental and novelty-driven. Ironically it was also motivated, at least among evangelicals, by the desire to reach the nation's youth—who are now the parents/grandparents of these teenagers![22] As has been admitted, some have surely been brought within the orbit of Christ's teachings because of our half-century of worship experimentation. But evidence such as the NSYR suggests that something within church life remains puzzlingly inadequate.

A corroborating line of evidence comes from the growth of America's "nones," the "spiritual but not religious" persons who, when asked to identify their religious preference, enter the word "none." This group now numbers twenty percent of all U.S. adults—and among those adults under thirty, a third of them identify themselves in this manner.[23] Certainly generational change contributes to these disturbing percentages, as does the apparent secularization of our society, but it is clear that whatever evangelical churches have been or are doing to attract the populace—including market-driven worship services—is not stemming the tide of departure from evangelical churches or their Sunday gatherings. Surely, in light of information like this, a closer look at our fifty-year sojourn into worship innovation is not a witch hunt: it is justifiable.

In search of a word

Here, however, we encounter a first and fundamental problem that makes it difficult to proceed. Just what do we mean by the word "worship"? No word in evangelical Christianity's vocabulary is presently more garbled than this one. Like an old dime, its features have been rubbed almost indistinct by long use and current overuse. Obviously, it is still in circulation—like that old dime—but it has no corresponding value. As the examples from the earlier pages show, this word has become amorphous, gelatinous, foggy, fuzzy, muddled—choose your preferred synonym. This is no small matter! It means, among other things, that just about anything can be and is being called worship. But if that is so, then we are, to recall the words of William Nichols printed at the first of this chapter, in danger of defaulting on our "supreme and only indispensable activity."

It's obvious that we treasure worship—at least we treasure these meetings we call worship. It's a first thing start-up churches begin, and it's the last thing dying churches will relinquish. Without any theologian's coaching, we know intuitively that worship isn't just one of the nice programs churches offer. Nor is it just a weekly club meeting, the content and conduct of which aren't worth fussing over. To the contrary, we know this meeting is in some sense our life-line. Even so, we are far from united or clear about what this meeting is "for" and what God might actually be wanting from it.

For some of us worship is understood to be the songs, praise choruses, and prayers that begin the Sunday service. For others, worship includes everything that transpires in a church service, from the "Hello" to the "Good-byes." To some evangelical minds, worship has been offered if the prescribed prayers have been said, while worship for others hasn't been rightly offered if there isn't a sermon and an observance of the Lord's Supper. Not a few would question if worship has really occurred if no sign-gifts of the Spirit—e.g., speaking in tongues, words of knowledge, healings—have been in evidence. There are some for whom worship is so hardwired to the word praise that "praise-and-worship" is not three words, but one. In still other quarters, worship is a fancy word to indicate what their grandparents called "going to preaching." If the gathering isn't alive with excitement—or calming in its tranquility—some would judge it non-worship. Candidly, one could add variants to this listing for several paragraphs and not exaggerate.

Uniting noun and verb

Part of our confusion is inevitable, given the fact that in the English language worship is both a noun and a verb, a meeting and an act.[24] Even so, it's a plausible assumption that when this word appears before a reader's eyes—at least in this book—it will be understood to be a reference to an event, a "church service." This is quite understandable, and indeed all the examples of worship given in the preceding paragraph deal with "church services." But the consequence of this association—which is more wide-spread than just this instant of reading—is that it is often difficult to isolate and discuss worship as a verb. Our melding of "worship" and "church service" makes it difficult for us to think of them separately. (And ultimately the two must—or should—reconnect!) But this linkage means that most of our conversations about worship are more often conversations about church services, conversations which quickly degenerate into arguments about *your* "church service" versus *my* "church service." Thus, the needed conversation about the underlying, primary verb is lost in a debate about styles of church services. Worship as the purpose and essential act of the event remains unexamined. This, however, is the absolutely central issue! What is the meaning of this verb—biblically, historically, theologically—and what does it require of us in the meetings that bear this word as their name?

Until we come to grips with this neglected heart of the matter, all our debates about the style of our church services are quite pointless—and also threatening. For such explorations might lead to the unsettling discovery that *my* church service and *your* church service are both standing in need of prayer and revision if they are to be expressions of worship that's truly worship, that is, that's really about God.

So it's not surprising that worship-anxiety runs high among many. Pastors and laity see the array of expanding Sunday options—and the impressive attendance some of them garner—and begin to question the wisdom of their own worship patterns. Who among us wants, truly wants, to stifle our church's ministry—or Christ's continuing work on earth? So committees are appointed to study the issue and bring recommendations concerning the church's worship. But often as not, even before its recommendations are made, factions form. Pastors or musicians leave—or are asked to. Churches divide. And the culprit time and again is that we have no clear understanding about what this word "worship" calls us to do.

The rules of engagement

As every game player soon realizes, rules don't take the fun out of a game—they actually enable and enliven it. Rules establish the purpose and object of a game. Remove the rules and you don't know whether you're playing poker or Spades, dodge ball or soccer. Rules determine the boundaries that keep games challenging and interesting. Remove respect for rules and the game becomes a melee of frustrated, angry players and fans slugging it out. These same dynamics are also true of the game, the "play" of worship.

The urgent question then is where might we find these needed rules? As evangelicals, a study of biblical teaching on the subject is certainly essential and foundational. And, although this book doesn't survey those teachings it certainly attempts to build upon and honor them.[25] However, as many students have been surprised to learn, the New Testament, the one source we are most disposed to turn to as our ultimate authority, provides very few words that might fairly be termed "rules" concerning public worship. Its concern is to establish the gospel rather than to prescribe rules for corporate worship. This then means we must look to the worship practices of the early Church, specifically the Church of the first three centuries, to discover how the Spirit of God molded the worship of the infant Church. Here, thankfully, we can detect emerging, uniform practices and hear the admonitions of early leaders whose counsel and example give us helpful rules. Moreover, the ensuing centuries of the Church's life provide even more clarity about these rules. These sources, therefore, are where we must turn to find the needed guidance.

However, a warning is in order. The unwanted discovery that awaits us upon identifying these rules is that "all we like sheep have gone astray: we have all turned to our own way" (Isaiah 53:8). All present forms of evangelical worship can be critiqued and reformed by the Spirit-taught worship wisdom of the first three centuries of Christian faith—and be improved by learning how the later Church, at its best, implemented this wisdom. No group, no tradition, no style gets a pass here. Readers need not, therefore, fear that a hidden agenda of championing one form of worship is lurking here behind the seeming guise of objectivity. Instead, an early admission is made that, rather than being a seeking of God's face, all too often our worship suggests we have "forsaken the fountain of living water [God], and dug out cisterns for [our]selves, cracked cisterns that can hold no water" (Jeremiah 2:13).

"I hate, I despise your festivals"

At this point, it might actually be of some comfort (and profit) to recall the number of occasions when our predecessor's worship also went astray. That list begins as early as the days of Israel's nativity when she worshiped a golden idol at the very foot of Mount Sinai (Exodus 32). It continues in her temple's hymnbook (Psalm 15, 24, 50) and is there in the days of the prophets (Isaiah 58, Amos 5:21ff) as well as in the years of restoration (Habakkuk 2:18-20) and continues into the days of Jesus (John 2:13-22). Surely, however, the Israelites didn't sit down every generation or so and dream up new ways to botch their worship. No, it just happened—for whatever reasons, it just happened—again and again and again! Moreover, with the aid of historians and theologians we can also identify multiple times when the worship of Christ's Church has similarly lost its way through clericalism, excessive sacramentalism, minimal proclamation, liturgical fundamentalism, etc. This dismaying record indicates that vigilance and great spiritual discernment about worship are always in order. To cite William Nichols' words once again, worship must always "come under the criticism and control of the revelation on which the Church was founded," lest it become a profitless exhibition of anarchy rather than of Godly play.

The search before us
Our search for the needed "criticism and control" begins in the next chapter of this book with case studies of three influential models of corporate worship, the confluence of which in our day is largely responsible for our confusing worship situation. These studies help us understand more precisely our present context, an important first step. However, they do little to provide the constructive guidance we need to move forward into more fruitful and faithful worship. That assistance begins to surface in the last section of that second chapter when we turn our attention to the worship of the Church in the period between Jesus' resurrection and the political legitimization of Christianity three hundred years later. The third chapter then describes this early worship more closely, permitting us to see clearly the continuities and discrepancies between our worship and that of our founders. That comparison continues by describing how the Church in subsequent centuries, at its best, honored the rules sketched out first by the early Church. The fourth and final chapter details what a twenty-first century order of worship might look like, using the rules identified from within the Spirit's guidance of the Church throughout the past two thousand years. Finally, in the book's conclusion, a definition of worship is provided which distills the worship wisdom gained from all our searching.

The importance of this search

One of the New Testament's most significant and often undervalued admonitions is found in Hebrews 10:25: "Let us not give up meeting together" (NIV). Though much has changed within the Church since the days of that writing, the urgent necessity of our meetings abides. Worship remains "the supreme and only indispensable activity of the Christian Church." It is the originating, authorizing, galvanizing epicenter of the Church's existence, her hour of weekly rebirth, her most theological and doxological moment. Worship is the Church gathered from its many weekday locations for glad family reunion. Through worship the Church becomes visible and actualized—no longer a list of 'names' but real people with faces and stories and a Lord to acknowledge. Worship is the Church gathered in the presence of her Lord—assembled to seek God's face—and in that divine gaze to be incrementally transformed into a replica of God's own presence in the world. Worship therefore is a meeting of immense significance for the Church's life as well as for the life of the world. From this encounter with her Lord that we call worship all the rest of the Church's ministries flow. If worship doesn't happen, nothing else will happen well thereafter for it will lack the orienting, enlivening contact with the Church's Source. Worship is just this important for the Church.

Therefore, the exploration we are beginning is not "much ado about nothing." It is an inquiry about the quality and character of our weekly "seeking the face of God" and therefore a journey to the center of our faith. If anyone mistakenly minimizes the importance of this investigation, I can do nothing more than ask that they listen to the testimony of four separate witnesses, each from a very different context, yet all uttering a common conviction about the uncommonly important significance of our worship. First, there is Orlando Costas, a passionate theological spokesman for third world liberation: "Worship is not a mere function of the church, it is her *ultimate* purpose."[26] Second, there is South African Bishop Desmond Tutu who, from another continent and facing racist apartheid, adds his Amen to Costas' declaration, saying: "The church exists primarily to worship and adore God."[27] From Europe hear the voice of German theologian Karl Barth joining in, by adding: "Christian worship is the most momentous, the most urgent, the most glorious action that can take place in human life."[28] Last, a not-so-widely-known theologian from America's southwest, W. T. Connor, who most certainly raised eyebrows by writing the following words in 1945 to revivalist Southern Baptists:

> The first business of the church is not evangelism, nor missions, nor benevolence; it is worship. The worship of God in Christ should be at the center of all else that the church does. It is the mainspring of all . . . The whole life and organization of a church should spring from worship, center in worship, and end in worship.[29]

Although these voices all speak from the Church's twentieth century, their opinion is not a latter-day novelty. From every age and from every corner of the globe, thoughtful Christians agree that what happens—or doesn't happen—on Sundays is an important issue. It matters, and it matters supremely.

EXCURSUS: WORSHIP WORTHY OF THE NAME

If a picture is worth a thousand words, let me spare you two thousand words by providing two verbal pictures of two very different worship services, both of which thankfully managed to keep the verb and the noun of worship together. The first of them came as a gift on an Easter Sunday morning decades ago.

The dawn seemed to be debating its willingness to "get up and do it again" as my family and I made our sleepy way to the country home of friends who had invited us for an Easter sunrise service. There were actually four families invited to this gathering, all of us members of the same church—and all of us would later find our place within its time of

Easter worship. But for me, the later experience would play second fiddle to the one I was about to have.

Our hosts had steaming coffee waiting for those of us who needed wake-up help (and cups of fruit juice poured for the non-caffeinating sleepy-heads). Even so, the greetings among us were the muffled "g'mornings" of persons whose biorhythms were struggling to adjust. But once assembled we shuffled into the living room, which had a grand picture window opening to the east.

A child from among us had been chosen to read a short biblical passage as our call to worship. One among us had a splendidly-trained voice, and she began to sing a simple song about the death and burial of Christ, a song we had sung at church the evening before last, a song we now resumed, joining her as she sang in a pitch low enough that even early morning voices could join in. Then we listened as another, an older child, read a longer portion of scripture about women telling idle tales and of men running to a tomb to verify their wild stories. A prayer was then offered by one of the mothers present, a prayer of thanks for the blessing of another Holy Week, another Easter morning, another day of life, and especially for this moment of worship.

Perhaps he was the senior member of our group, but regardless of his age, one fellow had taken a corner chair so as to be able to see everyone in the room. He was a chaplain, though not of the hospital-hall-way-walking type; he was a chaplain who spent his days inside the walls of a nearby state prison. His world of work was foreign and frightening to me though he himself was as warm as the coffee cup in my hand. He'd been asked to speak to us about resurrection—impossible subject!—but his words came as easily as if his subject had been tomato gardening. He told us the story of dejected disciples on their way to Emmaus and of One who drew near—drew near even out of the abyss of death!—and whose presence transformed these disciples' defeat. He assured us this One was still with us, especially when our paths were walked in dejection and shadows, and as he spoke I got the feeling he'd walked in and through enough of those shadows to know what he was talking about.

Wondrously, as if by agreement with the Universe, his words were endorsed, paragraph by paragraph, by the eastern sky progressively filling the picture window with light. When he finished the sun wasn't yet fully visible, but the sky was bright with anticipation. So was I.

Our songstress had no difficulty now getting us to sing with her. "Christ the Lord is risen today, Alleluia! Sons of men and angels say, Alleluia!" As I recall, by the second stanza, and without any prompting, we were all standing. Who could stay seated in such a moment? Quiet sentence-prayers of thanksgiving—from children and adults—and some of intercession (even for a fellow on death row) followed as the sun's rays filtered into the room.

Then, as would befit good worship, we exchanged all manner of hugs and smiles as our hosts hurried to the kitchen. Within minutes, the aromas of welcomed food filled the house, and though no Eucharistic prayers as such were offered, I've seldom ever felt as much at the Lord's Table as I did that morning. Friends in Christ broke bread (and eggs and bacon as well), fresh in memory that He who once died was alive and with us in that happy dining room, in a simple country home, on a county road in rural Oklahoma—and would be with us and all humankind from there through eternity.

Many years later, a very different worship hour was given me under the vast arches of Duke University's Chapel. I was thankfully free from my own pastoral duties that Sunday, duties which at the time were giving me little joy and creating great anxiety. (Yes, pastors do "get the blues" and struggle to find spiritual equilibrium just like the rest of God's people.) The best word to describe my spiritual state that day would be the word numb.

Yet, there I was in church—and what a church it was and is! Patterned after several French cathedrals, the architectural and theological statement that building makes is overwhelming. In the best sense of the expression, one enters its spacious splendor and whispers, "OMG!" You do this in a whisper because the room itself sucks a reverent "Oh, my God!" out of you. And when any of its three majestic pipe organs begins to throw triumphant sounds against those interior stone walls you can almost feel them ricochet in delightful play throughout the room and then reach down and lead the processing choir of a hundred robed singers down the center aisle. So it was on that Sunday. I felt as though I was being swept up into a separate reality.

The congregational hymns we sang (one unknown to me) and the anthems the choir sang (one in a language other than my own), I heard as witnesses to a faith and a Church larger and older than my own little experience of it. The same was true of the several portions of Scripture that were read; more than I was accustomed to, but because they were read well, I listened to each with interest and profit. The sermon, understated and quiet that day, awakened personal inventory of my soul's emptiness and longing. Then there came the prayers, offered for so many different needs and groups—a feast of intercession, really—that they drew me out of my centrifugal self-concern into an elevating awareness of others and to the care of God for all us wondering, struggling sinners.

Communion was offered that day. It observance was more ritualized than my Pentecostal grandmother would likely have approved, but I heard and saw in it a declaration that here the body and the blood, the life and forgiveness of our Lord were to be handled with the greatest of care. As I walked down that long aisle toward where the servers waited to serve us all, I thought of the pilgrimage that had been mine thus far—and of how passionately I did want it to continue, though in a truer, deeper measure. Not being much of a wine drinker, even the burning sensation of the wine slipping its way down into my gut became a visceral vow about that desire and also a welcomed reminder of my Lord's "I in you, and you in me" promise of fruitfulness (John 15:5).

Then the recessional hymn—and this one I knew from childhood! I sang it heartily. As the choir recessed up the central aisle, singing it grandly and led by a golden cross held high, I wanted to elbow my way out into the aisle to join up—not as a choir member—but as a fresh recruit for the Movement, marching gladly into a wounded world and my own God-held future.

QUESTIONS FOR DISCUSSION

1. Do you think the multitude of worship forms available creates confusion? Among believers? Among the general public?

2. Do you share the opinion that much evangelical worship is not truly "about God"?

3. Recall some worship services that in your opinion were "worthy of the name," and identify the characteristics made them so.

4. If your church uses a worship folder or bulletin, review its content. What indicators are there that the worship service is "about" God?

Notes

[1]Guardini, *The Spirit of the Liturgy*, trans. Ada Lane, 2nd ed. (London: Sheed & Ward, 1937), 103.

[2]"Evangelical" is a notoriously slippery word to define, "but it is still possible to identify some generic characteristics: an embrace of the Holy Bible as inspired and God's revelation to humanity, a belief in the centrality of a conversion or 'born again' experience, and the impulse to evangelize or bring others to faith" (Randall Balmer, *The Making of Evangelicalism: From Revivalism to Politics and Beyond* (Waco, TX: Baylor Press, 2010). See Jon Butler, Grant Wacker, & Randall Balmer, *Religion in American Life: A Short History*, 2nd ed. (New York: Oxford University Press, 2011), chapter 9 for greater background. Accepting Balmer's definition, "evangelical" describes a mindset rather than a denomination and may include persons of various church traditions. One of those, the Free Church tradition (so named for its claimed freedom from hierarchical church authorities and creeds) is my own tradition, but Evangelical is the broader category addressed here, although Free Church concerns surface often.

[3]Scott L. Thumma, "The Shape of Things to Come: Megachurches, Emerging Churches, and other New Religious Structures," in *Faith in America: Changes, Challenges,*

New Directions, Vol. 1 Organized Religion Today, Charles H. Lippy, ed. (Westport, Connecticut: Praeger Publishers, 2006), 198.

[4]Bergler, "When Are We Going to Grow Up?" in *Christianity Today*, June 2012, Vol. 56, No. 6, p. 19.

[5]Wilson, *Setting Words on Fire: Putting God at the Center of the Sermon* (Nashville: Abingdon Press, 2008), 9.

[6]Noted in Robert D. Putnam and David E. Campbell, *American Grace: How Religion Divides and Unites Us* (New York: Simon & Schuster, 2010), 161.

[7]Constance Cherry, *The Worship Architect: A Blueprint for Designing Culturally Relevant and Biblically Faithful Services* (Grand Rapids, Michigan: Baker Academic, 2010), 222.

[8]Cherry, "Merging Tradition and Innovation in the Life of the Church," in Todd E. Johnson, ed. *The Conviction of Things Not Seen* (Grand Rapids, MI: Brazos Press, 2002), 19.

[9]Lester Ruth, "A Rose by Any Other Name: An Attempt at Classifying North American Protestant Worship," in Johnson, ibid., 33.

[10]One friend acidly summarized: "On any given Sunday you can find everything from a Group-hug of the Almighty (whose ego doesn't need it), to a Memorial to the Dead Deity (whose presence doesn't welcome it)."

[11]In this same period much of the rest of western Christendom engaged in a liturgical renewal movement which found resources in historic worship practices leading to a retrieval of discarded rites, an updating of language, greater lay leadership, a flowering of new hymns and service music, etc.

[12]The task of indigenization, or inculturation, i.e., the task of offering worship that is accessible to persons of varying cultures, is imperative, and more will be said about it later. The issue here, however, is whether today's scrambled scenario reflects legitimate inculturation or a do-it-yourself improvisation that is either ignorant of or consciously distancing itself from its own lineage.

[13]John Killinger, of the Divinity School of Vanderbilt University, was another influential Protestant champion of change in his *Leave It to the Spirit: Commitment and Freedom in the New Liturgy* (New York: Harper & Row, 1971).

[14]James F. White, *New Forms of Worship* (Nashville: Abingdon Press, 1971), 34, 36.

[15]Owens, *The Total Image or Selling Jesus in the Modern Age* (Grand Rapids, MI: Eerdmans Publishing Co., 1980), 62-63.

[16]One indication of this lack may be seen in the seventeen articles within Mark A. Noll and David Wells, eds. *Christian Faith and Practice in the Modern World: Theology from an Evangelical Point of View* (Grand Rapids: Eerdmans, 1988). This book, dedicated to Carl F.H. Henry, a god-father of modern evangelicalism, gave an overview of evangelical theology as presented by a "Who's Who" of British and American evangelicals at a 1985 conference held at Wheaton College on "Christian Theology in a Post-Christian World". One looks in vain through its three hundred plus pages for any mention of worship or the significance of worship in the theological formation of the Church. It is as though the every Sunday "practice" of the faith in the churches was irrelevant to "Christian Faith and Practice in the Modern World"! This theological blind spot was more the rule than the exception.

[17]Christian Smith & Melinda Lundquist, *Soul Searching: The Religious` and Spiritual Lives of American Teenagers* (New York: Oxford University Press, 2005). A subsequent volume four years later tracked the development of these teens: Christian Smith, *Souls in Transition: The Religious and Spiritual Lives of Emerging Adults* (New York: Oxford University Press, 2009). Kenda Creasy Dean, *Almost Christian: What the Faith of Our Teenagers is Telling the American Church* (New York: Oxford University Press, 2010) attempts proposals for counteracting the reality Smith described; Thomas Bergler, *The Juvenilization of American Christianity*, op cit., charts the fifty-year juvenilization of American Christianity stemming from evangelical's obsession to reach teenagers for Christ.

[18]Smith and Denton, *Soul Searching*, 137.

[19]Ibid., 166.

[20]Ibid., 162-163.

[21]Ibid., 166.

[22]Bergler's *Juvenilization of American Christianity* documents this well.

[23]See www.pewfourm.org/Unaffiliated/nones-on-the-rise.aspx.

[24]In broadest definition, Christian worship will also include daily life and personal pieties. Hence, holistically, worship is 1) a corporate event, 2) an individual's devotional practices (e.g. prayer) and 3) personal lifestyle (ethics). To ignore the interrelatedness of the three is fatal, but the focus of this book remains upon the corporate event.

[25]Of the many books available on Old Testament understandings Samuel E. Ballentine, *The Torah's Vision of Worship* (Minneapolis: Fortress Press, 1999) offers an excellent survey of the literature and of the subject itself. David Peterson's *Engaging with God: A Biblical Theology of Worship* (Grand Rapids: Eerdmans Publishing Co., 1992) provides guidance for both testaments. Robert Webber, ed. *The Biblical Foundations of Christian Worship*, Vol. 1 of *The Complete Library of Christian Worship* (Nashville: Star Song Publishing, 1993) gives easily accessible orientation and many bibliographical leads to the date of its publication.

[26]Orlando Costas, *The Church and Its Mission: A Shattering Critique from the Third World* (Wheaton: Tyndale House, 1974), 38.

[27]Desmond Tutu, *Hope and Suffering: Sermons and Speeches*, ed. John Webster (Grand Rapids: Eerdmans Publishing Co., 1984), 84.

[28]Cited by Ralph P. Martin, *The Worship of God* (Grand Rapids: Eerdmans Publishing Co., 1982), 1.

[29]Walter T. Connor, *The Gospel of Redemption* (Nashville: Broadman Press, 1945), 277, 279.

II

EVALUATING WORSHIP MODELS

In the spirit of Guardini's concept of worship as play, imagine with me a Sunday morning helicopter ride. Not as an excuse for skipping church, but for a bit of religious research. What is sought is a high-flying bird's eye view of worshipers as they make their way to church, to observe them in route to their place of worship. Observe those who descend from high-rise apartments and navigate city sidewalks, and those who pull into parking lots where the sound of gravel rises from their tires, and still others who follow uniformed greeters' instructions to Parking Lot A or C—and, of course, those who pass right on by to observe their own Sunday "holy meal" at IHOP. The point of this flight is to monitor this migration.

Is it not a remarkable moment each weekend when, even in this increasingly secular age, millions emerge from their separate cocoons and make their way to a place of worship? As they approach their chosen destinations, how might that appear from a distance? Would these worshipers in mobile array look like little ants in ecclesiastical queues?

And upon arriving and finding their place within the gathered assembly, one might wonder what was it, actually, that motivated them to get out of bed, forsake coffee cups and morning newspapers to seek this event? What was the magnet that pulled them away from solitude to community? What drew them here? In essence, what is this hour about?

These are questions that can't be discussed well in the noisy clatter of a helicopter hovering high above land. So, as fascinating as the perch might be, the pilot must return us to mundane earth so we can make a beginning by walking to a bookshelf.

Descending from a lofty perch

Open any English dictionary and turn to the entry for worship. It won't supply the stout boundaries and curious contours that we might find in the biblical Hebrew and Greek words, but even a dictionary will indicate a very fundamental point about worship that is also stressed in the Bible. Even in English (be it in the noun or the verb form) the word "worship" has reference to a person or Person deemed to be higher. (Only in a derivative sense do we speak of worshiping a thing, like money.) Your dictionary will talk about worship as paying great honor and respect, displaying great love and admiration to this worthy other. It will also talk about taking part in religious services that provide means to express this awe. The point will be that worship is first and foremost an action undertaken for, expressed to, and directed toward the object of one's worship. In our case, the object is none other than the Triune God. (And thus one hopes the answer as to what those spied-upon worshipers are seeking is—at least in part—God.)

The implication of this dictionary definition is that Christian worship is truly worship to the degree that it orients itself toward assisting the worshipers' response to God—to the God whose self-revelation has been seen in the face of Jesus Christ and whose presence has been sensed in the work of the Holy Spirit. Christian worship, in other words, has an inescapable vertical priority to it. It is a gesture, an act offered to God; it is about believers doing and saying things toward God and also listening to this God. In worship, it's all "about" God in the sense that God is the One to be sought, to be praised and thanked, to be prayed to and listened to. There is much more involved in this "about" character, but this alone is enough to require comment.

This understanding opens the discomforting possibility that a service that lacks this vertical-dialogical priority would be hard pressed to qualify as a worship service. It might qualify as a religious meeting or a church service—but not a worship service, per se. James Magaw revealed the difference even as he spoke for many when he confessed he "goes to church" for many reasons: to be with people whose company he enjoys, to show which side he's on, even to keep folks from asking why he wasn't in attendance. But he says the discussion rises to another level if he's asked why he worships, for "when I worship I expose myself to the power of God without any personal control over the outcome . . . ,[it] pushes me into uncharted territories. Going to church is easy most days. Worship is another matter."[1] Surely, the reason it is another matter is because worship is "about" God, and about engaging in the vertical-dialogical work that is worship.

The list of programs or causes or persons that Christians' gathering times can become "about" is endless—everything from pastoral anniversaries to Boy Scout Sunday to music appreciation—and consequently it is exceedingly difficult to keep the main thing the main thing. But failing in that attempt, God may be referred to or sung about in Sunday's meetings, but an impartial observer might say that though God received top billing, God was seldom front and center. In fact, God wasn't even talked to very much—or when talked to, that conversation didn't sound like the day's most important one. The biblical word for such a scene is idolatry.

Guess who's coming to dinner

Consider this story. A Christian organization announced they were giving a banquet to honor and celebrate the lifetime contributions of a distinguished leader. Admirers from far and near promptly bought tickets and drove good distances to display their respect. When the hour came, the banquet hall was filled with friends who'd come to celebrate this servant's steady hand and worthy accomplishments. It was a grand occasion—almost. The meal was excellent, the entertainment humorous, and the honorific speeches sincere and well done. But then the sponsors of the event cranked out a too-long video and a parade of endorsers for a new program they were premiering that night. A celebrative gathering to honor a patriarch was transformed into a sales pitch to a captive audience. One supposes—or hopes!—the honoree knew about this double agenda ahead of time, that he knew that he was essentially being "used" by the sponsors. If not, he had every reason to be furious or sick at heart as he headed home that night.

Could this possibly be a parable of what happens on many Sundays? One wonders how God feels when our church services are over. They have been held in God's name and were said to be an occasion to honor God. But is this the way the gathering actually played itself out? The question is: Where is God in these assemblies? Is God being "used" or worshiped in them?

Worship that is really "about" God will have God as the Subject (the content) and the Object (the recipient) of that worship.[2] In a search for "rules" to guide worship, this is unquestionably a first and absolutely fundamental one. Worship meetings must be about God in substantive ways or they ultimately discredit the very God they purport to honor. Ironically, as the next section of this chapter will show, this displacement of God from the very meetings convened in God's name has actually been done for imagined righteous reasons. In the name of God, God has actually been marginalized by his own friends!

This will become clearer in the next pages as we examine three dominant models of worship. Each, in my estimation, has minimized or forsaken the vertical-dialogical priority of worship in order to do something good in God's name. Lesser agendas, good enough in their own right, have unfortunately converted countless so-called worship meetings into something other than worship. Even so, these agendas are so all-pervasive that they now carry a holy aura. They dominate most every church's worship discussions, having become sacred assumptions, assumptions that are all the more powerful because they go without names or faces.

In the next pages names and faces are supplied for these influencers. We need to see them in flesh and blood historical dimensions rather than as shadowy, nameless ideas hiding behind the curtain of consciousness. I fear this sounds like an expose of dirty little secrets, but it is not. No vilification is appropriate or intended—these influencers are sources of worship confusion, not antichrists. Indeed, would that we today had the moxie brought to the Church by the movements and persons named here. In a very true sense, they are simply *us*, writ large. They symbolize the popular, collective evangelical mindset of yesterday and today, representing trends and opinions widely shared. By identifying and analyzing them we can "look at ourselves in a mirror" (James 1:23) and choose different paths—if we will.

So, with malice toward none, but with a desire to understand how we got to this season of stumbling about in search of guidance—and how we might get out of it—let's begin by turning the calendar back some two centuries and journey to tiny New Lebanon, New York.

1. WORSHIP AS EVANGELISM

Charles Finney and the Influence of Revivalism

Perched on the north-south line dividing the states of New York and Massachusetts—and just outside the reach of New York's capital city of Albany—sits the little village of New Lebanon, NY. It's a quiet town, the kind of idyllic Hudson River Valley hamlet sought by bed-and-breakfast tourists. Its best claim-to-fame today is as the historic site of one of the handful of Shaker communities that thrived in America's nineteenth century. The Shakers, through their fascinating celibate, utopian communities of simplicity, left an intriguing legacy within America's religious heritage. But far less known than the Shakers is another religious group which once met at out-of-the-way New Lebanon —with consequences still felt every Sunday morning in the vast majority of Protestant churches in America and the world.

In July of 1827 a group of eighteen Protestant clergymen assembled for a week in New Lebanon—it was located equidistant from the home-cities of most of the attendees—for a hoped-for meeting of the minds. Their differences had been simmering for at least fifty years, the sources of their discontent growing by the decade and, with alarming and growing frequency, boiling over into church splits, pastoral terminations, and name calling. In fact, despite the fact that all in attendance were men of piety, the brokers of the meeting felt compelled to obtain a pledge that participants would not engage in name-calling during the meeting. One side, known as the New Lights, swore they would not refer to their opponents as "cold," "dead," or "unconverted." And their opponents, the Old Lights, had to swear they would not refer to the New Lights as "heretics," "enthusiasts," or "mad."[3]

"I'll fight you every inch of the way…"

The principal antagonists for the meeting were Lyman Beecher (1775-1863) and Charles Grandison Finney (1792-1875), two men of larger-than-life reputation and ego. Beecher was known as New England Puritanism's "lion," its anti-Unitarian champion whose pastoral career in Connecticut and Boston was noted for its pugnacious, uncompromising intensity. The "Old Lights" looked to him as their champion. On the opposite side, Charles Finney was equally famous, but not for his pastoral leadership. In truth, he served as a pastor of only one church and that for only a brief period; he was preeminently a lawyer-turned-evangelist to astounding effect. Finney freely attributed his evangelistic success in part to the "new measures" he employed to secure conversions. He accordingly was the leader of the "New Light" faction and it was his "new measures"—and the ethos created by them—that finally made the New Lebanon meeting mandatory.[4]

Even in appearance and bearing the two leaders were strikingly different. Finney was slender and tall for his day, his clean-shaven young face revealing prominent facial bones and deep-set, penetrating eyes that bored soul-deep into any person beholding him. Even from the grainy photographs of that period his stare continues to be intimidating—had his been the age of Hollywood leading men, movie moguls would have cast him as a stentorian Moses. When he entered the pulpit even his detractors acknowledged the hypnotic power of his combination of a lawyer's erudition and an actor's grace. Beecher was equally unforgettable but in a very different way. He was as brusque and prickly as Finney could be smooth; his choppy pulpit gestures and backwoods mispronunciations were almost as legendary as his intelligence, zeal, and physicality—a descendant of blacksmiths, at age eighty he was still able to leap a five-rail fence without missing a running stride. Two of his children displayed a similar life force; a daughter, Harriette Beecher (Stowe), through her novel *Uncle Tom's Cabin*, threw the incendiary power of passionate "fiction" into America's pre-Civil War slavery debate, and her famous preacher-brother, Henry Ward Beecher, fanned the embers into full flame from his Brooklyn pulpit. But even before his children gilded his reputation, Lyman Beecher's opinions were sought and listened to in influential New England ecclesiastical circles. And in Beecher's opinion, Finney had simply pushed the envelope of propriety too far.

Curiously, for all their differences, the two men were in other and fundamental ways remarkably of one mind. Both were revivalists at heart, passionately concerned about the eternal destinies of the exploding populace about them—as well as the multitude of Americans migrating weekly into the nation's new western territories, where clergy were few and churches non-existent. As authentication of that concern, Beecher eventually would resign his Boston pastorate to relocate in "the west" (Cincinnati, Ohio) to be a teacher of preachers and president of Lane Theological Seminary. Finney would follow suit, settling in another Ohio city, Oberlin, to become a professor of theology and later president of Oberlin College. Both men were also kin in a shared determination to fashion from their Calvinist past a gospel message that would correspond more compatibly with the new American nation's fascination with the dynamic of self-determination. Out of the fatalistic implications of a theology of predestination, both were in search of a more inclusive and less passive message—a gospel of personal ability to grasp salvation now, this very hour. But, in Finney's case, this quest had led to the adoption of evangelistic methods or "new measures" which Beecher objected to so strongly that he warned Finney that if he dared to import these "new measures" into Beecher's Massachusetts, he would "meet him at the State line, and call out all the artillerymen, and fight every inch of the way to Boston, and then I'll fight you there."[5]

Thus they met, on the New York side of the state line—barely outside Beecher's line-in-the-sand—to engage in last-ditch diplomacy. For an entire week an assembly of nine New Lights and nine Old Lights struggled to find better light, daily engaging in earnest, but often futile negotiation and prayer. Their deliberations were of such public interest that three newspaper correspondents eagerly reported the proceedings to a curious readership.

No small amount of time was spent in establishing the facts about what "new measures" Finney and his followers actually did espouse and practice, and in refuting reports of behaviors not endorsed by them. Yes, it was true that they did not uniformly enforce the old pattern of separate seating for men and women and children. And, yes, it was true, that they didn't forbid women from speaking or praying aloud in their meetings, nor did they feel it inappropriate for the preacher or others to intercede publicly—by name!—for persons they sensed were under conviction of the Holy Spirit. Lay participation of many kinds—even lay exhorters (untrained preachers offering extemporaneous sermons, even approaching sinners one-on-one during the "invitation")—was welcomed. Moreover, preachers felt free to name names and call for repentance from individuals present. And, without question, the New Lights provided a reserved seating area—"anxious benches"—near the pulpit for those who, by sitting there, would declare that they were nearing conversion. Invitations to repent and be converted "on the spot" were also given—an alarming shortening of the time generally thought to be necessary for God's Spirit to convert—and these invitation moments were accompanied by the repetitious singing of emotion-laden invitation songs.

Finally, it wasn't uncommon for great weeping, falling, or even laughing in the Spirit to be in evidence during the revival meetings of Finney and the New Lights.

At the meeting's conclusion it was generally conceded that Finney and his partisans had prevailed. Beecher and the Old Lights had extracted a few concessions, but for the most part, as Beecher was reported to have told his party on the way home: "We crossed the mountains expecting to meet a company of boys, but we found them to be full-grown men."[6] Within five years Beecher —even if with a smattering of reluctance—was among a group of Boston clergy who invited Finney to preach in Boston.

Much ado about nothing?

It is tempting to categorize this New Lebanon meeting as only one of many skirmishes among American churchmen about evangelistic methods. Such a categorization is surely justifiable, for New Lebanon was this and much more. It was preeminently a symbolic tipping point for the weekly worship experience of American Protestantism. From this date forward revivalism would be a major factor in the Sunday morning diet of American church-goers. New Lebanon sealed it.

For decades American religious life had experienced revivalist surges. The colonial-era preaching of British evangelist George Whitefield and the theological, pastoral work of Jonathan Edwards had provided the kindling for the emerging nation's first great awakening in the 1730s and 40s. Although to its advocates the duration of the awakening was disappointing, its influence upon the worship patterns of American Protestantism was more durable. By the end of the American Revolution, a sedate and cerebral Sunday morning worship service was no longer the only option available to the new nation's worshipers. Lyman Beecher himself would be among those whose worship services were marked not only by rigorous doctrinal instruction but also by an unabashed, experiential "feeling" for the subject. However, with the westward expansion of Americans into and beyond the Appalachian mountains after the Revolutionary War, a second religious awakening erupted through the labors of zealous Methodist, Baptist, and Congregational/Presbyterian ministers who organized annual protracted, open-air camp meetings which attracted thousands of frontiersmen and yielded a comparable number of baptisms. Finney and his New Lights represented an urban adaptation and domesticating popularization of many features of those camp meetings—features now no longer to be marginalized as revival techniques but to be incorporated in varying degrees as Sunday worship expectations.

Thus, the New Lebanon outcome declared that revivalism had trumped "regular" church, that the era of worship as education[7] had been overtaken by the era of worship as evangelism. Or, to put it in lawyer-evangelist Charles Finney's frame of reference, worship would no longer be a schoolroom experience of being taught about the faith but would now become a courtroom experience of being challenged to render a verdict for the faith—today! The attractive vibrancy, as well as restrictive single focus of revivalism, would now be a trans-denominational, major influence in shaping American Protestant church life. The aroma of the camp meeting's sawdust trail would enter, and as often as not, permeate Sunday's sanctuary.

Finney realized and applauded this in his *Lectures on Revivals of Religion*, published eight years later. In the course of these lectures he held up to humorous scorn the protests of those who in earlier generations had been offended by such innovations as ministers clad in street clothing, the discontinuance of lining-out of hymns (a leader singing one line with the congregation then repeating that line), the introduction of choirs and pitch pipes and instrumental music, extemporaneous prayer rather than prayer-book prayers, and the like. Such innovations, Finney said, were piously bemoaned as the death knell of the Church. Obviously they were not, and, therefore, Finney scolded those who now opposed his "new measures." His contention was that the evangelizing mandate of the Church contained no directive about means or measures for its accomplishment. "No person can find any [prescribed] *form* of doing this laid out in the Bible," he insisted. "The fact is, that God has established in no church, any particular form, or manner of worship, for promoting the interests of religion. The scriptures are entirely silent on these subjects, under the gospel dispensation, and, the church is left to exercise her own discretion in relation to all such matters."[8]

Unacknowledged in Finney's remarks is the possibility that the assembling of God's people for worship might have some purpose other than the evangelization of the lost. This is implicit in his use of the word worship as essentially a synonym for an evangelistic meeting. To his credit, Finney provides an accurate interpretation of New Testament teaching when he claims that worship forms were left to the discretion of the Church. However, what he and his followers failed to note is that the New Testament does not authorize the conversion of church worship gatherings into evangelistic meetings. To the contrary, the repeated impression from every biblical glimpse into the gatherings of the earliest Christians is that these were meetings of and for the faithful, not the outsider.

The New Testament has only one verse that might even hint of such a conflation of purpose. In Paul's first letter to the calamitous church at Corinth he asks (14:23-25) if, when "the whole church comes together and all speak in tongues, and outsiders or unbelievers enter, will they not say that you are out of your mind?" Paul's unmistakable presupposition in this discussion is that the meeting's goal is the edification of the church, not evangelism; his repeated plea that all be done for the building up *of the church* (14: 4, 5, 12) can only mean that he saw this meeting as being for the church, not the world. The entrance of outsiders or unbelievers is a happenstance, not a sought-after objective. In other words, worship, not evangelism, is the purpose of this gathering. Of course, it must quickly be added that as a consequence of observing the church's orderly worship, "the secrets of the unbeliever's heart [might be] disclosed" and the outsider might then "bow down before God and worship him, declaring, 'God is truly among you.'" Nonetheless, evangelism is seen as a possible outcome of maintaining the integrity of the church's worship, not the reason for the assembly. It is indeed curious that the evangelical tradition, which prides itself on biblical moorings, has mostly ignored this clear New Testament distinction. Sadly, this oversight is one reason we find ourselves in worship confusion today.[9]

Nonetheless, there is in the Revivalist tradition no hint that worship might be a distinct calling of the Church, separate from evangelism or that worship might be a spiritual discipline not subject to the yardstick of evangelistic usefulness. The New Light concept of worship as evangelism became established as a basic evangelical expectation and, due to evangelicals' effectiveness in shaping American religious life, this understanding has influenced every Protestant tradition in America. For this reason a leading worship scholar, James F. White, believed Finney "may be the most influential liturgical reformer in American history."[10]

How great a forest is set ablaze by a small fire!

Revivalist themes had, as noted, been evident within American church life for decades prior to New Lebanon, but with the 1827 ratification these themes reshaped Sunday practices. A notable first example was in the pulpit itself. *Pastors* whose strength was as teacher or resident scholar or gentle shepherd were now less favored than preachers who could preach without notes, stir listeners' emotions, and effectively exhort sinners to "come to Jesus." *Sermons* also changed. Preachers now began, for the first time, to speak of a "plan of salvation," that is, a sequential list of theological affirmations that, when believed, assured one of eternal salvation. The sermons in which this plan was advanced began to be drawn from a narrower list of biblical texts that lent themselves easily to evangelistic use, although, regardless of the originating text, sermons consistently deposited listeners at a crossroads of salvation decision. Exposure to the entire canon of scripture and the wide range of Christian doctrine was thereby diminished in deference to the new evangelistic mandate. This homiletical trend was appropriately supplemented by an enabling change in *the order* in which worship was conducted—a concluding song of evangelistic invitation now became expected. This novelty was only one of many adjustments, if not abandonments of historic denominational orders of worship to accommodate the three-phase revivalistic order of singing, preaching, and inviting. In its crudest form this new order amounted to a format of *preliminaries* (heartfelt singing and short prayers done in the service of preparing listener's spirits for the sermon), *preaching* (generally of the character just described), and *pressure* (an extended invitation to "accept Jesus" today). *Music* underwent a change as well. The theologically instructive poetry of previous days (hymns), typically set to sedate European tunes, was supplemented or supplanted by more recently written poems of personal testimony, religious experience, and evangelistic appeal (gospel songs), set to tunes with memorable refrains. Choirs, where existing, had previously been situated in a balcony or corner of the church as reinforcers of congregational singing. They were now relocated to the front of the worship space, directly behind the preacher and facing the congregation as, in effect, performers as well as additional exhorters during the invitation songs. Gospel soloists also made their debut as a part of this shift. Music, in whatever expression, was chosen not for the tutelage it offered in theological understanding but for its ability to stir worshiper's hearts.

Seating was also changed. The established pattern of church seating had been boxed seats (an enclosed rectangle with interior seating on three sides), or the more recent introduction of open-ended pews. Occasionally one might even find a box equipped with a folding writing desk to facilitate sermon note-taking for later study. Both boxes and pews were annually rented as a means of church financial support, with none but the renters permitted to occupy these seats. But box seating made it possible that at least some worshipers might have their backs turned to the preacher and also made evangelistic response difficult, and the practice of renting pew or box was a deterrent to advertising that the "seating is free and open to the public." So pew rentals and boxed seats were phased out, and free, slip pews became the expected norm. 'Free' meant anyone could sit anywhere and the open-ended 'slip' pews allowed persons to slip from their pew and easily make their way to the altar during the invitation period. The *pulpit* itself, whether a massive speaker's podium or, as

Finney preferred, a simple waist-high wooden stand to hold a glass of water, was always stage-center. Removed from any true visual significance was the *communion table*, which, if retained, was usually located on the floor level beneath the pulpit. *Baptismal fonts* or *baptisteries*, for those practicing immersion baptism, were variously placed.

Whenever new church construction was needed or possible, the new building often departed from liturgical *architectural patterns* of the past and featured designs with sloped floors directing the worshipers' eyes to a stage area, the back wall of which was centered by tier-seating for the relocated choir. The entire stage area was often set within an artfully decorated proscenium arch resembling performing arts theaters. In the one worship building Finney had a hand in designing (in New York City), all the slip pews were curved in nature, creating a theater-in-the-round effect and lessening the distance between the preacher and his audience. Additionally, all supportive pillars were placed so that no person's view of the preacher was obstructed. This design, therefore, provides justification for one contemporary scholar's designation of this as being "when church became theater."[11]

These new worship spaces obviously were not meant to be "worship" environments in historic senses, that is, to be "sanctuaries" of retreat and prayer, or "temples" of residence for God. Rather, they were "auditoriums" for the word to be preached and physically responded to. They were constructed to carry out the Finneyesque program of evangelism. They telegraphed to those in attendance that the primary action was on stage, not in the pews; laity came to be moved by the power of the presentations coming from the stage.

And the point of all this is . . . ?

For most evangelical readers all this sounds familiar because these are the buildings and the practices that characterize our recent history. They represent an understanding of worship that is the native habitat of millions of evangelicals. Put in today's terminology, this is the homeland for what is currently called "traditional" worship—even if today's expressions of "traditional" worship are usually lukewarm digressions from Finney's impassioned practice of it.

The more significant point is that, as the previous paragraphs have attempted to show, this so-called "traditional" worship is less than two hundred years old—a blink of an eye within Church history, and an American novelty at that. It represents only the legacy of Charles Finney's "new measures" program of evangelism, not the Church's historic norms of worship. In cold historical fact, "traditional" worship is best understood as nineteenth century American revivalism institutionalized. When placed up against the long history of the historic Church, "traditional" worship is a Johnny-come-lately with scant resemblances to what Christians across the previous 1800 years would have recognized as worship.

The Creation of the Land of Confusion

This understanding of worship as evangelism represents a fundamental reshaping of the goal of worship. Worship in this new construal is not a high and holy hour for the faithful to draw near to God in renewing thanks, attentive listening, priestly intercession, and glad communing. It is an occasion for the congregation to appeal to the outsider. This shift of goal and focus conflates, and therefore confuses, two essential but distinct tasks of the Church. The two are better seen as sisters, not Siamese twins. As sisters, they assist and complement one another, but when they are equated with one another both suffer a blurred focus—a confusion.

This differentiation of worship from evangelism is best understood as one aspect of the holistic mission of the Church. In that understanding, the Church has a five-fold missional purpose in the world: 1) to proclaim the gospel, 2) to teach the way of Christ, 3) to provide Christian community, 4) to serve the needs of others, and 5) to worship God. All of these, seen together, constitute the overall mission of the Church, a mission that must not be reduced to any one of these tasks. Each task has its own distinct identity and role to play in the forming of a full-orbed witness to Christ. Each complements the others and is to work synergistically with the others. But if any one of them begins to be conflated or confused with another, the wholeness of the ministry and mission of the Church is diminished.[12]

Specifically, when worship and evangelism are commingled in intent and in implementation, worship then becomes a meeting that is focused on converting "them," rather than a meeting in which "we" ourselves encounter God and, transformed by God's mercies, live the light of Christ into the world. When worship and evangelism are conflated evangelization is transferred from its best arena—the world—and is relocated to an arena—weekly worship—meant for a very different purpose. In this rearrangement, evangelism and worship and laity all lose. Worship is evicted from its proper home, evangelism is imprisoned within walls, and the ministry of the laity is essentially reduced to that of a supporting role for the "on stage" ministry of the evangelizing musician and the preacher/pastor.[13]

One man's story

Every person's story is somewhat different, so I can only offer a portion of my own at this juncture. But such as it is, here is one person's testimony. From my infancy, a revivalist-traditioned Southern Baptist church was my twice-on-Sunday and most-Wednesday-nights home away from home. My parents were both Sunday School teachers who took no sabbaticals and gave none to their children. Therefore my memory is filled with scenes and sounds of church-going, and fortunately, the vast majority of them bring a smile—including my own boyhood conversion and baptism. Indeed, going to church—even to worship—was usually an interesting experience. For me, the excitement focused on the invitation songs, on waiting to see who and how many might "go forward." That was church-stuff even a little boy could always anticipate with relish. However, there came a day when I became aware I was not enjoying it as much as in times past. That day came in the same period when my adolescent mind began to say: "Now that I'm saved, there's not a whole lot to look forward to in this church-going stuff other than being 'good' for the rest of my life. The 'big show' is over, kid; from here on out, it's just a matter of keeping your nose clean 'til you die."

Yes, there's a lot of shallow theology in that adolescent pool, but I'm now persuaded that one cause of the shallowness was that worship was unknown to me. Worship was in essence a church meeting we went to in order to be the cheering squad for the preacher/evangelist and to provide "crowd cover" for the lost until they singled themselves out by walking an aisle. All those hours in worship were really about "them," not us, and certainly not about me—at least, not since I'd been saved. Consequently there really wasn't much reason to keep on going to church after this realization, other than to conform to my parents' expectations, to be a loyalist for the incumbent pastor's efforts, and to manfully soldier on in the truly depressing prospect of being "nice" all the rest of my life—which at the time seemed like an eternity. (And inherent within this "nice" mandate was the imperative of being a personal soul-winner whose effectiveness would be measured each Sunday during the invitation song, transforming even my exciting moment into an excruciating moment of judgment for failure once again to be a good and faithful servant.) Any idea that those services might be about "us," the saved, and about our need to sit at the feet of our Master in reverence and to be molded through these moments into a group that looked and acted like Him— this may have been on somebody's screen but it certainly didn't filter down to a youngster like me who, believe me, was all ears and eager heart.

Again, one person's story doesn't make an irrefutable case for anything. But I do think my experience is indicative of the shallow discipleship rootage that is predictable when revivalism overwhelms worship's contribution to Christian identity. When evangelism and worship become conflated, when worship is planned primarily for evangelistic purposes, when human brokenness is addressed more than divine resourcefulness, when the time of worship even subtly shifts to an expectation that this is a time for "others" to get right with God more than it is a time for the Church to engage in her own corporate vertical-dialogical work, the negative consequences for the Church are deep.

Perhaps in some quarters of the evangelical world one can still hear the story which preachers—evangelists, usually—used to tell in order to inflate their own importance. That story was about "the little old lady" who went to England and took a tour of one of its many massive cathedrals, a building so different from her small-town Baptist church house. She took it all in and then asked the tour guide, "Excuse me, sir, but, when's the last time somebody got saved in here?" Those who told this story always got a laugh because the story served to pat the backs of his evangelical audience—as well as to pour scorn on those who didn't worship as they did. But in the longer sweep of Christian history, they were the Johnnys-come-lately, the children of Charles Finney who likely needed to have laughed less and wondered more about what riches might be being forfeited by confusing corporate worship with the laudable goal of getting someone saved.

Having said all this, and even while insisting upon the distinction between evangelism and worship, it must also be added that worthy worship always has an evangelistic function. If the glory of God is extolled, if the story of God's goodness is rehearsed, if the lives of the worshipers in any sense reflect the God they worship, how can worship not have evangelistic fruitfulness? In the earlier story of my own worship experience at Duke Chapel, I told of my desire to jump into the aisle as a fresh volunteer as the service ended. Good worship always has evangelizing power. In a sense every worship service is a re-evangelizing of the Church as well as an occasion for any unbeliever to hear and see the gospel portrayed and voiced—and to respond in faith. This comes, however, as a by-product and not as the goal of worship. If the focus is where it needs to be in the Church's worship, the complementary ministries of evangelism, teaching, service, and fellowship become nurtured and nurturing facets of the Church's holistic mission.

Still, an adequate understanding of our present worship confusion requires consideration of influences other than revivalism. Today's situation can't be laid at the feet of just one nineteenth-century meeting in upstate New York and the revolution it symbolized. The situation is much more complex than that. So to a second major influencer we now turn, and once again our case study begins in a little town off the beaten path.

2. WORSHIP AS INSPIRATION

Robert Schuller and the Influence of Entertainment

In 1926 the northwest Iowa farming community of Alton boasted a population of less than four hundred persons, the majority of them being of sturdy Dutch immigrant stock. Though the soil surrounding the town was rich and fertile, the same could not be said for those who worked it. Sioux County Iowans were mostly hardworking, God-fearing farm folk whose wealth was in spirit, not in cash.

One of them was Anthony Schuller, a ram-rod straight, reed-thin six-footer of few words and deep piety. Although he'd grown up in the area as an orphaned farm hand, by the time of the Depression Schuller (locals pronounced it Skull-er) had impressively managed to marry well, buy his own farm and build a Sears Roebuck kit home for his family. The house had no indoor plumbing but it provided a living and dining room and three bedrooms, one for his wife Jennie and him, one for his three daughters, and another for his two sons.

The second son, the last of the Schuller children, was given the name Robert Harold on the day of his birth, September 16, 1926. Harold, as he was called by the family, would continue his father's remarkable pattern of achievement but in a profession quite different from his father's. Through hard work, ingenuity, persistence, and good fortune—especially the emergence of television and cable and satellite broadcast technology—Robert H. Schuller became one of the twentieth century's most famous clergymen.

"You can go anywhere from nowhere"

Schuller began his autobiography, *My Journey*, with a sentence that captures his rags-to-riches life story and the gospel he loved to preach. He wrote: "You can go anywhere from nowhere." In his case, nowhere was his father's prairie farmhouse "at the dead-end of a dirt road that had no name and no number,"[14] and anywhere was Robert Schuller's position as the founding pastor of the 10,000 member Community Church in Garden Grove, California, conceiver of and fundraiser for its signature "Crystal Cathedral," and the star of an internationally televised worship service, "Hour of Power."

Schuller freely admitted the grandiosity of his Crystal Cathedral (journalist Norman Cousins teased that it was "the kind of church building God would build, if He could afford it")—but in typical "possibility thinking" mode, Schuller saw it as a twentieth-century American counterpart to Europe's historic cathedrals—plus, it provided a magnificent setting for his television program. At its highest point the "Hour of Power" telecast was watched by more than two million Americans each week, enjoying a fourteen-year run as either the first or second most-watched religious program in the nation. It also was the only religious broadcast regularly available on the Armed Services Network and became a staple feature of the European Broadcasting Network. Add to this globe-encircling television presence Schuller's string of best-selling books and annual Successful Church Leadership Institutes in which he taught thousands of pastors how to copy his "nowhere to anywhere" formula, and it's clear that Robert Schuller's stature was huge among clergy and laity in the late twentieth century.

His influence was felt "everywhere"—particularly in American church-goers' expectations for worship. Of the few televangelists[15] of that day who were actually pastors, Schuller televised an entire worship service—most of the other television "pastors" televised only crusade events they had led or excerpts of their weekly services (usually a musical selection and their sermon—plus a financial appeal), and all built their telecasts on the revivalist model of Finney. Schuller, however, chose to sculpt a worship service not built upon the revivalist order and to broadcast "the whole thing," carefully edited to be sure, but viewers were intentionally led to believe they were watching a worship service being conducted at the Crystal Cathedral—and it was impressive! From the opening panoramic views of the lush trees and sparkling fountains on the $30+ million campus, to Schuller's joyful greeting, to the sprightly congregational hymns and stirring anthems sung by a huge choir accompanied by instrumentalists and a world-class pipe organ, to the much anticipated celebrity interview/testimonies and the energetic 'possibility thinking' sermons of Schuller himself—the "Hour of Power" was both fascinating and inspiring! What was there not to like? Americans clearly did like it and for decades they sent in millions of dollars to insure that Robert Schuller's worship services stayed on the air and in their living room.

For this reason this ministry provides an entrance into a consideration of a second dominant model for evangelical worship today, namely worship as inspiration—for inspiration is precisely what Schuller desired to provide.

In a strictly analytic sense, however, this model is not a separate, distinctly new confusion—it is more accurately understood as an extension and new iteration of Finney's evangelism model. During his seminary studies Schuller had made a careful study of the ministry of Southern Baptist pastor George W. Truett, a princely revivalist, who had presided over the phenomenal growth of the First Baptist Church of Dallas, Texas. Schuller found in Truett a pastor-hero who modeled urban church growth. Throughout his Garden Grove ministry, Schuller understood himself to be an urban evangelist, a pastor-salesman for God. To be sure, in good Finneyesque tradition, he chose to develop new measures for his evangelistic efforts—he wouldn't scare the hell out of people; he would inspire them into heaven. But in this endeavor he was continuing the revivalist tradition, even as he gave it a new look and sound. Through this "new measure" Schuller, the good pastor, tied the knot between inspiration and American consumerism, officiating a marriage that seemed to have been made in heaven.

It bears repeating that this judgment is not offered as an indictment of Schuller as a bad guy. Not at all. He simply did splendidly what the evangelical and wider culture itself esteemed most highly—he succeeded! He dreamed big, located well, worked hard, and saw his dreams come true.

We must remember that it is only in recent years that consumerism has become a whipping boy of social criticism. In Schuller's formative years, the enabling action it required, namely hustling to connect customers with the goods you had to sell, was just quintessential Americanism. The concept wasn't difficult to grasp. The basic premise was that there were customer/consumers, and there were suppliers. In America's free-market system, the supplier who knew how to attract customers and meet their needs was certain to do well. Countless companies demonstrated the truth of this during the post-World War II years when Schuller was a searching seminarian. These companies blossomed and became known brands and franchises due to their shrewd meeting, if not creation, of consumer desires. So it is not surprising that a seminarian with Robert Schuller's poverty-marked background, searching for a successful ministry strategy, might be drawn to this understanding. In his religious adaptation of this scheme, the necessary task for an up-and-coming young clergyman was to find a need and fill it.

"It was the best of times, it was the worst of times"

To quote a popular folksong of the time, the needs Schuller found were "blowing in the wind" of that period of American history. His California ministry began in 1955 as a mission endeavor of his Reformed Church in America denomination, which deputized him to begin a church in the booming area of southern California. Unknown to the eager young church planter or his sponsors, decades of horrific social eruptions were looming. They were marked by deadly racial riots, assassinations of political leaders, presidential impeachments, disgust with an endlessly protracted war in Vietnam War, and the appearance of a drop-out generation of LSD-using "hippies" repudiating all authorities and questioning every tradition. The churches themselves seemed disoriented by the chaos: theologians made headlines declaring "God is Dead," pastors and priests were arrested in political protests, and spirituality was said to be dead. It was, in a very true sense, the worst of times to be peddling religion in secular southern California. But week after week Schuller reframed it as the best of times to mold a fantastic and fulfilling life. This was the need he identified—the deep yearning of beleaguered Americans to be inspired, to possess a self-esteem that was more than sufficient for the day's challenges, to be lifted up above the nowhere of disturbing societal upheaval. This was terrain Schuller knew well, it was his life-path, and in the Christian story and the ethos of positive-thinkers of the past such as Norman Vincent Peale, he found resources to meet the need of inspiration.

It is outside the concern of this discussion to assess the ways he also reframed his inherited Reformed theology to do this.[16] Our concern here is more limited; it is restricted to describing and assessing the weekly format of worship he developed as the setting for his message. This is where the strengths as well as the inadequacies of confusing worship with inspiration can most clearly be seen.

"Retailing religion"

For Schuller as for Finney, worship as a distinct and separate activity was apparently unimaginable. Sunday's activities had to be planned with the unchurched in mind, planned as outreach events that would attract and inspire any and all persons—especially the non-believer. "For 30 years my ministry has been a mission to unbelievers," Schuller explained, adding that "I have seen my calling as communicating spiritual reality to secular people, people who aren't ready to believe in God."[17] To that end he designed spirited religious services built around topics of broad personal interest rather than Christian doctrine or expositions of scripture which he believed "would . . . turn off many people who do not yet believe that the Bible is the Word of God."[18] He approved secular songs within worship rather than restricting the musical menu only to songs that "contain references to God or Jesus or the Holy Spirit, or to sin or salvation."[19] "The parish church is in the business of 'retailing religion'"[20] he contended, and therefore churches that are "so dignified they're dull," with their "quietly meditative and perfectly tranquilizing" mood, and sermons that aren't "enthusiastic, exciting, and dynamic" were doomed to dwindle.[21] His counsel to pastors was to "Let your Sunday morning services aim at inspiration, entertainment, and a basic commitment to Jesus Christ."[22]

Consider how this understanding worked itself out in weekly practice, in a package that arrived in millions of living rooms each weekend for the better part of twenty years.

Worship according to Schuller

First, this is worship characterized by *joy and celebration*. Contrary to the restrained mood of many evangelical churches of the period, and certainly differing from the urgent solemnity of his televangelist cohort, the "Hour of Power" was upbeat and cheerful in every way. Although his Reformed tradition had a historical worship identity with the psalms of ancient Israel, many of which are laments, only Israel's joyful words were heard by "Hour of Power" worshipers. Never before had his tradition's opening psalmic words of worship ("This is the day the Lord has made. Let us rejoice and be glad in it.") found such exuberant expression as they did from always ebullient Bob Schuller at the top of each week's service. The man himself was a crucial part of the package—slender and enviably photogenic, blessed with a Hollywood smile and elegant silver hair. Then there was his manner of dress. He usually appeared in a grey clerical robe with doctoral stripes and a bluebird-colored hood, thereby providing a perfect human complement to the sparkling fountains and sun-bathed brilliance of the Cathedral's interior.

Having established this ambiance, nothing in the following fifty-plus minutes was allowed to destroy it—certainly no psalm of lament.

The organ and the choral and congregational music were all of the joyful genre—the words of all anthems and hymns having been carefully vetted by Schuller's wife, Arvella, in order that no negative thought or puzzling word might trouble or perplex the worshiper. Schuller's sermons always majored on the challenging rather than the threatening. Billy Graham might dwell on the nuclear "Doomsday Clock," but Robert Schuller would insist, "It's a great time to be alive!" Worship acts such as pastoral prayers and scripture readings were kept short and chosen for their inspirational potential. Silence, in which sobering thoughts might emerge, was avoided as being just what radio broadcasters of old called it: dead air.

This was worship that was joyful and celebrative from start to finish. This was worship that cheerfully excluded intrusions from worrisome threats; it offered a retreat from the 'world' into the cubicle of the self and its yearnings. This worship wasn't concerned with teaching the faith as a body of thought or even with pressing for decisions about the faith; the purpose of this worship was celebrating the joyful potentials and personal applications of this faith. This it could do very effectively because of a second characteristic.

This is worship that was *accessible to the novice*. Schuller began his Garden Grove ministry in a drive-in theater, preaching from the flat rooftop of the concession stand to worshipers who never had to leave their cars. This same kind of user-friendly strategy continued as a hallmark of his ministry in the elegant Crystal Cathedral. This building featured a parking lot with audio/visual access to the inside goings-on for those who didn't even want to leave their automobile. But those who walked into the 3,000-seat sanctuary were also made as at-ease as possible. There was no expected dress code—southern California casual was just fine. One need not be familiar with any off-putting rigmarole of "stand-up, sit-down, now kneel-and-say-Amen"—the simplest of instructions were given for a non-stuffy protocol. No memorized creeds were in evidence, no catechism classes presumed. There were educational opportunities available at other times, but the worship service was intentionally a low-demand, dummies-are-welcome affair. Walk in (or drive in), take a seat (or stay in your car), and relax. No one is going to make you feel uncomfortable. Indeed these worship leaders are going to do everything possible to make you feel very much at ease.

A third characteristic is that this is worship skillfully *designed to be attractive.* In blunter, terms, it can be called worship as entertainment—Schuller himself said so.[23] Among other things, its leaders knew very well that they were going up against Disneyland. One must not overlook the fact that Schuller's Community Church in Garden Grove was begun in 1955, the very same year as the opening of Walt Disney's first gigantic amusement park in Anaheim—and that the two are separated only by a freeway. Adjacent to Disneyland, there would soon be major league baseball's Angel's Stadium and Knotts Berry Farm, entertainment attractions of the highest caliber. Even if these neighbors weren't always on Schuller's mind, he clearly recognized that his service had to be as professional and inspiriting to people as were the hundreds of destinations people might choose. He recognized as well that his television audience was only one click of a remote control button away from more appealing shows. The "Hour of Power" had to have a large dose of entertainment value. As Schuller's TV producer Mike Nason, said: "If you are going to do television, you had better be television, you had better give the viewer what he has come to expect from television . . . [and] they expect it to be fast paced, entertaining, and colorful."[24]

This requirement dictated the previous two characteristics and also mandated that "Hour of Power" services must *conform to the passive expectations* of the entertainment consumer. This must be a low-demand, high-yield experience.

An earlier entrepreneurially-minded preacher-pastor, Aimee Semple McPherson, had known the same challenge in the 1920s in this same southern California locale. To meet that challenge she had built the 5,300-seat Angelus Temple in nearby Los Angeles where she staged elaborate religiously-themed services. One of her most famous sermons, "Stop! You're Under Arrest!" was preached in a policeman's uniform as she stood next to a police motorcycle with recorded sirens providing a background soundtrack.[25] Schuller, in less flashy manner, was every bit as good a showman as McPherson and surely surpassed her in the Hollywood-quality Christmas and Easter productions he produced. In the annually-performed "The Glory of Easter" pageant, a pastiche of Jesus' final days was dramatized by professional actors and church-member extras with professionally-designed sets and live elephants, camels, and donkeys adding a Bible-lands touch. Even the crucifixion was re-enacted (via a filmy curtain lifted for a ten-second glimpse of an actor on a cross) followed by a much longer resurrection scene in which, as one observer described it, "white-robed women wearing angel wings [shot] forth from the rafters, suspended by wires, and perform[ed] a synchronized, midair ballet. Triumphant music and a laser-light show announce that Jesus is risen."[26]

This, then, is worship that is intentionally striving to deliver an emotional wallop to passive consumers. It is worship that is audience-centered, striving to offer spiritual inspiration to those in attendance, without requiring anything from them other than attendance.

Fourth, this is worship that offers *few sacramental acts*. The observance of holy communion or the Eucharist—so central to historic Catholic and Protestant liturgies—was omitted for obvious reasons: it is pokey and therefore is poor television material and, like its sacramental twin, baptism, is doctrinally divisive among the potential pool of viewers and attenders. Thus, both were eliminated. Historic reverential postures such as kneeling or raising one's hands were also eliminated as being potentially divisive. Lengthy readings from scripture or prayers of more than a sentence or two were likewise jettisoned. Though ostensibly representing mainline Protestantism, this worship eliminated several other staples of the worship practices of many of those churches, such as confessions of sin, recital of creeds, multiple readings from scripture, or responsive readings.

Perhaps less easy to detect is the fifth characteristic of *individualism*. The difficulty applies because the malady of individualism actually

pervades American society as a whole and Schuller's worship was notable
only in the degree to which it elevated it. Individualism in this context
means that the pitch in worship is consistently made to the "I" in the
audience, rather than to the "we" of the gathered assembly. Individualism
seeks to exalt the individual rather than to locate the individual within
community. It plays to "me" and to what "I" can obtain rather than
remind "me" of "us" and of our shared brokenness and responsibility for
one another. In this worship a viewer can even sit at home, never enter a
local church door, yet be aglow with spirituality—all by oneself.

A sixth characteristic is that this is *high-tech* worship. "Hour of
Power" worship utilized every cutting-edge technology known at the
time. Its television production quality was state-of-the-art, using equipment so costly and rapidly evolving that it was rented—and trucked
in each weekend—rather than purchased. The studio/Cathedral was
an architectural masterpiece of light and sound. After an acoustically-
embarrassing introductory concert by Metropolitan Opera diva Beverly
Sills (before the building was completed), the acoustics of the room were
consistently praised. The pipe organ was a marvel of its craft and perfectly pitched to the room. Long before most athletic stadiums featured
jumbotron screens, Schuller had one in use within the Crystal Cathedral,
using it to project hymn lyrics as well as a magnified image of the day's
performers and preacher.

Finally, this was *gate-way* worship. A next generation of worshipers, dubbed "Jesus Freaks," who cared not for cathedrals, choirs, pipe
organs, or clerical gowns, was already on the southern California beaches
in flip-flops singing guitar-chorded neo-pentecostal praise songs to the
Lord who'd saved them from drug addictions and promiscuous sex. But
for all their apparent difference from Schuller, this emerging, iconoclastic
crew was not stupid. They knew Schuller, and when they came to prominence, they followed his lead in all six of the identified characteristics
of "Hour of Power" worship—though infusing them with more overtly
evangelical theology.[27] By the early 70s their new-sound Christian music
was becoming such a commercial success that annual Dove Awards were

begun by Nashville recording executives and picked up by TV bosses who saw enough audience/market in the Awards program that they began televising the event nationally. At the same time other young viewers, coming from a more traditionally-churched orientation, also went to school on the success of the "Hour of Power" inspirational model of worship. Youth ministers like Bill Hybels in Chicago launched "seeker friendly" services for the unchurched and saw his concept mushroom into a megachurch (Willow Creek) and a national movement, a success that Schuller applauded and even showcased in his Successful Church Leadership Institutes.[28] Thus, even as Schuller's personal star began to dim, his worship philosophy informed the ministries of a rising generation who built upon Schuller's model of worship as inspiration.

Positives to be gained from a Possibility Thinker

Whatever criticisms may be leveled against the Schuller phenomenon, his positive contribution to America's religious life must not be forgotten. In an era when the institutional church was on the ropes Bob Schuller provided a weekly window into church experience that was affirming, encouraging, and yes, inspirational. His challenge to church leaders to discover fresh ways to reach the unreached was sorely needed. Moreover, unlike several of his televangelist cohort, Schuller actually established and led in the growth of a real congregation that had a profusion of vital educational and community service ministries—and he remained above the scandals of immoral or unethical behavior that marred many of them. Whatever deficiencies one may identify within his theology or methodologies, one can still admire his spirit and his timely witness to the uplifting power of faith. Even those of us who decry features of the worship model he popularized must applaud the masterful way in which he demonstrated that worship itself does not have to be conducted in funeral parlor black. In living color he modeled for us the vitality that should be a part of Christian worship.[29]

The point, however, still must be made

Nonetheless, some concluding observations about this understanding of worship are essential. Some of them, admittedly, have as much to do with the mixture of television and worship as with the confusion of worship with inspiration. Schuller, in fact, melded all this together—since every Sunday's services were televised, you could not worship at Crystal Cathedral without doing so as part of a TV audience. This fusion only deepens the dilemma faced today by evangelical congregations as they attempt to find their way through worship's Land of Confusion.

Consider the television-and-worship connection first. In 1985 Neil Postman, a professor of communication arts and science at NYU, published a disturbing assessment of the impact television was having on Americans. His conclusion was well-stated in his book's title: *Amusing Ourselves to Death: Public Discourse in the Age of Show Business.* Among the spheres of public discourse Postman analyzed was the phenomenon of televangelists who included, for his sampling, Oral Roberts, Jimmy Swaggart, Jerry Falwell, Jim Bakker, Pat Robertson, and Robert Schuller. (Schuller himself, as previously stated, would like to exempt himself from this grouping, but Postman did not do that.) After watching forty-two hours of the telecasts of this group, Postman concluded: "On television, religion, like everything else, is presented, quite simply and without apology, as an entertainment. Everything that makes religion an historic, profound and sacred human activity is stripped away; there is no ritual, no dogma, no tradition, no theology, and above all, no sense of spiritual transcendence. On these shows, the preacher is tops. God comes out as second banana."[30] Whatever one may make of that judgment, it must be coupled with Postman's ultimate worry, expressed in the final sentence of his discussion: "The danger is not that religion has become the content of television shows but that television shows may become the content of religion."[31]

This last concern—that television shows might become the content of religion—is a most fruitful one for exploration. This concern becomes of colossal importance once one places a premium upon the vertical-dialogical priority within Christian worship. If worship is about enabling this kind of God-ward action, then one needs to ask if television can facilitate it. My own conclusion is that it is extremely difficult, if not impossible, to do so. The accommodations that must be made to the medium of television are too many and too basic.

For one thing, the God of Christian revelation is a God of mystery, while television is a medium of clarity. TV doesn't do subtlety well. Christian theology, on the other hand, has always insisted on the subtlety, the faith nature of our religion; it has understood with the Apostle Paul, that our knowledge is "in part" (1 Corinthians 13:12)—that mystery pervades even our most cherished faith assertions. God, in other words, is not reducible to clichés and sound bytes. However, television craves such simplicities; it is at its best in delivering snappy certainties, not mystery. Therefore, those TV preachers who are most assured in their firm pronouncements come across well; those who remind us a God "who hides himself" (Isaiah 45:15) speak to dwindling audiences.

Also, Christian theology has always recognized that God is not in a hurry, that patience and "line upon line" forbearance are inherent in God's manner of dealing with humankind. The faith itself is drawn from revelatory events and encounters gleaned across thousands of years. But television, in contrary fashion, is in a hurry; it demands rapid delivery and constant movement. Although silence and meditative brooding have a revered place in Christianity's worship history, within the world of television silence and inaction are archenemies.

Thus it is that no commercially-successful televised worship service features the church's historic ritual actions. Baptism is too divisive or wordy; communion is far too slow. Likewise, congregational prayers are suspect—eavesdropping on intercessions for a needy world will bury one's Nielsen ratings in a nano-second. So essential and historic dialogical acts with the Eternal One must be edited. The 'slow" God of Christian revelation is a poor match for an impatient TV camera.

Moreover, the God of Christian revelation and worship is a jealous God—an assertion that is often and easily misunderstood. In essence, however, it means God doesn't like it when humans or human constructs presume to take God's place. God alone is ultimate, a foundational truth that worship is intended to underline for us in an emphatic manner. Even so, once the cameras start rolling, someone has to take the stage, and—assuming the invisible God of the Bible chooses not to respond to the camera's curtain call—the superstar preacher or gospel singer or megachurch ministry becomes, as Postman put it, "the top banana." The show no longer is really about God—it's about the performers.

This brief digression is sufficient to demonstrate that television may deliver "religion" or a "religious show" to a TV audience, but that it is a poor vehicle for communicating the communal act of Christian worship.[32] Supremely, it is the inability of television to create community out of dispersed and isolated viewers, that is, to make a congregation out of an audience, that exposes its weakness as a helpful worship aid. What TV can do well is to provide religious shows that one writer has blisteringly characterized as "a popular music concert or variety show with a sermonette."[33] However, if there is anything more to worship—as I claim there is—TV is incapable of transmitting it. What, in fact, is being offered is religious inspiration, or what Schuller would call pre-evangelism. It is an appetizer, an appetizer which, unfortunately, is so high in sugar content that the more nutritious meal of Christian worship can easily be passed up.

The larger issue here, however, is that when such an attractive dish is placed on a nation's table each weekend for decades, viewers cannot help but compare its sparkling professionalism with the more mundane religious services available at their local church. The difference between the polish of the televised package and the plainness of the parish church was both obvious and disappointing. The showmanship displayed by Schuller created a growing desire for pastors to sound more like Schuller and for the local church's worship to feel more like the "Hour of Power." Many parish clergy felt this dissatisfaction as failure on their part (regardless of their context or spiritual gifts) and younger ministers, seeking keys to rejuvenate churches and expand small flocks,

found Schuller's model most appealing—especially when the burgeon-
ing Church Growth movement insisted numerically-growing churches
all provided worship services that were welcoming, curb appeal events,
designed to speak to and attract the unchurched.

The tap-root error here, however, is that what is seen on television
is not holistic worship; it is made-for-TV pre-evangelism entertainment,
it is faith-based inspiration. What is seen on TV isn't even "real" church
as it must be encountered, "real" church with its history, its budgets, its
"little old ladies," its potluck suppers, its baggage, its anniversaries, its
funerals and baptisms, and its less-than-Schulleresque pastors. However,
in consumerist America, television's "virtual church" became the model
church and the worship ideal for thousands of pastors and millions of
church goers. Thus, Postman's fear that television shows might become
the content of religion became a fact in countless locales.

In one of his famous parables, the Danish writer Soren
Kierkegaard (1813-1855) suggested that Protestant worship had become
all theater—and that the play had been tragically miscast.[34] He said that
we have cast ourselves as being the audience, the patron-consumers who
take our seats in the sanctuary with the hope that we will be moved
by the performance of the clerical or musical professionals "on stage."
These worship leaders are presumably getting their cues and coaching
from the Resident within the prompter's box—God, and if they follow
God's directions well, we in turn will be moved and inspired by the performance. This set-up, though well known to Kierkegaard (and to us),
was faulty—then and now! He said what must become our practice was
for worshipers to realize that God is the audience and that we are the
actors on stage. We, not the paid professionals, are the performers, and
the leaders' task is to provide direction and feed us our lines occasionally
from their prompter's box.

Within such a reconfigured situation it is most obvious that worship becomes not a show or an event anyone attends with the purpose of
being inspired. No, in this recasting we go to weekly worship in order to
play our hearts out to God whose mercies have nourished and sometimes

even overwhelmed us. We go to remember and to say and sing "thank you." We go to join the great company of players throughout the ages who didn't go to *get* anything, but to *give* something: themselves.

Indeed, one of the complete disappointments within the worship-as-inspiration concept is that it is ultimately so selfish. It fosters the expectation that worship is supposed to inspire "me." Thus, an action meant to be about and for God becomes about and for "me." Charles Finney's model of worship as evangelism at least has the merit of displaying concern for the welfare of others' spiritual condition. Worship as inspiration, however, can't even claim that virtue.

To summarize: When the worship of God becomes a platform for anything other than worship, it becomes something less than worship. It becomes a rally, a show, a spectacle, or a production designed to impress or excite or inspire an audience. Not that inspiration is an evil; it is not, it only becomes so when it becomes the goal of a service of Christian worship. When this happens the horizontal usurps the vertical. Worship leaders become more performers than priests, and worshipers are demoted to consumers rather than honored and led as worshipers. Worship then becomes utilitarian and worshipers are deprived of the opportunity to be "lost in wonder, love, and praise" of God alone.

Notwithstanding all of this, I must close this discussion by repeating that worthy worship does have high inspirational potential. The crux here, as in the earlier discussion about evangelism, is whether the priority remains upon the worship of God or is shifted to "using" God as a means to an end. When God, in the grandness of the story of revelation and redemption is the subject and object of the gathering, how is it possible not to come away without being "bright with anticipation"—as I was during that Easter sunrise service (and have been countless times throughout my lifetime)? It is unimaginable to me that worship of the living God doesn't regularly yield a grand lifting of vision and life—even if it often involves, like Isaiah, a shattering and cauterizing "Woe is me!" component. That elevation, however, requires the focus to be kept, as it was in Isaiah's case, upon seeing "the Lord . . . high and lofty" (Isaiah 6:1ff), whose glory fills the whole earth.

EXCURSUS: 'SISTER ACT' AS WORSHIP MODEL

The amazing degree to which Christian worship has become thought of in entertainment categories may be seen in a plea issued by a noted professor of evangelism and missiology. He pleads with the church to accept "a challenge from Hollywood," noting that "even Hollywood seems to be challenging the church to forsake its cultural captivity, to identify with unchurched people and their struggles and their community, and to offer culturally-relevant indigenous worship and music that will actually *attract* unchurched secular people."[35]

He sees Hollywood's challenge in the 1992 movie *Sister Act*, starring Whoopi Goldberg and Maggie Smith. In this movie, Goldberg plays the role of a nightclub performer who as a witness to a murder is placed under witness protection in a convent. There she is disguised as a Roman Catholic nun and is under the supervision of the Mother Superior, played by Maggie Smith. When the convent's choir is placed in Goldberg's charge she leads the nuns to sing the music for mass in the Las Vegas show-style she knows best—an alteration that proves attractive to the parish's people but appalling to the Mother Superior. The movie's "most important moment," according to the missiologist, occurs after the mass in which Whoopi Goldberg has led the choir to sing a pop love-song (with God being "my guy") in show-biz style. She is immediately confronted by Smith.

> **Smith to Goldberg**: "Boogie Woogie on the piano! What were you thinking?"
>
> **Goldberg**: "I was thinking more like Vegas; you know, get some butts in the seats."
>
> **Smith**: "And what next? Popcorn? Curtain calls? This is not a theater or a casino!"
>
> **Goldberg**: "Yeah, but that's the problem see. People like going to theaters, and they like going to casinos. But they don't like coming to church. Why? Because it's a

drag. But we could change all that see. We could pack this joint!"

Smith: "Through blasphemy? You have corrupted the entire choir!"

The parish priest (overhearing this exchange, enters the room and says to Smith): "Reverend Mother, I just wanted to congratulate you. I haven't enjoyed mass this much in years. What a marvelous program—innovative, inspiring—you are to be commended. I can't wait until next Sunday when the choir performs again. Did you see the people walk right in from the street? That music, that heavenly music! Reverend Mother, it called to them."

Smith: "It . . . it did?"

The professor says that in this exchange the Reverend Mother is "beginning to get in touch with the discovery that could transform thousands of congregations." The discovery he refers to apparently is that the worship of the Church ought to be more accessible to the culture in which the church is located—a principle with which I completely agree. But this Hollywood example provides an extremely poor illustration of this needed cultural adaptation. It says that the way to do this is by adopting Hollywood's entertainment model "to put butts in the seats" and thereby "pack this joint."

This, however, is a strategy many churches have, in good faith, adopted. But in doing so they have enrolled Christian worship as a competitor with the entertainment industry, and therein have tasked themselves to produce, as the parish priest calls it, "a marvelous program—innovative, inspiring" every Sunday, with limited budget and volunteer labor.

In invoking this Hollywood challenge no recognition is made of the possibility that worship might be about something other than an attractive program of toe-tapping inspiration or that only megachurches can successfully staff or fund such an approach. Count the number of times show business terms and expectations appear in the dialogue above; its "challenge" may more fairly be termed a temptation to "think more like Vegas" than Calvary. *Sister Act* as a movie is a delightful spoof that rightly calls into question the isolationist mindset strangling too many churches; but as a model for better worship it is seriously flawed.

3. Worship as "Experiencing"

Pentecostalism and the Influence of Feelings

No discussion of today's evangelical worship scene can ignore one more powerful shaper of it. In a measure it is an extension of the previous two, yet it has a distinctive history and character to it that requires a separate consideration as a third model influencing today's evangelical worship. For lack of a better term I call this third influential stream the confusion of worship with "experiencing."

In its most familiar form "experiencing" means "experiencing God," and in its Sunday clothes "experiencing" expects worship to offer just that: an experience of God. Presbyterian Robb Redman says that "experiencing God in worship is the key issue confronting Protestants," and suggests that the question 'Will we experience God here?' is not a [worship] question mainline Protestants usually ask of themselves."[36] Culture-savvy Leonard Sweet insists that anyone who wishes to connect with a postmodern culture—meaning anyone who wishes to be relevant today and tomorrow—must offer experience-rich worship since postmoderns "are hungry for experiences, especially experiences of God."[37] While the counsel of these two must be heard appreciatively, I will nonetheless argue that "experiencing" is a questionable goal for worship. It is a third confusion, which, like evangelism and inspiration, too easily diverts us from the vertical-dialogical priority of true worship.

To be sure, the desire for worship to be more than an exercise in cold religiosity is as valid and ancient as it is deep. The psalmists leave us in no doubt that the worship they commend is worship that stirs the peoples' soul. The primary Protestant reformer, Martin Luther, though he had some shocking denunciations of and reprisals against the "enthusiasts" of his day, nonetheless was no stranger to religious experience, having had his own defining religious moments during a lightning storm, at the altar table, and even on the commode![38] John Wesley's "strangely warmed heart" is only one of countless other exemplary testimonies to the reality of God becoming real through experience. Even Jonathan Edwards, the stern Puritan intellectual par excellence, saw the inadequacy of mental assent alone and became a champion and interpreter of "religious affections." Some of the repercussions and aberrations of his ideas were central to the 1827 New Light/Old Light summit at New Lebanon. Today any discussion of evangelicalism would have to include terms such as "experience," "heartfelt," and "zeal" as characteristics of the evangelical orientation. So I am not attempting to deny this experiential element within the evangelical tradition as we know and practice it. Nor am I ignorant of the excellent work of scholars such as Kenneth Leech, whose theologically rich 1985 book *Experiencing God* sought to respond to "the loss of any sense of a living experience of God,"[39] especially in Leech's British context.

However, it is one thing to be given experiences as a serendipitous gift from God, and it is a very different thing to understand them to be an essential criterion of worship.[40] To say it differently, to receive such "sweet meats," as Wesley called them, is one thing, but it is a far different thing to assume they are to be every Sunday's entrée. Yet this expectation has now become a virtual demand, meaning that worship planners and leaders must labor under the unwritten-but-real mandate to "create powerful God experiences" Sunday after Sunday for their congregations.[41]

This expectation is a logical extension of Schuller's consistent weekly offerings of winsome optimism—but now the product is no longer Schuller's package of self-esteem and inspiration. Now the product is the Ultimate Inspiration, it is no less than God! This mandate means worship planners and leaders are charged to engage in a weekly "all-stops out" effort to produce the Real Deal—or worshipers will travel down the freeway to another vendor whose "God" arrives on time each week in a consistently-thrilling manner.

However, rather than present a critique without specifics, a third case study can help us see the real difficulties that follow when worship is closely identified with "experiencing." In this instance there can be no question that Pentecostalism has been the dominant player on the field—at least in the last half of the twentieth century. So let's look at it.

In doing so, however, I need to repeat the proviso made earlier about the previous models. Persons or movements are not studied here in order to vilify anyone, but to see the problems as well as the contributions they brought. Accordingly, although Pentecostalism is the case study for this model of worship, Pentecostalism must also be given great credit for restoring the missing vertical-dialogical priority to evangelical worship, and not to evangelicals only; every Christian worship tradition has felt its enlivening impress either as threat or blessing. Therefore it must be applauded and thanked for having powerfully addressed a lamentable deficit. Nonetheless, I have qualms about the way in which Pentecostalism has done so and about the way others have appropriated its "experiencing" tradition of worship. Like every historical phenomenon, Pentecostalism's correctives have also birthed perplexities. We need to understand both.

The 'experiencing' phenomenon of Pentecostalism

Historians may very well record the twentieth century as being the Pentecostal century of Church history. Within those ten decades Pentecostalism grew from non-existence to become a major global influence, especially with regard to worship practices. Pentecostalism, in its multiple forms, has modeled and taught an "experiencing" form of worship that's found deep resonance around the world.

By most accountings Pentecostalism now includes at least one-fourth to one-third of all the world's Christians. A survey conducted in 2006 by the Pew Forum on Religion in Public Life, revealed that twenty-three percent of America's Christians were within this column. Its influence is even greater in other parts of the world. Fifty-six percent of Kenya's Christians are Pentecostals of some form. In Brazil the number is forty-nine percent, and in Guatemala it is sixty percent. The number crunchers within missionary organizations say that while most missionary efforts are at a statistical stand-still, Pentecostals continue to attract converts in astounding numbers—some estimates yielding as many as 35,000 converts per day! Arguably ninety percent of America's television preachers represent some form of Pentecostalism, e.g., Benny Hinn, Joyce Meyers, Creflo Dollar, Fred Price, T.D. Jakes, Joel Osteen, Kenneth Copeland, et al. Additionally, the billion dollar Contemporary Christian Music industry, so influential in many evangelical worship venues, is a child of and dominated by artists from the Pentecostal tradition.

"We're not in Kansas (only) anymore"

The beginning of Pentecostalism as an identifiable ongoing movement may be traced to a prayer service on New Year's Eve of 1900 in a small Bible college in Topeka, Kansas. As a part of that service Charles Parham, a former Methodist pastor and holiness teacher, laid hands on and prayed for one of his students, Agnes Ozman. "I had scarcely completed three dozen sentences when a glory fell upon her," he later wrote; "a halo seemed to surround her head and face, and she began speaking the Chinese language and was unable to speak English for three days." Parham and his followers were certain they had witnessed a repetition of the miracle of the gift of 'tongues' reported in the second chapter of the Book of Acts. As they reassembled the following day it didn't escape their attention that this was the first day of a new century. For a group predisposed to see divine signs and wonders, the timing of Miss Ozman's experience was fraught with significance. Later voices would claim Parham's act was "the touch felt round the world," but at that moment the tiny Topeka group was voiceless before the larger world and impotent before that world's predisposition to laugh disdainfully at the beliefs and deeds of religious "nuts."

However, a scant six years later these "nuts" gained a west coast microphone that had a global reach. Another of Parham's students, an African-American preacher named William Seymour, had by April of 1906 attracted several hundred black followers to a residence on North Bonnie Brae Street in downtown Los Angeles, California. A revival then broke out that provided more unusual manifestations of spiritual presence than those in Topeka. One evening ecstatic worshipers even spilled out onto the street speaking in tongues, at which point summoned police arrived and arrested a sizeable number of them on a 72-hour psychiatric hold. The loss of the incarcerated brothers and sisters proved less bothersome to the faithful than the fact that the same night the porch of the Bonnie Brae residence collapsed under the weight of many jubilant dancers-in-the-Spirit. Seymour and his followers had to relocate their meetings to a former AME church building on nearby Azusa Street. A week later the Los Angeles newspaper could ignore the story no longer and, on April 18, it published an article, "Weird Babble of Tongues" and, in the journalistic style of the day, this title was followed by a three bullet-point summary of the story: "New sect of lunatics is breaking loose," "Wild scene last night on Azusa St.," and "Gurgle of wordless talk by sister." The unimpressed reporter went on to declare that "the night [was] made hideous by the howlings of the worshipers."

R.G. Robins provides another description of the Azusa Street services in his excellent historical study, *Pentecostalism in America*. He reports that these earliest services bore three characteristics. The first two of these were intertwined: *spontaneity* and *emotional intensity*. The conviction was that "if the Holy Spirit were truly in charge . . . worship would give no visible sign of human orchestration," but abundant human participation would be evident. And indeed it was: "boisterous and simultaneous prayer, fervent testimony, rituals of healing, outbursts of holy delirium like 'shouting' or 'dancing in the Spirit,' and the trancelike experience of being 'slain in the Spirit.'" Others "might play musical instruments under the power of the Holy Ghost or break forth in synchronized melodies known as the heavenly chorus." There was "no regular order, and yet perfect order," according to one reporter, who judged the free flow of worship to be a proof of God's presence.

A third characteristic of Azusa Street worship Robins termed *"divine surprise"* and by it he refers to the egalitarianism present specifically in the earliest days of the movement. Worshipers as old as one hundred and as young as seven preached impromptu sermons. Frank Bartleman, an evangelist and sometime-reporter, reported that at Azusa Street, "no one knew what might be coming . . . the Lord was liable to burst through any one," regardless of race, class, gender, age, or occupation, "from the back seat or from the front. It made no difference." Still, this radical openness wasn't universal even in the earliest days, according to Robins and "soon weakened in the face of pragmatic concerns for efficiency and order. Nevertheless, the remembered or imagined past cast a long shadow . . . "[42]

The negative publicity coming from these explosive services did not in the least deter the Azusa Street crowds. They continued to come in astounding numbers and to depart in wet-eyed wonder. And, if their experience on Azusa Street did not assure them that this phenomenon was of God, a tragedy then unfolding in San Francisco was a sign from God none of them overlooked. For the very day the Los Angeles newspaper reported the Azusa Street revival—April 18, 1906—San Francisco suffered its historic 8.3 Richter scale earthquake, destroying 514 city blocks and taking more than 700 lives. Miraculously, as all the Azusa Street faithful knew, two days previously one of their number had prophesied that God was about to cause a mighty shaking in San Francisco. For them, such prophecy and "shaking" were mutually-corroborating evidences of a fearsome work of God afoot.

The Azusa Street revival continued seven days a week for almost three years, with hundreds of visitors from across the nation coming to sample its electricity and departing with no small amperage, catapulting a derided, back-street ensemble onto the national and eventually the global religious stage. On the 100th anniversary of the Azusa Street revival in 2006 an article in the *Los Angeles Times* (the successor publication of the one that had scoffed at the Azusa St. revival) offered this sadder-but-wiser reassessment: "Pentecostalism may surpass the movie business as being Los Angeles' most influential export."[43]

"He touched me . . . something happened, and now I know"

Within Pentecostal thought "experiencing God" is the ultimate good. Feeling one's religion, and being touched and filled with the Spirit are baseline concerns. This concern, as the previous sections of this book document, surely isn't unique. The distinction in Pentecostalism arises only from the theology informing it and the ultimacy that it places upon an affectively-experienced work of the Holy Spirit.

In classical Christian thought, the Holy Spirit of God is imparted to the individual at the time of baptism or conversion. In distinction, Pentecostals insist there is a subsequent baptism of the Holy Spirit. In their thought the presence of the Holy Spirit granted via baptism or conversion is but an introductory step; what is essential and available is a second impartation of the Holy Spirit. Only when the believer experiences this Spirit baptism is he or she really Spirit-filled, only then is there full assurance and access to God's abundance. As expressed in an early and beloved refrain from a Gaither Vocal Band song (and later canonized by Elvis Presley's recording of it): "He touched me, O He touched me! And oh, the joy that floods my soul; something happened and now I know! He touched me and made me whole."

Also, in classical Pentecostal doctrine, the sure and certain evidence of this second work is when one speaks in tongues. Other manifestations of the Spirit may also be experienced, such as the gift of prophecy, words of knowledge, or healing, etc., but these are subsequent to the certain evidence shown in speaking in tongues. Among the many Pentecostal groups that have emerged in the past century there are those that downplay the significance of tongues as the certain evidence.

Nonetheless, among Pentecostals there is an unbudging belief in a second work of grace, a baptism of the Spirit that must be sought if the individual is to experience all God desires to give. Once this second-work is experienced, the individual will be introduced to spiritual realities unknown to the merely water-baptized; they will experience the power of "the full gospel."

Strangers to this tradition often ask, 'Where do they get these ideas?' Well, not even the most strident opponent of Pentecostalism can erase the reports of speaking in tongues found in the New Testament books of Acts and 1st Corinthians (albeit even classical Pentecostals now agree that the tongues are not foreign languages such as Parham mistakenly thought Miss Ozman was speaking). So, speaking in tongues—however one interprets this phenomenon—is within the New Testament portrait of the early Church.

As for the two-stage bestowal of the Holy Spirit, it turns out that one of the primary sources is none other than John Wesley, the founder of Methodism. In Wesley's writings on Christian sanctification there is a strain of teaching regarding a second experience of God's Spirit that introduces believers to a deeper dimension of personal holiness. Wesley did not, however, link this to speaking in tongues or the like; his thought remained focused upon the growth of Christlikeness in the believer. Nonetheless, his two-step suggestion unlocked a theological door which was pushed wide open by some who followed him. (On the American frontier, this open door to the work of the Holy Spirit led to some of the very unconventional and emotion-laden actions displayed in Finney's revivals and, of course, in later Pentecostalism.)

Those who appropriated Wesley's hint of a higher plane of spirituality included many of nineteenth-century America's social reformers, intent as they were with infusing holiness into the fabric of the nation. Witness the number of utopian-minded groups and social experiments that appear in that century: the previously mentioned Shakers, the Oneida Community, the Salvation Army, the abolitionists which Finney championed, and still others who fused bodily health and healing with the broader yearning for the end of the domination of sin, death, and the devil. All of these seekers, however, understood that such dramatic reversals would come as much by the Spirit of God as by their human efforts. The Pentecostalists therefore easily discerned in Asuza Street's stunning twentieth-century-opening events, the dawning of this yearned-for new era. Indeed, could Christ's second coming be long delayed now? To the Pentecostal mind, the answer was a resounding "No!"

Thus, Pentecostalism united many desires for a spiritual "more" and did so by means of offering palpable evidence of miraculous power, religious ecstasy, bodily healing, and the hope of a world reborn—soon. It was a potent formula, especially to the materially dispossessed, the poor of the United States in the 1920s and 1930s—and subsequently among similar populations throughout the entire world.

The Charismatics and the Third Wave

For some thirty years the movement remained a backstreet, black folks' and poor white folks' religious expression, mostly ignored or condescendingly smiled at by the established denominations and religious hierarchies. But a strange thing happened in this nation on its way to the sixties. Black America began to assert itself. A rejection of authority and revered institutions flourished across all races and especially among the young—"Don't trust anyone over thirty!" became a watchword. Prudery gave way to expressivity—"Let it all hang out!" became a way of life. "Country" became cool, and Elvis and rockabilly music became king. And in its wake, shocked mainliners awakened to discover that Pentecostals were everywhere!

By the sixties, however, Pentecostalism itself had begun to undergo change. Out in its California birthplace, the change was surfacing in a manner so distinct that it merited a separate label: the Charismatic movement. It began first among "Jesus Freaks," whose drug-saturated life-style required a high-octane conversion, and then among less-desperate Episcopalians, showcased by a priest in Van Nuys who declared he'd received the second blessing. These neo-Pentecostal Charismatics were less insistent upon the necessity of speaking in tongues as evidence of the reception of the Holy Spirit's fullness, and they also saw no need to continue the plain dress, tight hairbuns, and even tighter morality of the holiness roots of their Pentecostal forebears. Many of them established new churches that featured worship services that blended traditional evangelical elements with Pentecostal fervor and stylings. However, many other Charismatics migrated into or returned to existing Protestant and Roman Catholic churches, yearning to renew them with their new-found experience, but often as not splitting rather than renewing them—this was especially so among the Protestant congregations. It was an unsettling, divisive era for many evangelical churches as they struggled to handle the Charismatic passion for "experiencing God."

More recently, Pentecostalism has seen a "third wave" arise, an ingress of persons of all socio-economic strata and education, many of them disenchanted with the culture of modernity and its messianic claims for rationality, science, and technology. These expatriates find in "third wave" churches an undiluted spirituality that bypasses the obstacles of modernity.[44]

A principal expression of this spirituality is in the distinctive music of these and the Charismatic churches, a type of music that became known as Contemporary Christian Music and which became enormously popular especially among younger evangelical worshipers who had little if any knowledge of or interest in its Pentecostal theological rootage. They simply found the music compelling.[45]

"Experiencing" in Praise & Worship format

Because Pentecostalism has become such a diverse and universal presence within Christianity, and because (at least theoretically) every Pentecostal service's worship order is left open to rearrangement according to the movement of the Spirit within it, it is impossible to offer a one-size-fits-all characterization of its worship patterns. However, since the majority of Americans will most likely encounter Pentecostalism in the worship form followed in neo-Pentecostal Charismatic and "Third Wave" churches (or those intimating them), their virtually standardized form will be illustrative. This form of worship is usually called "Praise and Worship," and it is this form that many evangelical churches have appropriated and adapted under the general label of "contemporary worship."

The term "contemporary worship" is most unfortunate in at least two respects. First, its introduction created unnecessary resentment by the implication that other ways of worshiping were now no longer contemporary, having been rendered archival and irrelevant by the arrival of the new. Second, "contemporary" masked the more substantive issue of the neo-Pentecostal origin of this way of worship. Consequently, when it was introduced into churches that had theological moorings in non-Pentecostal traditions, the reaction was understandably sharp and critical—an expression of the initial confusion created by Pentecostalism.

When one explores the "Praise & Worship" (hereafter referred to as P&W) tradition,[46] it quickly becomes apparent that *a unique differentiation of worship* is operative within it. Specifically, the P&W tradition does not understand the entire congregational meeting time to be worship. Instead, it understands worship to be only that portion of the meeting in which God is praised and believer's emotive expressions of love for God are offered. In Sunday-by-Sunday practice, this means "worship" is understood as the musically-driven (and typically, the first) portion of the congregation's meeting time. All other historic worship acts (e.g., the sermon, monetary offering, intercessory prayer, communion) are removed from worship, per se, and conducted at a later time during the meeting.

This identification of worship as only one portion of the meeting time leads to the creation of *a new three-part order* for the congregation's gatherings: first, the worship time; second, the teaching time ("teaching" is often preferred over the historic designation of "sermon"); and finally, the ministry time (prayer, one-on-one expressions of care).[47] In effect, within the P&W tradition these are three discrete "times" within the longer meeting time with three very different foci and moods and with little attempt typically made to orchestrate these parts into a unity or to achieve a sense of drama or flow to the whole. To summarize, P&W functions with a very high value given to music, so much so that worship is nominally restricted to the musical component of the service alone. All other historic worship acts are declassified as worship acts, per se. These are significant shifts and represent a clear departure from previous norms. But departure from historical precedents is not an evident concern for practitioners of P&W.

Indeed, within the literature of the P&W movement there is little evidence that historical continuity or tradition is to be valued greatly. Judson Cornwall, an early and respected patriarch for the P&W movement, asserts that "all religious heritages that were birthed in revival have experienced days and even years of vital worship," and then laments that "all too frequently it is the doctrine rather than the experience that is passed on to succeeding generations." Thus, it is imperative for these traditions to be open to new means of experiencing the Spirit "for worship is always a NOW activity."[48] Bob Sorge, a popular conference leader and writer within the P&W movement, reveals a similar anti-historical tilt when he contrasts the shocking worship of the sinful woman who washed the feet of Jesus with her tears, hair, and costly perfume ("not following the conventional forms of worship") with the behavior of the Pharisees who criticized her actions. He says the Pharisees "could represent a non-worshipping church—perhaps a church that takes greater pleasure in its historical roots than in its expression of worship."[49] Darlene Zschech— composer, author, noted recording artist from the Australian Hillsong Church, and a leader of this tradition—offers a variation on the same theme when she urges worship leaders to "build a culture that embraces the new" and, citing Isaiah 42:10 (sing new songs), Isaiah 62:2 (called by a new name), and Ezekial 11:19 (put a new spirit in them) she pleads with them to prize the new: "new songs, new day, new start, new hope, new mercy, new possibilities, new ideas, new ways, new people, God says 'new heaven and a new earth,' 'new covenant,' 'new self,' 'new heart,' 'new command,' 'new creation,' . . . new, new, new!"[50]

Here is a passion to elevate the latter-day, fresh work of the Spirit rather than the Spirit's cumulative work as expressed especially in older patterns of worship. This concern is in keeping with Pentecostalism's historic ties to a belief in an imminent second coming of Christ. In their view we are living in history's last moments and the ecstasy of the soon-to-be-raptured Bride of Christ has little need for a backward glance. Historical continuity and tradition are therefore of no deep importance; readiness and participation in the new and imminent are the greater good. Curiously, however, Cornwall is not reluctant to point to church history as an endorser of some of P&W's worship actions. He contends that, "while it may be necessary to seek out [this] history in a used book store, *uncensored* church history records singing, dancing, shouting, weeping, and even glossolalia as a normal part of the response of the founders of our Christian heritages."[51] Countless church historians might wish to refute the sweeping nature of Cornwell's claim but the intensity of his belief is irrefutable.

It is fitting that Cornwall's itemization of the components of worship names singing first, since within the P&W tradition *music and song become the dominant expression of worship.* Like its Pentecostal parent, P&W places enormous significance upon praise—especially musical praise.[52] Calvin Johansson, professor of church music at Evangel College, an Assemblies of God school, explains that "the aim of worship" in historic Pentecostal worship "was the passionate arousal of feeling" in order to create "the right atmosphere for the exercise of [the *charismata*]," and that key to this was "emotion-driven participation. Music was boisterous, physically stimulating, emotionalistic, highly repetitious, and generally accompanied by hand-clapping."[53] This understanding is extended into P&W services as well.

A prized, key biblical text in this regard is Psalm 22:3, which, in the New American Standard Bible, says "God is enthroned on the praises of Israel." Sorge explains that this means God loves our praise and "is so pleased with our praise that he literally surrounds himself with and bathes in our praise"[54] and that when such praise is offered, "the Holy

Spirit begins to stir our hearts, and we become more conscious of God's presence."[55] He links this high estimate of the significance of praise with statements in Isaiah 60:18 and Psalm 87:2 to suggest that through our praise the gates of heaven are opened and full interchange between God and the "praisers" is made possible. Thus, praise is the key to heaven. In some expressions of P&W this idea is recast as worship being a praise-led processional of the people of God from the outskirts into the Temple and its inner courts and finally into the Holy of Holies, God's own throne room. Musical praise provides the vanguard and the authorizing key for this advance from the world's periphery to the center of God's dwelling place.

Although in P&W services praise may be expressed in multiple ways, for example through the lifting and clapping of hands, playing musical instruments, standing, kneeling, prostration, or dancing, it's clear that singing and song are supreme. As Sorge puts it, when we simply say "Allelulia, Alleluia, Alleluia!" it doesn't do much for any of us, but when we pair these words of praise with great melody "our hearts are lifted to the Lord, and our spirits are moved in the presence of God." This phenomenon is an "ultra-rational experience in which one plus one equals three, in which words plus music equal 'more' than just words and music."[56] Although he insists that "worship is not a musical activity but a function of the heart,"[57] this is a distinction that is lost in actual practice. The P&W tradition, like its Pentecostal parent, can't disassociate worship from music. In previous times and other settings its "worship leaders" would have been called "ministers of music" or "choir directors." The baseline for a P&W worship leader continues to be her or his ability to facilitate the peoples' praise and worship through music. This explains why more than half of Sorge's 287-page "practical guide" to P&W provides guidance for music leaders. Music is unquestionably the signature of the P&W tradition.

This music explosion was greatly aided by the emerging technologies of the period. The sheer volume of "new" songs emerging from the P&W movement made it impossible for any bound hymnal to keep pace. So, overhead projectors, which teachers had been putting to good use in classrooms for the previous two decades, were introduced to worship. Simply by projecting the lyrics of a new praise song on a wall or screen worshipers were able to sing it—without any need for hymnals. Their hands were also free to be raised in praise. Of course, the loss in this exchange was the theological and devotional treasure within the hymnals, but at the time the gain seemed to far outweigh the loss.[58] With each passing year the ever-expanding computer and internet capabilities made inter-church sharing of new songs and visual aids for worship a commonplace. Emerging from that same interconnectivity, a greater commonality in the worship time began to be observable.

In the majority of services, the opening praise songs call for a wide span of notes, and they are sung with great volume, vigorous rhythms, and rapid tempos. They'll be led by a "praise team" (a small ensemble of enthusiastic, encouraging singers spread across the stage, each with a standing floor microphone) and will be accompanied by a "praise band"[59] with percussion and electronic keyboard instruments and various kinds of guitars. These musicians' intent is to elicit praise—excited, full-throated praise of God. Those in attendance will be expected to stand (sitting is too passive a posture, unless physically impaired), lift hands, dance, sing, shout, or engage in other physical expressions of God-directed praise during the course of this twenty to forty-plus minutes of the service. Often the intensity of the praise will increase with each passing minute.

But at some point the musicians, led by the "worship leader" or "worship pastor," will transition from praise music to worship music. The lyrics of the songs will shift from jubilant "Alleluias" to more intimate expressions of personal love for God, themes of adoration and submission will appear, the tempo of the songs will slow, the volume of the singing will subside, and the range of notes being sung will narrow. "Soft" music may be heard as worshipers kneel, prostrate themselves, speak in tongues, or weep in ecstasy. This is the Holy of Holies moment for the P&W tradition, the moment when believers have been led through the gates of praise into the presence of God; and there they worship God.[60] Only after this worship time has been sufficiently honored will the congregation recompose itself for the next event of the service, the teaching time. And, once again, this transition is facilitated by the musicians.

"Good meat makes its own gravy"

Appreciation has already been expressed for the way in which Pentecostalism has highlighted worship's vertical-dialogical nature. Though many quarters of Christendom have received it as an unwanted noisy child, this powerful antidote to dead formalism and lethargic congregational participation has been, on balance, a blessing to the Church. Even the most stately of worship traditions has felt its impress. However, its strong emphasis on "experiencing" is ultimately an unsatisfactory answer to the question of worship's meaning. Confusions enter here, even as they do with revivalism and inspiration. More specifically, the confusions within Pentecostalism's Praise & Worship expression, are both terminological and foundational.

The first terminological matter concerns the restriction of a "worship" service to just the musically-driven "praise and worship" portion of the meeting. This is a shrinking of the word's meaning that finds no precedent within Christian history and can be sustained only by a strained interpretation of select scriptures. This constricted understanding is understandable given the Pentecostal origins of P&W, but it does raise significant questions.

One question concerns the severing of the hearing and exposition of the Bible from worship, as P&W has redefined worship. Attention to the words of scripture is delayed and relocated to another segment of the gathering, a segment not classified as "worship." This relocation is significant because it suggests that "worship" is primarily the believer's words addressed to God rather than listening to God's word addressed to us. Minimal listening and receptive discipline is expected during P&W "worship" because in the actual moments of its "worship" the primary speaker is the worshiper, not God. To the degree that this is ever so, the dialogical pole of worship's vertical-dialogical nature is jeopardized.[61]

In that same vein, one wonders if this narrowed definition of worship does not teach believers that worship is loving God with only one's heart (affections), rather with the more holistic "heart, *mind*, soul, and strength" commended by scripture. Rational reflection upon scripture is surely as essential to true worship as is cathartic expressions of adoration. This objection may be met, of course, by saying the scriptures are not omitted, they are simply relocated and encountered in a later portion of the meeting. But the removal of the designation of "worship" from all acts of worship except praise effectively weds worship only to the expressive dimension of worship. Such jiggering with the historic meaning of the word worship creates confusion, if not spiritual error.

A second consequence of this restrictive definition of worship is that worship, as so defined and practiced, is wholly dependent upon music. Although music in some form has almost always been a component of Christian worship, in this tradition music is absolutely essential. Music and worship are so intertwined in the P&W community that they are unwittingly spoken of as one entity. It is customary, for instance, to hear P&W worship leaders speak of the "worship set" ("set" likely being a term borrowed from the world of secular bands,[62] but here meaning the list of songs to be sung during the worship time) as a synonym for worship itself. While this unification slides by unnoticed in today's musically-saturated society, it presents significant questions from the standpoint of Christian worship.

As omnipresent as music has been within the history of worship, music and worship ought not be considered as an indissoluble unity. Worship is more than music. (In fairness, worship is also more than preaching and liturgy, etc.) To be sure, worship without music would be greatly diminished, but it would be possible. After all, there are Christians among us, notably The Society of Friends, or Quakers, who worship in silence and do so with great effect. Music aids our worship, beautifies our worship, and certainly facilitates our worship, but music is not the same thing as worship. An over-reliance upon music, whether composed by J.S. Bach or Paul Baloche, poses a profound challenge to the larger significance of worship.

Throughout Christian history, music has frequently been a source of contention within worship. As the next chapter will show, early Christians were actually very wary of the charms of music and accordingly placed clear restrictions upon its use in worship. Later Christians often found the concerns of the early Church justifiable and prudent. In the fourth century St. Augustine, being very aware from his earlier days of philandering of the seductive power within music, as well as the power of hymns he'd heard in Milan, struggled with the appropriateness of its use in worship.[63] The Roman Catholic Church of the sixteenth century, in recognition that its worship music had become too ornate and attention-attracting, reined it in and insisted upon simpler musical forms. Thoughtful persons like John Calvin found music to be a double-edged sword and, in Calvin's case, permitted only versified psalm-texts to be sung *a capella* to tunes that had been carefully selected for their appropriateness in worship. His contemporary, reformer Ulrich Zwingli, a most competent musician himself, actually banned music of any kind from worship, finding it a reminder and a temptation of the flesh. Extreme? Yes, but these are only the more prominent expressions of the controversy over the extent, the kind, and even the presence of music within worship that continues to this day. This long song of conflict ought to warn us—unless we choose to turn a deaf ear to it—that music is a glorious gift that must be used wisely. Consequently, when music becomes the driver of an entire tradition's worship, legitimate caution signs are appropriate. In the longer history of Christian worship, music has typically been called a "servant of the Church," and a "humble handmaid of the liturgy," never its ruler. As Joseph Gelineau says, "For the handmaid to become the absolute mistress is a phenomenon only of recent times."[64]

Turning now to foundational questions, one must ask if this tradition's praise priority is fully justified. The question arises first from the seeming struggle to distinguish between praise and worship. Sorge, for instance, is insistent that the two are "mutually cooperative activities and are frequently very similar in the way they are outwardly expressed, but they are not one and the same. Each has its own nature and purpose."[65] But the offered distinctions do not offer much help, as the following statement shows:

> Praise is largely horizontal in its purpose, while worship is primarily a vertical interaction. Much happens on a horizontal level when we praise; we speak to one another, and declare his praise before each other. But worship is more private and is much more preoccupied with the Godhead. Praise does have some vertical functions, and worship has some horizontal elements, but these are not their primary directions.[66]

But when praise is said to be "largely horizontal," this seems to say that it isn't really expressed as a Godward action after all, but is more of a witness to others about God. If this is so, then the very vertical-dialogical priority that is thought to be P&W's genius is clouded.

A related question also arises from the use of praise as a functional synonym for worship. This is a marriage that wasn't made in heaven. For worship is infinitely more than praise. If we had nothing more than the psalter of Israel to be our teacher, we would note that although praise is in the forefront, lament also has a prominent place in worship. Laments of both individual and national character can be found on virtually every page of Israel's "worship book." Through these laments Israel was schooled in honest expression before God, encouraged to seek God's face through the darkest as well as the brightest of her moments. Weeping her rage as well as shouting her joy she made it through. African-American spirituals continued this same tradition with soul-stirring laments, and one may well wonder if "the stony road that was trod" would ever have been survived without a melodic means to moan her plight before God—in worship. Pastorally, I must add that some of the most profound expressions of praise I've ever witnessed came from believers who were so stricken by life's blows that they could barely speak. Yet, they brought their broken hearts to the time of worship. For them to have shouted for joy in that hour would have been dishonest. But their presence, and the bruised-faith lament which their silent presence spoke, rattled the rafters of the meeting place with the sound of believing praise.

Finally, it must be asked if the "God" dimension of "experiencing God" gets lost in P&W's quest of "experiencing." When goosebumps are what a worship leader feels obliged to deliver on Sundays, it is very understandable if that leader becomes as attuned, if not more so, to psychology than to theology, perhaps more sensitive to the emotional flow and "kick" of a certain "worship set" than to the content of the songs themselves. The co-pastors of a church that used this format for years speak of the *tyranny of the sincere* that lurks as its persistent danger. As they put it:

> Since our worship services aren't centered on content that is true regardless of our engagement, we make up for this by demonstrating that we "really, really" mean what we are singing. This can be a heavy burden not only for the worshiper, but also for the worship leader. Nobody can worship with that intensity every week. The danger of feigned sincerity becomes very high.[67]

It must quickly be admitted that this is not unique to the P&W tradition. Musicians within the revivalist tradition have long faced the expectation to deliver a rousing choral anthem or dramatic solo—with great feeling!—just before the preacher steps to the pulpit. The P&W tradition doesn't challenge this expectation of a musically-induced "high," it simply extends it. The question must be raised once again—is this about God or about generating experience, about seeking God's face or about our feelings?[68]

Keith Getty is a composer and performer well-known within the P&W tradition, and is also one who recognizes the dangers lurking here. In an interview for Southern Baptist Theological Seminary's alumni magazine, he says:

> The modern interpretation of worship music is, for the most part, pithy reflections of what God is doing. If we go back to the Psalms as the biblical songbook and look at the characteristics of the God of the Bible, I doubt if even twenty percent of the Psalms even mention that aspect . . . which is a frightening thing.
>
> What has happened is, by [a] very slight change of vocabulary, having encountered God has become synonymous with a quiver of your liver when you sit in a worship service. The flip side of that is if for some reason people don't get that feeling, then they didn't meet with God. In a sense, the worship leader has become the modern priest who brings people into the presence of God. Music, rather than accompanying the congregation in singing to the Creator of the Universe, has become level-one marketing. This "dodgy" or vulnerable generation is walking away from Christianity because they think it's manipulative. And frankly, if people have been told that a quivering liver equates to the presence of God, they deserve to think Christianity is manipulative.[69]

I repeat, "experiencing" is not the enemy; the enmity arises only when "experiencing" becomes the *goal.* How the service of worship 'plays' before the people is of course a legitimate concern—and tragically, too much traditional and liturgical worship has been offered with a lifelessness and sometimes even with a contempt for affect that it is appalling.

But when major attention is given to affect rather than substance, a secondary concern has idolatrously become a major concern. Constance Cherry has rightly said: "When all is said and done, worship *is* about experiencing the living God." But then she adds an all-important definition in the next sentence: "To experience God is to participate in a conversation with God."[70] It is not just to "feel" God—or whatever one may infer to be God.

Reference was earlier made to Jonathan Edwards' insistence upon the legitimacy of "experiencing." Specifically, Edwards contended that the scriptures "do everywhere place religion very much in the affections; such as fear, hope, love, hatred, desire, joy, sorrow, gratitude, compassion, zeal." But this was not the whole story for Edwards, nor for the practice of the faith as he understood it. He also said: "Holy affections are not heat without light; but evermore arise from the information of the understanding, some spiritual instruction, that the mind receives, some light or actual knowledge."[71]

Or, to express Edwards' thought more colorfully, the African-American preaching community has a saying meant to redirect any preacher who neglects nutritious biblical content in favor of theatrics or a staged "whooping" to an emotional climax. They remind the preacher that "good meat makes its own gravy." The saying has multiple applications.

A baseline question for worship is: Are our feelings, our emotions to be our primary means of acknowledging our relationship with, knowledge of, and love for God? The history of Christian thought gives a resounding "No" to this question.[72] But it is not incomprehensible why so many believe otherwise. For at least half a century now there has been a relentless erosion of confidence in all authorities and institutions previously thought to be trustworthy. Today's younger generations, especially, have witnessed a steady stream of failed heroes—in sports, commerce, politics, science, and even religion. The result is a populace that's now resigned to a world of "spin," a populace that despairs of getting the "truth" about anything and actually expects to be lied to. In such a context, is it any wonder that the only truly trusted authority is one's own experience? And if it can be religious experience, that is the ultimate authentication! Unfortunately, many haven't yet awakened to the fact that religious experiences can be induced just as surely as tears can be induced in a sappy melodrama, or fanatical loyalty can be induced by an Adolph Hitler using thrilling pageantry, song, and oratory.[73]

The expression "experiencing God" may actually be a notably modern one. Previous generations might speak of "encounter" with God or a "sense of the presence of God" or "walking with God" or of a quest to "know God"—but not necessarily of "experiencing" God. To use but one example, when one studies the passionate pursuit of God carried on by the Desert Fathers and Mothers of the early Church[74] and considers the discipline, the austerity and intensity of their quest, it is surprising to discover how little they trusted their "experiences." They pushed beyond their "experiences," having found them a quicksand of emotional and psychological confusion, and continued to empty themselves for years before entering a level of communion with God that beggared human speech. In contrast, how easily God is "had" by this generation—a rousing quick-fix worship service grants all the experience our small souls desire or can handle.

Since the value of all things in our times has become measured by their being interactive and experiential, God also must now be rendered as an experienceable phenomenon—and a rapid one at that. Whereas earlier generations seem to have acknowledged a modest reserve and respectful recognition of the mystery and otherness of God, the "experiencing God" model acknowledges little of this.[75]

A fundamental concern here is the character of the God we worship. Is God really available to our beck and call, a phenomenon we can deliver on demand to a waiting audience each week? Leonard Sweet claims that "postmoderns literally 'feel' their way through life" and that "if postmodern worship can't make people furiously *feel* and *think*" (in the old 'modern' world we would have said only 'think')," it will be spiritually irrelevant; therefore he says wise preachers won't "write sermons," they will "create experiences" so that Sunday's worship "meets the 'wow' standard."[76] Once again, there is good counsel here—and great problems. For while it is always prudent to be interested in the affective dimension of worship, it is equally imprudent to place upon worship leaders the expectation to be miracle-workers who produce experiences of God each week, or to imagine that the God of the Bible can actually be served up "wow-fully" by anyone! To engage in such pursuits is to revisit the debacle at Sinai when the Hebrews, tired of waiting upon Moses and his slow god, Yahweh, requested Aaron to "make gods for us, who will go before us" (Exodus 32:1). When "out came this calf," it handsomely met the peoples' desires, for it was a god to their liking—a "wow-ful," experiential god of joyful dancing and feasting. But it was an idol, an idol that Moses ground into a powder that he commanded them to drink—and therefore inevitably excrete as the waste matter it was. With legitimate grounds, therefore, wise worship leaders will wonder how different they are from Aaron if meeting the people's "wow desire" becomes their accepted assignment. God is not a bunny to be pulled on cue from the priest's or worship leader's hat. Moreover, regardless of our immediate emotional impressions, it's often the case that "The Lord is in this place—and I did not know it!" (Genesis 28:17). We walk by faith anchored in biblical facts, not by feelings.

"Experiencing God," for all its commendable intentions, actually suggests a God much more accessible and survivable than scripture itself describes. When Isaiah "experienced God" in Jerusalem's temple, he feared for his life; when Jacob "experienced God" at the River Jabbok, the encounter left him limping for a lifetime; when Israel "experienced God" at Sinai, she begged for no encores (Exodus 20:18-19); when Peter, James, and John "experienced God" on the Mount of Transfiguration, they were "terrified" (Luke 9:34); and when the NT letter to the Hebrews bids believers to "experience God" by approaching God's Holy of Holies with boldness (4:16), it also reminds them that "it is a fearful thing to fall into the hands of the living God" (10:31) because the God they will encounter is "a consuming fire" (12:29). Consequently, even though scripture is replete with assurances of God's nearness and grace, the theme of trembling reverence before the holiness of God persists as a caveat against the presumptuousness of any who would imagine that this wonder authorizes chumminess—or indifference.

Applying a Pentecostal patch

One curiosity in the current swap-shop of evangelical worship practices is that countless non-Pentecostal churches have taken up the three-part P&W order and its upbeat, stirring praise songs but have left its informing theology alone. Thus a "Pentecostal lite" brand of worship has become a frequently seen form of "contemporary worship." But lacking its theological base the form itself feels somewhat rootless. Mostly what comes across is an explosion of high-decibel songs of praise (deleting, of course, the to-be-avoided Pentecostalist worship climax), followed by a retreat to limp acts of traditional evangelical worship. The thunder is borrowed, but the lightning remains within P&W's homeland.

Unquestionably the P&W pattern lends an attention-getting, acoustical shot-in-the-arm that provides a different energy level for a few minutes. But divorced from an informing charismatic theology as its base, this benefit easily becomes just a change in musical "sound," not necessarily an improvement in worship per se. Certainly, there is an inner integrity and coherence within Pentecostal worship when practiced by Pentecostals. But when non-pentecostals dip indiscriminately from that tradition, they introduce doctrines and assumptions that may actually be at loggerheads with the ethos and theology of their own church.[77] What is needed is the sober work of developing a coherent understanding of what the time of worship really is to be about for their church and for the greater Church.[78]

A.W. Tozer (1897-1963), a much-respected evangelical teacher and writer continues to be read eagerly by evangelicals half a century after his death. One excerpt from his writings may be a fitting conclusion to this discussion of "experiencing." In his classic 1948 book *The Pursuit of God*, Tozer expressed his yearning for worshipers to have "an intimate and satisfying knowledge of God, that they might enter into Him, that they may delight in His presence, may taste and know the inner sweetness of the very God Himself in the core and center of their hearts." Such was his evangelical language for "experiencing God." But only a paragraph away he wondered "if there was ever a time when true spiritual worship was at a lower ebb." Within great sections of the Church, he said, "the art of worship has been lost entirely, and in its place has come that strange and foreign thing called the 'program.' This word has been borrowed from the stage and applied with sad wisdom to the type of public service which now passes for worship among us."[79] One wonders how Tozer would view today's "experiencing" worship model.

∽

My hope is that the foregoing survey of the three dominant streams swirling within today's evangelical worship illustrates why Tozer's concern regarding worship is justified, and why we have good reason to share it. The confusion resulting from these streams and their twentieth century confluence is real. In marvelous mercy God has and is unquestionably working through all of these streams, and others not considered here. To deny this would be both untrue and a needless offense to those who regularly worship within them. But it is also clear that their colliding emphases and differing goals are central to our current worship confusion and to the fatigue and anxiety of worship leaders. The environment they create means that in the majority of evangelical churches worship planners confront the requirement that next Sunday's worship "program" must be: 1) evangelistically clear enough to lead many to give their heart to Christ (Finney); 2) appealing and inspirational enough to draw in the outsider (Schuller); and 3) sufficiently emotional to demonstrate the presence of the Holy Spirit (Pentecostalism). This is a most demanding if not impossible assignment, especially when it is understood that no two weeks' "programs" are to be alike. Novelty has now become mandatory—a development which goes a long way toward understanding why large churches with multi-staff and deep-pocket resources get larger and larger while small churches with limited resources get smaller and smaller. Little guys just can't compete in this league!

But is the worship of God really meant to be a matter of competition between ecclesiastical units fighting for market share? Is it the calling of God's leaders to be innovative producers of weekly spectacles for spiritual consumers? As prevalent as this pattern presently is, I must register a firm and heart-broken protest. I can find no warrant anywhere within the Bible for worship or for worship leaders to be such captives to the culture. As well-intentioned as our journey to this confused and confusing scenario may have been, evangelicals need to awaken to the fact that wrong turns have been taken, and that we who started out to win the world are now its hostages, vainly attempting to attract it by satisfying its religious hankerings with Christian programs inaccurately called worship. Our understanding of worship must be reconceived.

Thus, I return to the primary thesis of this book that worship is about God and God alone. It is not about selling God, nor is it about inspiring people with God-ideas, or generating electric moments when God may be experienced. These, however, are the ends to which we often turn corporate worship. The revivalist model uses worship to evangelize and therefore it tends to be not as much about God as it is about conversions and numerical church growth. The entertainment model uses worship to inspire and entertain and therefore it tends to be not as much about God as about attracting people to its productions. The experiencing model is a definite improvement over the other models, but by placing human emotions in the driver's seat, this model tends to become less about God than about creating feelings. Unquestionably, each model can offer its own rationale for doing what it does and can rightly claim that this is being done to serve God. But to serve God and to worship God are not identical. In service we go in God's name to the world of God's creation and care. In worship we come in Christ's name to the God of all and are ourselves made whole.

The detour we have taken has actually brought about a diminishment of worship. We have, in effect, valued worship as a means to other, defensibly-righteous purposes. This, however, is a fatal wrong turn. Worship cannot be "used" for any purpose other than its vertical-dialogical heart. Whenever it is "used" for any other purpose, regardless of the nobility of that purpose, things fall apart. Idolatrous tendencies are afoot. Some goal, some good has been placed as being of greater importance than the goal of "seeking God's face."

This is why some say worship is inherently useless—at least in the world's scheme of things. It isn't good for anything measureable or quantifiable by human criteria. To return to Guardini's "play" analogy which introduced this book, worship is not to be assessed by its pragmatic usefulness. Making it utilitarian is to convert the soul's love-language into a businessman's balance sheet. Harnessed to purposes other than offering ourselves in non-calculating sincerity to God, our gatherings become something less or other than worship. Unquestionably, such a seemingly pointless activity—in a world driven by bottom lines, efficiency, and productivity—may strike many (even within the Church) as being a purposeless expenditure of our time, a waste of time, really. But it is a sublimely "royal" waste of time.[80] How that might be so, is the subject of the remainder of this book.

RESOURCE: AUGUSTINE ON CHURCH MUSIC

Though the great North African bishop Augustine of Hippo (354-430 C.E.) wrote decades later than the period used as an exemplary worship model in this book, his comments about music in worship merit inclusion here. He expressed the dilemma faced by his predecessors as well as by him and, curiously, a dilemma that has reappeared in relation to the great importance given to music in today's worship. In this famous excerpt from his *Confessions* Augustine has been discussing the senses, especially the sense of smell, but now he turns his attention to hearing and sound.

I used to be much more fascinated by the pleasures of sound than the pleasures of smell; I was enthralled by them, but you [God] broke my bonds and set me free. I admit that I still find some enjoyment in the music of hymns, which are live with your praises, when I hear them sung by well-trained, melodious voices, but I do not enjoy it so much that I cannot tear myself away. I can leave it when I wish. But if I am not to turn a deaf ear to music, which is the setting for the words which give it life, I must allow it a position of some honor in my heart, and I find it difficult to assign it to its proper place. For sometimes I feel I treat it with more honor than it deserves. I realize that when they are sung, these sacred words stir my mind to greater religious fervor and kindle in me a more ardent game of piety than they would if they were not sung; and I also know that there are particular modes in song and in the voice, corresponding to my various emotions and able to stimulate them because of the mysterious relationship between the two. But I ought not to allow my mind to be paralyzed by the gratification of my senses, which often leads it astray. For the senses are not content to take second place. Simply because I allow them their due, as adjuncts to reason, they attempt to take precedence and forge ahead of it, with the results that I sometimes sin in this way but am not aware of it until later.

Sometimes, too, from over-anxiety to avoid this particular trap I make the mistake of being too strict. When this happens, I have no wish but to exclude from my ears, and from the ears of the church as well, all the melody of these lovely chants to which the Psalms of David are habitually sung; and it seems safer to me to follow the precepts which I remember often having heard ascribed to Athanasius who used to oblige lectors to recite the psalms with such slight modulation of the voice that they seemed to be speaking rather than chanting. But when I remember the tears that I shed on hearing the songs of the Church in the early days, soon after I had recovered my faith, and when I realize that nowadays it is not the singing that moves me but the meaning of the words when they are sung in a clear voice to the most appropriate tune, I again acknowledge the great value of this practice. So I waver between the danger that lies in gratifying the senses and the benefits which, as I know from experience, can accrue from singing. Without committing myself to an irrevocable opinion, I am inclined to approve of the custom of singing in church, in order that by indulging the ears weaker spirits may be inspired with feelings of devotion. Yet when I find the singing itself more moving that the truth which it conveys, I confess that this is a grievous sin, and at those times I would prefer not to hear the singer.[81]

4. WORSHIP AS SEEKING GOD'S FACE

God as the Object and Subject of Worship

I now want to introduce a fourth model that is, in my opinion, truer to the biblical intent of worship and also more attuned to the long history of Christian worship. Its primary features, however, are drawn from characteristics of the worship of Christianity's first three hundred years. I call this model "seeking God's face."

Stated in the tersest of terms, this model understands corporate worship to be *a spiritual practice engaged in for God's glory.* The balance of this book is an explanation and description of this conception of worship,

but in order to place the gist of it into immediate contrast to the foregoing models, here are several indications of why it is offered as a model
that is more "about" God than the options just surveyed.

First, by categorizing corporate worship as a spiritual practice
it is placed within the long tradition of spiritual formation, a tradition
that honors discipline and intentionality as intrinsic to spiritual maturity.
This tradition says that our worship is an expression of our yearning for
God—it is a response to the overtures and revelation of God and is an
expression of our longings to draw near to God. Worship, therefore, has
God as its Object; it is entered because we desire to "lift up our hearts" to
the eternal God in gratitude and wonder. It has no pragmatic, utilitarian
"use." This tradition insists that God is not "had" easily or quickly, never
by microwaved tactics. Thus, the path to "experiencing" God is one of
faithfully following spiritual practices—corporate worship being one of
them.

Second, corporate worship in this construal is not planned with
novelty, surprise, inspiration or entertainment as a goal. There is an
essential sameness, a ritual character to spiritual practices, just as there is
a ritual character in every other kind of practice, be it musical, medical,
athletic, etc. Accordingly, the practice of corporate worship will not be
attractive to all persons nor should it be planned as a religious or church
program to appeal to the "world"—though anyone from the community
is welcome to attend. This is a gathering of those who, similar to devotees
of regular gym-workouts, choose to engage in a weekly corporate spiritual discipline. (It actually might be quite helpful to think of worship
leaders as more analogous to personal trainers than platform performers.)

Moreover, the goal of this prayer meeting (for what is worship
if not an enacted prayer?) is to "seek God's face." It is engaged with faith
that this turning toward God's face brings joy to God and with hope
that, through seeking God's face, we might be transformed into a people
whose face reflects the face of God as we have seen it in the face of Jesus
Christ. The latter part of this is a longing, not a hidden utilitarian goal.
It is a selfless hope, a yearning that something of God might "rub off"

on us—to God's greater glory. Thus, such worship is not an enterprise of vanity or even a "useful" pursuit in terms of individual holiness; it is an indication that all is being done solely in fascination with the beauty of God and a realization that no one can gaze upon the beauty of the Eternal without being changed.

Worship as "seeking God's face" also means God is the Subject of this worship; God is its content and curriculum. It is "about" God in an obvious, substantive sense, its constituent parts and actions speaking to and being attentive to God. The "story" of God through scripture, God's mighty acts, God's mercies, God's will, and God's future are its recurring and unifying themes—not our programs, or our institutions (which would make worship to be "about" us).

"Seeking God's face" also suggests a humility that is essential to worship, for seeking underlines the truth that God is not in our possession; the phrase preserves holy mystery at the heart of our faith. It affirms that the Holy One is indeed Wholly Other and, though approachable with boldness, must still be sought respectfully rather than presumptuously taken for granted. A shouted hint is also here, a hint that worship requires work: seeking cannot be done lazily. There is a requisite focusing and involvement of mind and will and body that is inherent within seeking (just as in the practice of prayer that it represents) that makes it impossible to imagine worship as a passive, to-be-observed program performed by others.

It is reasonable to anticipate that some readers, upon reading these words, will be disappointed. Chief among these might be believers who are understandably committed to the propositions that worship must be turned outward—toward the world of God's concern. They worry that this re-conception is actually an unfortunate turn inward—toward the Church rather than toward the world. However, in reality, "seeking God's face" turns worship neither inward nor outward; it turns it upward—toward God, in whose care both Church and world abide. (I would, however, ask any unconvinced reader to read on and discover the prominence given to an outward orientation within the discussion of worship's Jerusalem and Olivet moments.)

The specific phrase "seeking God's face" is drawn from Psalm 105:4, which in the Latin Vulgate version reads: "Seek his face always." Robert Louis Wilken, in his profoundly helpful study of how the earliest Christians thought about what they believed, says this verse (a favorite of Augustine), "more than any other verse in the Bible . . . captures the spirit of early Christianity."[82] In the same volume Wilken also demonstrates and repeats as a matter of first importance, that early Christian thinking arose from and always was in the service of the Church's worship. Thus "seeking the face of God" is a symbol that puts us in touch with a worship and theological heritage far older than any of the options we have surveyed. It points us to a wisdom found within the worship of Christians of the first three centuries and a wisdom that's traceable throughout the subsequent history of our faith. Hence, "seeking God's face" provides an apt metaphor for better worship. Like a steady north star, it is an orienting guide for Christian worship. To understand it more fully, the next chapter will survey the worship of the early Church—which first demonstrated this kind of worship—and will specify enduring worship landmarks that preserve, interpret, and develop this model for our appropriation today.

QUESTIONS FOR DISCUSSION

1. Were you introduced to Christian worship via one of the models described? What valuable facets of it do you cherish? If this model is no longer the one in which you participate, what led you to change?

2. Is "seeking God's face" a helpful metaphor for worship? Is there another biblical metaphor that better captures your understanding of Christian worship?

3. Are there other models of worship you wish had been included? In what ways do you see them influencing evangelical worship today?

4. Do you see similarities in the models? In the arguments made for and/ or against their use?

Excursus: The Faith that Worship Shaped

(Lex orandi, lex credendi)

It isn't always appreciated or even understood that the approximate 14,500 Sundays between the birth of the Church and the date (312 C.E.) when Constantine legitimized the Christian faith had an enormous impact upon the doctrinal faith we consider as orthodox and thus who we are today.

First, consider that every time we open the New Testament we open a gift given to us by Christian worship. During the first centuries many writings circulated among Christians. But only twenty-seven of them were ultimately selected for use within the New Testament. All twenty-seven owe their place within the New Testament in large part to the fact that the churches across those centuries found these particular writings to be their best worship material. As these specific Gospels, letters, histories, and sermons were read and expounded upon in worship services, church people consistently heard the ring of truth in them and received through them the blessing of maturation. Thus, whatever other criteria were used to determine which writings "made the cut," their beneficial weekly usage in Christian worship was a most important winnowing factor. Our New Testament was cradled in worship.[83]

Consider also that worship may be understood as the womb of the Church itself. The social reality we call Church was nurtured and shaped through the weekly meetings of these followers of the Way. Beginning with the earliest believers in Jesus-Messiah who "devoted themselves to the apostles' teaching and fellowship, to the breaking of bread and the prayers" (Acts 2:42), corporate worship was a determinative influence on the life of the Church. Its survival as a distinct faith-people can be attributed in no small measure to these regular gatherings. In them the Lord's ways were learned and practiced. He himself in Spirit-form was among them, teaching them, sculpting them into a community that would "body" Him forth before the world. So it may be said that the Church itself is, in a sense, the product of its worship.

The instruction, the encouragement, the discipline, the joy and strength received when the Church-scattered became the Church-gathered was crucial to the Church's survival and identity. What believers saw, heard, prayed, ate, felt, and thought in Sunday's meetings molded them into the people they were before the world.

Finally, one must underline the fact that central Christian doctrines are also traceable to the worship life of that early Church. As but one example, we today accept as baseline theological orthodoxy the idea that God is a Trinity.[84] But, like the New Testament's table of contents, an historical process also lies behind this. In the case of the Trinity, it was as the Church offered its prayers in worship that the question arose as to whether it was permissible to offer prayers only to God, or could prayers also be expressed to Christ, or spoken to the Spirit of God whose presence in the gathering none could deny. The same question arose from the Church's baptismal practice. Following the command to baptize "in the name of the Father, the Son, and the Holy Spirit" (Matthew 28:20), they regularly used baptismal words that spoke of God in a tri-fold manner. But these worship practices created a difficulty. These Christians were monotheists (believers in one God alone), yet their worship life suggested they were serving three gods. As the Church wrestled with this dilemma, not wanting to renounce its Jewish monotheistic roots nor to endorse the idea that there were actually three gods, the inescapable conclusion was that the Church had already, in its worship, come upon a new conception of God as a Trinity. There was, in other words, a functioning worship-understanding of God as Trinity long before there was a doctrinal declaration. The hammering out of those doctrinal statements consumed several succeeding centuries. However, the necessity and truth of those statements was first established through the Church's worship practices, not by professional theologians' philosophical arguments.

This same kind of developmental process occurred often enough in the Church's early years that by the fifth century it was even given a Latin slogan: *lex orandi, lex credendi,* or "the rule of praying (worshiping) [sets] the rule of believing." Put into today's vernacular, this may be understood as saying: "What happens in worship sets the pattern for what is believed by the worshipers." This insight has had subtle and multiple ramifications throughout the history of Christian doctrine and therefore it is essential not to dismiss it as simply a museum curiosity. To this day, it's what people hear, see, do, feel, and are challenged to think and pray about in worship that sets the pattern for what they believe about God, themselves, the world, and life itself. If what has been established in worshipers' minds through their worship experiences is erroneous, it is difficult to dislodge regardless of the collective efforts of pastors, theologians, Bible teachers, and all the weight of scholarship. Thankfully, the corollary is also true. If what has been formed through worship is sound and nourishing, that deposit also remains as an asset buffering against the cruelties of life and the shifting winds of opinion.

Lex orandi, lex credendi reminds us of the formative significance of worship in the Church's past. It also may serve as a wake-up call to today's Church concerning the continuing power of worship to shape our faith, worldview, and ministry. Surely, it ought foster a hope within us that a similar kind of positive, unifying power might characterize worship today—a blessing not to be discounted as we increasingly confront a pluralistic, non-Christian world-culture unlike anything seen since those first three centuries.

Notes

[1]James Magaw, "The Power We Invoke," *Alive Now*, May-June, 1988, 60.

[2]Marva Dawn uses the evocative expression of God as the Infinite Center of our worship as another way of stating this imperative. See her *A Royal "Waste" of Time: The Splendor of Worshiping God and Being Church for the World* (Grand Rapids, MI: Eerdmans Publishing, 1999), 10, 149ff.

[3]Daniel Walker Howe, *What Hath God Wrought: The Transformation of American*, 1815-1848 (New York: Oxford Press, 2007), 173, provides these epithets and historical context for the meeting. A good source for understanding the "New Light-Old

Light" struggle is Edwin Gaustad & Leigh Schmidt, *The Religious History of America*, rev. ed. (New York: HarperSanFrancisco, 2002) and the bibliographies found within it.

[4]The standard biography of Lyman Beecher is Stuart C. Henry, *Unvanquished Puritan: A Portrait of Lyman Beecher* (Grand Rapids: Eerdmans, 1973), and Finney's career is well-surveyed in Charles Hambrick-Stowe, Charles G. Finney and the Spirit of American Evangelicalism (Grand Rapids: Eerdmans, 1996).

[5]Cited by James F. White, "Evangelism and Worship from New Lebanon to Nashville" in his *Christian Worship in North America: A Retrospective* 1955-1995 (Collegeville, Minnesota: The Liturgical Press, 1997), 155-172.

[6]Quoted by Keith J. Hardeman, *Charles Grandison Finney 1792-1875* (Grand Rapids: Baker Book House, 1987), 144.

[7]Protestantism's worship origins are to be found in a commitment to teach/ preach the Scriptures. Believing the Roman Church had neglected the teaching of Scriptures and the act of preaching, the Reformers placed great emphasis upon these, moving worship "from the eye (beholding the performed Eucharist) to the ear (listening to the word taught)." The sermon therefore became all-important, and sermons were both lengthy and didactic. Thus, the aura of a schoolroom characterized early Protestant worship and prevailed among America's Puritans who believed themselves to be bound in covenant with God to establish on the new continent a society governed by the word of God. America's first Christian worship, accordingly, was decidedly educational in intent. Even so, it was still worship that, through listening and through prayer, was marked by a vertical-dialogical priority.

[8]Finney, *Lectures on Revivals of Religion*, ed. William G. MeLoughlin (Cambridge, Mass: Belknap Press of Harvard University Press, 1960), 251, 276. Italics in original.

[9]James Emery White, *Opening the Front Door: Worship and Church Growth* (Nashville: Convention Press, 1992) is representative of the many who believe otherwise: "Such a view is not in accord with the biblical material or even with current practice" (p. 15), he says. However, I will argue throughout this book that the biblical material does distinguish evangelism from worship, and that "current practice" is precisely what must be challenged by the biblical material as well as by the theological formulations built upon it and the longer tradition of the Church.

[10]White, *Protestant Worship: Traditions in Transition* (Louisville: Westminster/ John Knox Press, 1989), 176. White labels Finney's influence "The Frontier Tradition" and offers an analysis of it here and in others of his writings.

[11]Jean Kilde, *When Church Became Theater: The Transformation of Church Architecture and Worship in Nineteenth Century America* (New York: Oxford University Press, 2002). In fairness, medieval Catholicism might also be characterized as Grand Theater, albeit in the service of a very different liturgy and theology.

[12]An accessible primer in this understanding of the Church's mission is Maria Harris, *Fashion Me A People: Curriculum in the Church* (Louisville: Westminster John Knox, 1989).

[13]One might also note that the triumph of worship as conceived by Finney and his descendants represented an alignment of church life with America's emerging free-market economy. Those churches that sought and attracted the most people were considered successful, a criterion taken more from the world of commerce than of scripture. This shift matched the culture, implementing a pattern of entrepreneurial competition among churches that continues to thrive. See Nathan O. Hatch, *The Democratization of American Christianity* (New Haven: Yale University Press, 1989) for other aspects of this accommodation.

[14]Robert H. Schuller, *My Journey: From an Iowa Farm to a Cathedral of Dreams* (New York: HarperSanFrancisco: 2001), 3.

[15]Although often considered a televangelist, Schuller disliked the label and bristled at comparisons with his more political and/or fundamentalist counterparts. In contrast to several of them, he had received a seminary education from an accredited seminary and never disparaged education. Nonetheless, he utilized the same technology and market techniques as the televangelists and thus may be studied as part of the televangelism phenomenon.

[16]A critical, but kind review of Schuller's theology written by Dennis Voskuil, a professor at Sculller's alma mater, Hope College, in Holland, Michigan, is in Voskuil's *Mountains into Goldmines: Robert Schuller and the Gospel of Success* (Grand Rapids, MI: Eerdmans, 1983).

[17]Schuller, *Your Church Has a Fantastic Future* (Ventura, CA: Regal Books, 1986), 92.

[18]Ibid., 334.

[19]Ibid., 94.

[20]Ibid., 245.

[21]Ibid., 261.

[22]Ibid., 317 In a strange twist of fate, Lyman Beecher's preacher-son, Henry Ward Beecher, using essentially these same tactics, became during the Civil War-era, "the most famous man in America." See Debby Applegate's, *The Most Famous Man in America: The Biography of Henry Ward Beecher* (New York: Doubleday, 2006).

[23]See page 48, footnote 22.

[24]Michael & Donna Nason, *Robert Schuller: The Inside Story* (Waco, TX: Word Books Publishers, 1983), 132-133.

[25]Richard Wightman Fox, *Jesus in America: Personal Savior, Cultural Hero, National Obsession* (San Francisco: HarperSanfrancisco, 2004), 344. McPherson often provided happy religious lyrics for her crowds to sing to well-known tunes; "It's a Long Way to Tipperary" became "It's a grand thing to be a Christian, It's the best thing I know . . . ," and another favorite was "We're a happy lot of people, yes we are! We're a happy lot of people, yes we are! For our sins are all forgiven, And we're on our way to heaven; We're a happy lot of people, yes we are!"

[26]Fox, ibid., 10.

[27]See Donald E. Miller, *Reinventing American Protestantism: Christianity in the New Millennium* (Los Angeles: University of California Press, 1997) for this trend as seen through the stories of three California charismatic churches: Calvary Chapel, Vineyard Christian Fellowship, and Hope Chapel.

[28]These Institutes were both an expression of and a model for the Church Growth Movement centered in nearby Pasadena, CA. This movement, emerging in the 1960s, noted Schuller's 1957-1967 growth rate of 765% and widely promoted his philosophy and Institutes. C. Peter Wagner, a foremost leader of the movement, wrote a glowing Foreword for Schuller's *Your Church Has Real Possibilities* (Glendale, CA: Regal Books, 1974). Mainline denominations also were drawn to his example through the widely-read books of United Methodist Kennon Callahan, especially *Twelve Keys to an Effective Church* (New York: Harper & Row, 1983). Callahan's third "key," following "Specific, Concrete Missional Objectives" and "Pastoral and Lay Visitation," was "Corporate, Dynamic Worship." Callahan's near cultic following among mainliners led to a sequel, a Manual for Strengthening the Worship Life of Twelve Keys Congregations, titled *Dynamic Worship:*

Mission, Grace, Praise, and Power (San Francisco: HarperSanFrisco, 1994). In all of this literature worship is promoted as being inspirational and evangelistic in purpose.

[29]It is a sad irony that Schuller's success did not extend beyond the ministry of the man himself. Upon his retirement disastrous intra-family squabbles about succession ensued which, coupled with declining viewership and a changing demographic, brought about the termination of the television ministry, the sale of the Crystal Cathedral campus, and eventually even the departure of Schuller from the bankrupt church's membership.

[30]Postman, (New York: Penguin Books, 1985), 116-117.

[31]Ibid., 124.

[32]This critique in no way is meant to disparage the value of many local church's televised worship services, which are typically telecast for the benefit of their homebound members as an extension of fellowship.

[33]Quentin J. Schultze, *Televangelism and American Culture: The Business of Popular Religion* (Grand Rapids, Michigan: Baker Book House, 1991), 214.

[34]The "parable" is worked out in Kierkegaard's *Purity of Heart is to Will One Thing* which is available in many editions and formats.

[35]George G. Hunter III, *Church for the Unchurched* (Nashville, TN: Abingdon Press, 1996), 79-80 (italics in original).

[36]Redman, *The Great Worship Awakening: Singing a New Song in the Postmodern Church* (San Francisco: Jossy-Bass, 2002), 43.

[37]Sweet, "A New Reformation: Re-creating Worship for a Postmodern World," in *Experience God in Worship: Perspectives on the Future of Worship in the Church from Today's Most Prominent Leaders* (Loveland, CO: Group Publishing, 2000) and reprinted in Tim Dearborn & Scott Coil, eds., *Worship at the Next Level: Insight from Contemporary Voices* (Grand Rapids, MI: Baker Books, 2004), 104.

[38]See the biographies of Luther which tell the stories of his "call" to priesthood via the lightning incident, his "breakdown" attempting to perform the Mass, and his bowel "release" when perceiving the primacy of faith and grace.

[39]Leech, *Experiencing God: Theology as Spirituality* (New York: Harper & Row, 1985), 1.

[40]William James' classic *Varieties of Religious Experience* remains a helpful introduction to this subject and Ronald A. Knox, *Enthusiasm: A Chapter in the History of Religion* (London: Clarendon Press, 1962) provides a historical overview of it throughout

history. According to Howard L. Rice, *Reformed Spirituality: An Introduction for Believers* (Louisville: Westminster John Knox Press, 1991), 24, "From its inception, the Reformed tradition [that is, Calvin's descendants] has been highly ambivalent about the role of experience in the Christian life." Nonetheless, Rice says conversion, ecstatic, visionary and auditory, intuitive, transcendent, and incarnational experiences are all legitimate. However, he describes "healthy spiritual experiences" as having four characteristics: they are unsought, unsettling, demanding, and confirmable by others. (This terminology is mine, interpreting Rice's discussion on pages 30-39. I would especially highlight the first characteristic.)

[41]Note, for example, the title of this book by Kim Miller: *Redesigning Worship: Creating Powerful God Experiences* (Nashville: Abingdon Press, 2009).

[42]R.G. Robins, *Pentecostalism in America* (Santa Barbara, CA: Praeger, 2010), 28-29. The complete Bartleman text, "Power in a Pentecostal Congregation," may be read in Richard Lischer, ed. *The Company of Preachers: Wisdom on Preaching, Augustine to the Present* (Grand Rapids, MI: Eerdmans Publishing, 2002), 417-422.

[43]All statistics and newspaper citations are taken from transcripts and data from an April 24, 2006, centennial program concerning global Pentecostalism sponsored by the Pew Forum on Religion and Life, available at www.pewforum.org/Politics-and-Elections/Moved-by-the-Spirit-Pentecostal-Power-&-Politics-after-100-Years (2). aspx. Accessed July 30, 2012.

[44]Some within the "third wave" movement now wish to distance themselves from that name because of its politicized, secular associations; one self-preferred name for these separationists is "empowered evangelicals."

[45]A sympathetic, though critical, assessment is found in Chapter 3 "The Contemporary Worship Music Industry," in Redman, *The Great Worship Awakening*, 47-71. Also see D.L. Alford, "Music, Pentecostal and Charismatic," in Stanley Burgess, ed. *The New International Dictionary of Pentecostal Charismatic Movements*, rev. and expanded ed. (Grand Rapids, MI: Zondervan, 2002), 911-920.

[46]Lester Ruth, "Praise-and-Worship Movement," in *The New Westminster Dictionary of Liturgy and Worship*, ed. Paul Bradshaw (Louisville, KY: Westminster John Knox Press, 2002), 379,, offers this brief definition: "A Praise-and-Worship approach to corporate liturgy sequences the order of worship, using contemporary Christian music to lead participants through a series of affective states. This sequencing serves as a kind of

long entrance rite, with worshipers ushered into an ever more strongly felt sense of God's presence. No physical movement through space is involved; the progression is inward and affective. Music is used sacramentally in that the worship created by the music enables the worshipers to experience God's presence."

[47]The pastor of a British "third wave," Vineyard Fellowship church documents this three part order even as he jokes that although his church looked askance at the liturgical captivity of their Anglican neighbors, the services in his own church "were regularly the same: a welcome, a worship time with the band, some notices [announcements], a conversational teaching time, and then prayer for people in response." He says he followed that pattern for nearly twenty years and that in his opinion it "qualifies as a liturgy" even if unacknowledged as such. See Jason Clark, "The Renewal of Liturgy in the Emerging Church," in *Church in the Present Tense: A Candid Look at What's Emerging*, Scott McKnight, Peter Rollins, Keven Corcoran, Jason Clark, eds. (Grand Rapids, MI: Brazos Press, 2011), 77.

[48]Cornwall, *Let Us Worship: The Believer's Response to God* (Plainfield, NJ: Bridge Publishing, Inc. 1983), 41-42.

[49]Sorge, *Exploring Worship: A Practical Guide to Praise & Worship*, revised and updated (Grand View, MO: Oasis House, 2001), 95. One must also gratefully note the appearance within *Worship Leader* magazine, a primary journal for P&W leaders, of occasional short articles introducing historic patterns and liturgical traditions.

[50]Darlene Zschech, "The Worship Pastor: 10 Worship Essentials," *Worship Leader*, Vol. 21, No. 3 (May, 2012), 14. In a subsequent article ["Then Sings My Soul," *Worship Leader*, Vol. 22, No. 1 (January/February, 2013), 16.] Zschech softens the newness counsel by also encouraging worship leaders "to always honor the past while pioneering into the future," because "our more contemporary songs of worship would not have been created if not for the amazing foundation of these legacy-carrying hymns."

[51]Cornwall, *Let Us Worship*, 41, italics added for emphasis.

[52]D.L. Alford says "It is not unusual for up to two-thirds of worship services to be given to music performance." Alford, "Music, Pentecostal and Charismatic," in Burgess, *New International Dictionary*, 916.

[53]Johansson, "Pentecostal Worship," in Bradshaw, Paul (ed.), *The New Westminster Dictionary of Liturgy & Worship* (Louisville, KY: Westminster John Knox Press, 2002), 370.

⁵⁴Sorge, *Exploring Worship*, 7.

⁵⁵Ibid., 72.

⁵⁶Ibid., 20-21. There is in this work a discernible preference for the power of music over the spoken word as a vehicle of God's communication. This low rating for speech is likely influenced by the fact that in this tradition the sermon or teaching is not considered a part of worship itself; it is a separate entity.

⁵⁷Ibid., 70. In the same paragraph Sorge says music is a "catalyst" for worship and that "It in no way guarantees or even denotes worship." At the same time, the union of the two seems inseparable.

⁵⁸A frequent complaint that these praise songs lack the theological substance of the older hymns, while valid, is actually beside the point. The new praise songs were never meant to be didactic; they were the musical literature of "experiencing" and were and are meant to function solely as praise songs

⁵⁹The terms "praise" band and "praise" team reveal the singular focus upon one genre of worship music.

⁶⁰One model of P&W (John Wimber's Vineyard movement) taught a "psychological shape" for sequencing worship that, according to Barry H. Liesch, *People in the Presence of God: Models and Directions for Worship* (Grand Rapids, MI: Zondervan Publishing House, 1988), 91-93, "operate[s] much like the dynamics of love-making." Wimber, previously a musical arranger for singers such as the Righteous Brothers, used a five-phase [1) invitation, 2) engagement, 3) exaltation, 4) adoration, and 5) intimacy] progression of worship songs with rising and then subsiding emotional intensity. The last phase, intimacy, was likened to "the kiss" which Liesch says corresponds to "one meaning of the Greek word for worship *proskuneo* [meaning] 'to turn toward to kiss,' as in kissing the feet, the hands, or the lips." However, this imputation of romantic/erotic notions into *proskuneo* finds no basis in the exhaustive study of that word by Heinrich Greeven published in Gerhard Friedrich, ed., *Theological Dictionary of the New Testament*, Vol. 4 (Grand Rapids, MI: Eerdmans, 1968), 758-766.

⁶¹Sorge does encourage P&W worship leaders to provide time for worshipers to receive God's message during the actual moments of worship, explaining, however, that such messages are most powerful when they come by means of song itself, through Spirit-inspired 'words' given in the moment via song—a "song of the Lord," not spoken words as in a sermon or even as in scripture being read. The question may still be raised if the

restrictive definition of worship doesn't (perhaps unintentionally) "say" that worship is in essence, "experiencing" God rather than being confronted by God. The long tradition of the Church, however, says that hearing the objective, written word and its preached interpretation is an essential component of the peoples' true worship of God. To sever worship of God from listening to God is a questionable practice.

[62]Barry Liesch, in his 1988 *People in the Presence of God*, 91, referring to the "long worship song service," says that John Wimber and Eddie Espinosa of the Vineyard in Anaheim, California, "term it, 'worship set'" and thus the term may come from the entertainment background of Wimber.

[63]Read his memorable comments on this in the Resource: "Augustine on Church Music" at the conclusion of this section.

[64]Joseph Gelineau, S.J., *Voices and Instruments in Christian Worship: Principles, Laws, Applications* (Collegeville, MN: The Liturgical Press, 1964), 50.

[65]Sorge, *Exploring Worship*, 1.

[66]Ibid., 69.

[67]Kent Carlson & Mike Lueken, *Renovation of the Church: What Happens When a Seeker Church Discovers Spiritual Formation* (Downers Grove, IL: IVP Books, 2011), 157.

[68]Ever since Krister Stendahl's ground-breaking essay, "The Apostle Paul and the Introspective Conscience of the West," (*Harvard Theological Review*, LVI [July, 1963], 199-215.), declaring that our interpretations of Paul (the dominant voice in Protestant theology) had been excessively influenced by western, psychologized, emotion-imputing presuppositions, scholars have been wary about imputing feeling states to reported experiences within the New Testament. See Luke Timothy Johnson's *Religious Experience in Early Christianity* (Minneapolis, MN: Fortress, 1998) and Klaus Berger, *Identity and Experience in the New Testament* (Minneapolis, MN: Fortress, 2003), for recent studies on this theme.

[69]See "Toward depth and beauty: Keith Getty talks about hymn writing," *Southern Seminary Magazine* Vol. 80, no. 4 (Fall, 2012), 25. It is likely that P&W music will be the characteristic "sound" of twenty-first century evangelical worship just as the gospel song was of the nineteenth and twentieth. This is all the more reason that P&W urgently needs to expand its content beyond its present limited focus upon praise alone.

[70]Cherry, *The Worship Architect: A Blueprint for Designing Culturally Relevant and Biblically Faithful Services* (Grand Rapids, MI: Baker Publishing, 2010), 270, italics added for emphasis.

[71]Edwards, "Concerning the nature of Religious Affections and their importance in Religion," in *The Select Works of Jonathan Edwards*, Vol. 3 (Edinburgh: Banner of Truth, 1961), 31, 192.

[72]The problem of authority in religion has a long and contested history, with experience usually appreciated as only one source of religious authority—in Wesleyan theology it is one pole of a quadrilaterally conceived authority of scripture, tradition, reason, and experience. In no theological schema I know of is experience granted a determinative voice. A helpful discussion of what he terms the "sources" or "formative factors" of theology (experience, revelation, scripture, tradition, culture, reason) and their interrelationship is in John Macquarrie, *Principles of Christian Theology*, 2nd ed. (New York: Charles Scribner's Sons, 1977) 4-18.

[73]According to *The Christian Century*, "Megachurch worship offers a spiritual high" (Sept. 19, 2012, 18-19), reporting a 2012 University of Washington study of megachurch worship services, it was determined that these services "can trigger feelings of transcendence and changes in brain chemistry—a spiritual 'high' that keeps congregants coming back for more." The report theorized its occurrence to be an "oxytocin cocktail," a combination of "shared transcendent experience and the brain's release of oxytocin, a chemical that is thought to play a part in social interaction. Emotion and group experience have been shown to raise levels of oxytocin." As one worshiper explained, "God's love becomes…such a drug that you can't wait to get involved to get the high from God," and another reported, "You can look up to the balcony and see the Holy Spirit go over the crowd like a wave in a football game." Thomas Bergler's previously cited *The Juvenilization of American Christianity* says: "Adolescent Christians [a term not restricted to teen years] are drawn to religious commitments that produce emotional highs and sometimes assume that experiencing strong feelings is the same thing as spiritual authenticity" (13).

[74]Belden Lane, *The Solace of Fierce Landscapes: Exploring Desert and Mountain Spirituality* (Oxford: Oxford University Press, 1998), esp. 11ff.

[75]See William C. Placher, *The Domestication of Transcendence: How Modern Thinking about God Went Wrong* (Louisville, KY: Westminster John Knox Press, 1996).

[76]Sweet, "A New Reformation: Re-creating Worship for a Post-Modern World," in *Worship at the Next Level,* ed. Dearborn & Coil, 106.

[77]Borrowing from other worship traditions has long been practiced, most notably in the transplanting of hymns from one tradition to another. But, as Christopher Ellis notes, the theological/spiritual strain of Pentecostalism is so distinct that "the *use* of charismatic worship songs will have an effect on the host liturgical structure through their spirituality as well as their musical style." See Ellis, *Gathering: A Theology and Spirituality of Worship in Free Church Tradition* (London: SCM Press, 2004), 64. An example might be Charismatic pastor Jack Hayford's popular song "Majesty," now widely sung in many non-charismatic circles without noting the significance of its refrain, "Kingdom authority," a pivotal theological concept in charismatic practice. On another point of the worship spectrum countless evangelical churches have borrowed from Catholicism the ritual of the Advent wreath but ignored Catholicism's historic accompanying Advent spirituality of penitence and austerity; thus the wreath may become little more than a reminder of the number of shopping days left until Christmas.

[78]Depending upon one's vantage point, there is either the promise of great gain or loss expressed in the title of Donald E. Miller's previously noted study of three charismatic/third-wave churches: *Reinventing American Protestantism.*

[79]Tozer, *The Pursuit of God* (Harrisburg, PA: Christian Publications, Inc.), 9, 10. Tozer, who had many probing observations about worship, is the source of the often quoted sentiment that worship is "the missing jewel of evangelicalism."

[80]Marva Dawn, *A Royal "Waste" of Time,* 1, explains that the reason for our worship isn't that it is useful but that "God deserves it." "It isn't even useful," she says, "for earning points with God, for what we do in worship won't change one whit how God feels about us. We will always still be helpless sinners…and God will always still be merciful, compassionate, and gracious…ready to forgive us as we come to him."

[81]Augustine, *Confessions* X, xxxiii, 49-50; trans. by R.S. Pine-Coffin, Agustine of Hippo, *Confessions* (Hammondsworth: Penguin Classics, 1961), 238-239.

[82] *The Spirit of Early Christian Thought: Seeking the Face of God* (New Haven: Yale University Press, 2003), xxii.

[83]The immense influence worship also played in the formation of the Old Testament is summarized well in Samuel E. Balentine, *The Torah's Vision of Worship* (Minneapolis: Fortress Press, 1999).

[84]It is helpful to know that the word orthodoxy initially referred more to worship than to doctrine. The Greek word *ortho* (meaning 'correct'), when combined with the word *doxa* (meaning 'glory'), denoted right glorying or right worship, not majority theological opinion. Geoffrey Wainwright's *Doxology: The Praise of God in Worship, Doctrine, and Life* (New York: Oxford University Press, 1980), re-presents this worship priority in a complete systematic theology (correct thinking) perceived through the lens of worship (correct glorying). Additionally, a worship-based (especially the Lord's Supper) survey of Christian Ethics is provided in Stanley Hauerwaus and Samuel Wells, *The Blackwell Companion to Christian Ethics* (Malden, MA: Blackwell Publishing, 2004).

III

RETRIEVING WORSHIP WISDOM

"Remember the days of old, consider the years long past;
ask your father, and he will inform you;
your elders, and they will tell you."

Deut. 32:7

☞

Earlier I made the bold statement that Christians of the previous 1800 years would hardly recognize much of the worship of American evangelicals as being worship. Such a verdict demands evidence—and this, I believe, is available through a survey of the long history of Christian worship. However, even a quick summary of that fascinating history isn't within the scope of this book.[1] I must therefore reluctantly rely upon just one snapshot from the history of Christian worship as representative of what might also be documented through images from other times. That one snapshot is the worship of the post-New Testament era Church (ca. 80-312 C.E.). Admittedly, this snapshot cannot prove my claim for the entire sweep of Christian history, but I trust it will dramatically document how different many of our worship assumptions and patterns are from those of our founders. It clearly lets us see Christian worship before categories like Catholic, Protestant, or Orthodox begin to complicate our understandings. It shows us Christian basics that time and personalities have diminished. Most significantly, for reasons to be specified later, it gives us a benchmark that can be most clarifying as we seek "rules" for Christian worship.[2]

This, however, immediately places a psychological challenge before us. That challenge is to entertain the possibility that long-ago people possessed knowledge and wisdom as rich if not richer than our own. We must, in other words, be willing to consider the past as a source of valid help for today's dilemmas. Ours is, after all, an age that is exceedingly impressed with itself, and for justifiable reasons. Who can deny that our recent advances in understanding and mastering our planetary home are stunning—so much so that we're often dumbfounded when we hear of a technique, practice, or insight that ancient peoples had in place thousands of years ago. Such discoveries confound our belief in inevitable progress, for surely everyone knows that what is newest is the best!

In some cases, this dubious tendency comes much closer; it appears as a question mark placed over what even one generation can helpfully transmit to the next. Marketers, demographers and sociologists have so effectively described the generation gap between, say, Baby Boomers and Millennials, that it may seem to be a Grand Canyon, a separation so severe that "the fathers have nothing to give to the sons, and the sons have no use for what their fathers can give them."[3] In such a context it is not astonishing that some doubt that those who dressed in togas or wrote on parchment have much to teach us.

Of course, this psychological challenge certainly finds a sharp focus within worship discussions, for it is often here that the clash of yesterday vs. today, of tradition vs. innovation, of young vs. old is glaring. In countless instances our clashes over worship are a contest between "the church of what's happening now" vs. the church of our ancestors, whether those ancestors are from the second or even the twentieth century. A dismaying example of this was given to me while watching a television commercial for one church's Easter morning worship service. The service was to be held at a local high school football stadium and the on-camera, thirty-something lady who voiced the church's invitation concluded by wondering why anyone would want to worship in "some old brick building where they sing hundred-year-old hymns." Stunned by her contrasts, I wondered how she, so obviously enamored by the new, managed to tolerate a two-thousand year old Savior, let alone a God whom scripture calls the Ancient of Days.[4]

We will not advance far if we do not advance together—or if we ignore the church of yesterday. The experience of the Church across the past two thousand years is the story of the Holy Spirit's steadfast work in every age. Therefore, to leap-frog from the New Testament to the twenty-first century is to forfeit centuries of Spirit-given treasure and to reduce ourselves to poverty-stricken orphans who are strangers to our own story.

Admittedly, a neglect of the "dead" past and making up our scripts as we go along has permitted evangelicals to be, if nothing else, extremely light on our feet and able to adjust to all manner of cultural shifts.[5] And, if one judges only from our present position of numerical dominance, it can be argued there's no reason to second-guess that strategy now.

Nonetheless, a yearning for truth and authenticity is also within our DNA. As much as we prize experiential faith, we do not want it to be a shallow faith. As much as we cherish freedom, we don't want it at the price of irresponsibility. To respond to this other dimension of our personality, however, means we must give attention to what the Spirit of God was doing before we showed up. It means letting go of the conceit that the Spirit was doing nothing of true importance until our immediate forebears came on the scene. It means we must identify the congruities and wrestle with the discrepancies between our ancient foundations and our present practices.

Of all people, we should know that the way forward often means a return to forsaken ways. But if there is no knowledge of or respect for these forsaken ways, there is no hope. Learning more about what the Spirit of God has done in ages past, we also become more attuned to what the Spirit may be saying to the Church today.[6]

So, in the following pages, I once again board the helicopter I imagined on earlier pages, but this time I do so in order to offer a fly-over of what Sundays were like long before there was a New Lebanon or a Garden Grove or an Azusa Street. I want to hover over the Mediterranean world of the first three centuries of Christianity—and to learn from the "Faith of our Fathers (and Mothers)" what worship once was, and to imagine from this vantage what it might be today. So, even if your personal inclination is to do a fly-over of the following section, please resist that urge. Walk through the very different worship world described in the next pages. "Discover, if you will, what you cannot remember."[7]

1. OUR FOUNDERS' PRACTICES AND PURPOSE IN WORSHIP

Learning from the First Three Hundred Years

A first and most important question is: Why select this particular era of Christian history as a potential benchmark? Why not select a later period when Christians finally came into their own and freely worshiped in church buildings with services more recognizable by us? Why not select the age of the classic Protestant reformers who, after all, are the pacesetters for Protestant understandings and traditions? Why select the Church's most ancient period to address a most pressing current problem? There are three reasons this choice has been made.

A first reason is because it is the period closest to the founding years of our faith. The persons and practices of this era are as chronologically close to the New Testament era and culture as we can get. Presumably, an Italian convert to Christianity in 250 C.E. was still better able to grasp the cultural and theological nuances of the Galilean original than those who lived centuries later. Yes, reorientations of the faith surely took place as Christianity spread across the Mediterranean basin and into multiple Gentile settings, but to the historian's eye, those seem to be minimal in comparison to the ensuing centuries of change, adaptation and adulteration. Hence, I look to this era to gain wisdom about worship and in doing so I once again rely upon the judgment of James F. White who says: "As so often happens in Christian worship, if we understand the experiences of the church's first four centuries, we have gained the heart of the matter."[8]

A second reason is that this is the era when the Church's scripture and doctrines were being determined. It was the period when the principle presented in the Excursus concerning *lex orandi, lex credendi* (see previous pages) was most operative. The precise lists and statements and enduring formulations came in the next decades, but the essential sifting and discernment of the spiritual essentials belongs to the Church of the first three centuries. It is to the wisdom being accrued by the Church of these years that the later Church has always looked for so much of its later life. Therefore, if we grant to the Christians of this era such a determinative status in our canonical and theological standards, are we not justified in examining closely the worship practices that sensitized and prepared them to be such a judicious people? If such treasures as the twenty-seven documents of the New Testament and primal Christian doctrines were baked in the "oven" of early Christian worship, we would be most foolish to dismiss the oven itself as inconsequential.

A third reason is that this was the age of martyrs. This era was more than a period of chronological proximity and theological lucidity; it was supremely a period of repeated bravery. In the following pages I will cite the words of many writers and documents of this era. What must be stressed even before hearing their voices is the fact that very few of these writers lived out their years in peace and devotional quiet. Not a one of them was "playing church" when writing about the Church's meetings, indeed, many of them paid for their faith with their life. Hence, they wrote not as liturgical scholars but as believers reporting life and death matters, they spoke of meetings that put steel into the backbones of worshipers during the most arduous centuries of the Church's long history. What they tell us about those Sunday activities is of more than historical interest. It provides a solid foundation for a durable model of worship.

The world of early Christianity

A first fact essential to know about the Church that emerged from the pages of the New Testament is that it was only one of a multitude of religious options available within the Roman Empire. Confronting religious pluralism is not, therefore, a new phenomenon for the Church. In fact it appears that the Roman world of early Christianity was much more religiously diverse and crowded than anything we can imagine. Archaeologists have unearthed the presence of multiple temples and shrines dedicated to the worship of innumerable gods in virtually every excavated city, amply documenting a thriving spiritual cafeteria operative throughout the Mediterranean region. This corroborates the Apostle Paul's observation that "the city [of Athens] was full of idols" and his subsequent words to them: "I see how extremely religious you are in every way. For as I went through the city and looked carefully at the objects of your worship, I [even] found among them an altar with the inscription, 'To an unknown god'" (Acts 17:22-23). The same could have been said of nearly every city of his and later Roman times. Sacred meals, ecstatic speech and frenzy, sacrifice, ritual, pageantry, public parades and festal days, memorials to cult-heroes, incense, and song—all of this could be found in abundance in the thriving pagan worship of the day.[9] There was no lack of religion! Most all of the acts we typically associate with worship were already well known and thriving when Christians entered the stream of history. Had it been their intent to find a niche in the religious market or to fill a spiritual vacuum through their worship program, theirs would have been a fool's errand. The market was already saturated.

A second fact we may profitably note is that the house churches spoken of within the New Testament (e.g., Acts 5:42; Romans 16:5; I Corinthians 16:19) continued to be the principal site for Christian worship for the better part of two hundred and fifty years. Only as the Church lived its way toward the 300s did it begin to acquire real estate, and most often this relocation was into an already existing public hall, known as a basilica, in which anything from a farmer's market to a local court hearing might be held. But for the preponderance of the time period we are concerned with, private residences were the primary place for Christian worship.[10]

Most significant, in this regard, is the size of these houses. The average home within the Roman world could accommodate only about ten people per room—particularly if it was a meeting where a meal was served and the Roman custom of lying down to dine was followed. Even among the wealthy, the room size would seldom double this capacity. Thus, as we envision early Christian worship, it is critical that we place it in this small-group context rather than imagine they assembled in coliseum-sized venues. (The remarkable house church discovered only in the twentieth century in the Euphrates River site of Dura-Europos[11] could perhaps accommodate some sixty persons, but all indications are that this one-time residence had been remodeled ca. 265 C.E. into a permanent worship space by the removal of partitions, etc.)

Thus, one must dismiss any notions of early worship being equivalent to a city-wide crusade to which all were invited, as well as any notion of early worshipers conducting a "bring a friend" service; there simply wasn't enough room for such public outreach endeavors. Other and more significant factors were also involved, as we shall see, but space considerations alone would have greatly militated against outreach-oriented worship services.

But what these house church locales lacked in spaciousness they more than compensated for in a strong sense of community and intimacy. These were assets of incalculable value for persons who often had been shunned by friends, business associates, or biological families because of their belief in Jesus as the Christ. The dining and living areas of host-homes provided a hospitable setting for the kind of worship early Christianity knew. Also, as an important historical aside, it was these domestic settings that gave to women a worship leadership role exceeding any they have ever known since. Indeed, one of the most frequent artistic symbols of the Christian movement in this era is of a female figure standing at a table with arms outstretched in prayer (a prayer posture now termed the *orans* position).

Virtually every record we have of this worship indicates that eating—especially the Lord's Supper—was the central act of their time of gathering. In the earliest years this was supplemented with an Agape Meal, sometimes called a Love Feast, which was similar to today's covered dish supper with worshipers bringing a dish to share with the others. For reasons not completely understood by us, the Agape Meal was in time discontinued, but the meal known as the Lord's Supper retained its highlighted place within worship. Absolutely nothing else from this period received as much written documentation as did this Supper.

"Once upon a time in Rome"
One description of such a service, written by a lay teacher named Justin and sent to the Roman emperor Antoninus for his study (and thus preserved among official documents), gives us a picture of a Christian worship service in Rome around the year 150 C.E. Actually, Justin, prepared two summaries—one of a typical Sunday service and another of a service that had been preceded by a baptism. The two complement each other nicely, though, and therefore it's possible to synthesize the two into one order of worship as I've done in the following, supplying subject headings in bold print. The words, which come from the baptismal account, appear in italicized print and are introduced with the letter *B*. Here then is what Justin tells us about worship about one hundred and twenty years after the resurrection of Christ.[12]

Gathering: "On the day that is called Sunday all who live in the cities or rural areas gather together in one place . . . " In another place Justin explains: "Sunday is the day on which we hold our common assembly since this day is the first day on which God, changing darkness and matter, created the world; it was on this very day that Jesus Christ our Savior rose from the dead."

Word: " . . . and the memoirs of the apostles and the writings of the prophets are read for us as long as time allows. Then after the lector concludes the president verbally instructs and exhorts us to imitate all these excellent things."

Prayer: "Then all stand together and offer prayers." (B) *". . . after those who are called brethren have assembled . . . we offer prayers in common both for ourselves and for those who have received illumination and for people everywhere, doing so with all our hearts . . ."*[13]

The Kiss: (B) *"When the prayers have concluded, we greet one another with a kiss."*

Offering: "When we have concluded our prayer, bread is brought forward with wine and water. And the president in like manner offers prayers and thanksgivings, according to his ability. The people give their consent, saying, 'Amen.'" (B) *"Then bread and a cup containing water and wine are brought to him who presides over the assembly. He takes these and gives praise and glory to the Father of all things through the name of his Son and of the Holy Spirit. He offers thanks at considerable length for our being counted worthy to receive these things at his hands. When the presider has concluded these prayers and the thanksgivings, all present express their consent by saying, 'Amen.' In Hebrew this word means, 'so be it.'"*

Communion: "there is a distribution, and all share in the Eucharist. To those who are absent a portion is brought by the deacons." (B) *"And after the presider has celebrated the thanksgiving and all the people have given their consent, those whom we call deacons give to each of those present a portion of the Eucharistic bread and wine and water and take the same to those who are absent."*

Collection: "And those who are well-to-do and willing give as they choose, as each one so desires. The collection is then deposited with the presider who uses it on behalf of . . . all who are in need."

Before considering particular items within Justin's account, I must repeat that this account was prepared for the eyes of the Roman emperor; it was an attempt to lessen the emperor's suspicions or hostility toward the rapidly-expanding religious group known as Christians. Unfortunately, Justin's desire was unsuccessful; he was killed for his Christian faith about a decade after writing this document, and for this reason he's commonly called Justin Martyr in historical writings

Therefore, it must be remembered that Justin's words—like all the others we will read—were written from a context of actual persecution or of imminent danger. These persecutions were not constant or universal—they were sporadic and varied in intensity and locale until their final termination upon Constantine's Edict of Milan in 312 C.E. Even so, the possibility—if not the reality—of bodily, social, and financial harm is the context for Justin's words, as well as the others we shall review. This underlying fact must be understood if we are to appreciate these documents as fully as we should.

To elaborate on this more bluntly, these words and those we will read throughout this section weren't written as exercises for a college class on Christian worship. What we read here is the literature of suspected enemies of the state, the testimony of marginalized and oftentimes outlawed persons. Through their accounts we eavesdrop on the weekly meetings of martyrs-to-be and sit within the circle of persons who were paying a very dear price for their belief in the Lord they are worshiping. Hence, Justin's account of Christian worship must not be read just as a museum artifact, a curious sample of what some ancient people did when they went to church. It must be read as an account of the kind of meetings that once nourished and sustained peoples' willingness to "deny themselves and take up their cross and follow Jesus." To us, perhaps, the proceedings they describe may seem bland if not boring—they hardly seem to set a precedent for what many today expect in a good worship service—but this only highlights how important it is for us to explore the instructive differences between then and now.

Perhaps it's not inappropriate to insert that the urgency of this exploration is pressed upon me personally almost daily as I drive past a church marquee (actually the sign doesn't use the word church; it declares it's a Christian Center, not a church). In bold colors this marquee invites passersby to "Come enjoy the excitement." This invitation strikes me as a lamentable contrast to Dietrich Bonhoeffer's well-known dictum: "When Christ bids a man, he bids him come and die."

Analyzing a First Century Order of Worship

Consider some of the features of Justin's description of the worship he knew. Begin with his statement that it is "those who are called brethren" who gather for worship. This is obviously exclusive in that the general public is not the audience anticipated for this meeting. If these meetings' location or times were broadly announced, emperor Antoninus would have had no need for an account from an insider like Justin; any deputy could have attended and given him a report. This is but one more indication that outreach/evangelism was not an intended purpose of the worship meeting—this worship was a gathering of the sisters and brothers of the faith.

Inclusivity, however, is also evident here, for the assembled are called "brethren"[14] and at a significant transitional point within the service the brethren "greet one another with a kiss." In some places within the New Testament this is called a "holy kiss," presumably to distinguish it from the erotic kiss of lovers, but hugs and kisses were as much a part of family life in that day as in ours. Hence, a kiss as an expression of inclusion within the family of faith (which would have been for many of them a surrogate for forfeited biological families) was fitting. Unfortunately, to the imaginations of suspicious outsiders, a "kiss" in the "secret" meetings of a religious sect where women as well as men were present, led to accusations of incest and immorality—not that sexual purity was at all prominent in the ceremonies of other religions of the time. But Justin makes no attempt to conceal the intimacy and mutuality of the assembled worshipers. They were one body, a self-understanding also testified to by the deacons' taking the communion elements to those who were absent. In the bonds of Christ's family, each person was known and remembered; absenteeism did not go unnoticed.

Note also that the day chosen is Sunday, not the Sabbath. For Christianity's Jewish mother, the day of worship was the ten-command-ment-mandated seventh day. The Christians, however, chose the first day of the week in honor of the Genesis-identified day of creation and the resurrection-inaugurated day of new creation. This selection of a weekly day of assembly for worship is one of many examples of the way in which early Christians utilized the habits and words of synagogue and temple worship. Their worship day was different, but it was rooted respectfully in the Sabbath tradition. Centuries would pass, of course, before the Roman world would recognize this Christian Sunday as an official day of religious observance (381 C.E.). So throughout the period studied here, Christians contended with work schedules that often made attendance difficult, a difficulty that gives context to Justin's comment about taking the communion elements to those who were absent.

The first named activity of the assembly was to listen to "the memoirs of the apostles and the writings of the prophets . . . as long as time allows." It's estimated that no more than fifteen percent of the population of the Roman world could read—and copies of the Hebrew scriptures were not plentiful—so "lectors," or those who were able to read Hebrew scripture and also Greek writings (such as Paul's letters), were essential and honored. As the centuries unfolded, the importance of hearing the word of God read well in worship became so central that these lectors were even accorded clergy status. The "memoirs of the apostles" that were read seem to be the Gospels known to us today (or fragments of them) as well as possible other writings eventually not included within the New Testament. "The prophets" is surely a reference to the Old Testament. Extensive readings, therefore, from both Testaments, were followed by the "president's" verbal instruction and exhortations based upon the lec-tions or readings.

The Jewish synagogue services had a similar focus upon hearing and interpreting sacred texts. Historians generally say the Christian sermon is actually the child of the synagogue *darash* (searching), that is, the explanation and application of Old Testament texts that was a prominent component of synagogue worship. For our purposes, however, the important issue is the high priority given to listening to God's word, as written and interpreted orally. For Justin's church this was worship activity number one, and this was done as something "useful for teaching, for reproof, for correction, and for training in righteousness, so that everyone who belongs to God may be proficient, equipped for every good work" (2 Timothy 3:16-17). So well known was the Christians' fascination with texts and their meaning that in some places Christian meetings were rumored to be philosophical societies—a rough equivalent to today's book discussion clubs. This was worship that engaged the mind as well as the imagination, initiating the vertical-dialogical priority of worship by first listening to scripture "as long as time permits" and then receiving instruction and exhortation "to imitate all these excellent things."

The second activity of Justin's worship service was corporate prayer.[15] Justin's summarizing words, "Then all stand together and offer prayers" are supplemented by "we offer prayers in common both for ourselves and for those who have received illumination and for people everywhere, doing so with all our hearts . . . " Justin's described method of praying ("in common") has been interpreted by some to be a reference to the use of litanies, such as those known in synagogue worship, or to leader-led prayers to which all responded with an "in common" Amen. But it is just as likely that "in common" refers to many voices being raised simultaneously by standing worshipers. A cacophony of voices it perhaps was; but it also was a powerful means of encouraging each worshiper to speak his or her own prayers to God. This would be yet another way of orchestrating participation in direct dialogue with God. There were no critical ears monitoring the grammar or the content of the worshipers' prayers; these were simply offered "with all our hearts" to the present, living, and listening Lord. Yet Justin is clear that the expected and typical content of the prayers was not only for the welfare of the local assembly but also for the larger Church and "for people everywhere" regardless of their faith. There is a wideness and vision to these prayers; they are not selfish in character. One likely ought not make a great deal of it, but as a matter of mathematical calculation, Justin mentions intercessory prayer (for others) twice as often as he mentions supplication prayer (for self).

More prayers are offered in the next, the Eucharistic, act of this worship service, but only the "president" voices these prayers, speaking on behalf of all the assembly. Although, even in this period of prayer, all the assembly is expected to participate through active listening so as to add their "Amen" to what the "president" prays. Therefore it is still the entire congregation at prayer although in a different mode—and in different mood. These prayers offered at the Table by the "president" are distinctly of a praise and thanksgiving nature, a feature to which we'll turn our attention in just a moment. For the time being, however, do note the great significance this worship service has given to prayer—prayer offered by all the people for "all people everywhere." This is an assembly of priests, interceding for God's world and giving thanks to God for God's creating, sustaining, and redeeming works.

The service now moves to a very different activity, an offering of bread and wine (diluted with water) received with prayers of great thanksgiving and then shared with all present. This, obviously, is what we know as the "Lord's Supper." But the Greek word that is used by Justin (and uniformly by other writers of this era) is *Eucharist,* a word that means "thanks." Thus, the climactic act of this worship was a shared meal, participated in with great gladness and thanksgiving—note how Justin repetitiously uses the words praise and thanksgiving, for example "for being counted worthy to receive these things." This observance was also an act of great gravity and careful theology, for no less than the "president" presided at this meal, following a known and describable protocol, and using embryonic Trinitarian language in the prayer: "praise and glory to the Father of all things through the name of his Son and of the Holy Spirit."

Justin's account closes with the information that the worship service also includes opportunity to provide what Jewish piety would have called "alms for the poor." Through this note Justin provides a final confirmation that ancient practices are being extended into the corporate life of the new Christian community. The collection reminds this new community that just as compassion and justice are enduring concerns of Israel's God, they remain concerns of the people who now worship this same God through their Lord, Jesus Christ, and therefore the call to embody compassion and seek justice still has a rightful place within their worship. Any worship that fails to issue into tangible ministry is bogus.

The Apostolic Tradition
Justin's description clearly includes the Eucharist as a part of the service, but his words don't convey how central this act was to the service of worship. Other writers from the earliest Church era, though never disparaging any act of worship, greatly expand our insight into the supreme importance of this Eucharistic action. With amazing consistency and reverence, all of them devote major attention to it. Such fascination demands closer study.

One of the more well-known writings that aids us here is called the *Apostolic Tradition*, which for many years was considered to be the work of a bishop of Rome, Hippolytus (ca. 170-236 C.E.). Today it is more commonly thought that *Apostolic Tradition* represents the work of a group of conservative churchmen who issued it some fifty to sixty years after Hippolytus' death and attached his name to it to give it wider circulation. Authorship, however, is secondary to our search for early testimony about the Eucharist, and for this the *Apostolic Tradition* is a goldmine. (The document itself covers several subjects, but only its Supper instructions will be considered here.)

"Hippolytus" declares that the table portion of the service is to begin with a memorized exchange between worship leader and the congregation, an exchange which had been in use in Jewish worship long before and which still can be heard in many church-settings: the Salutation and the *Sursum Corda*, the lifting of hearts.

> The Lord be with you. *And with your spirit.*
> Lift up your hearts. *We lift them to the Lord.*
> Let us give thanks. *It is right and just.*

The *Apostolic Tradition* then provides this prayer to be voiced by the leader as the "thanks" of the people:

> O God, through your beloved Son Jesus Christ we give you thanks because in these last times you have sent him as Savior, Redeemer, and messenger of your will. He is your inseparable Word through whom you made all things and whom, in your delight, you sent from heaven into the womb of the virgin. Having been conceived, he was made flesh and showed himself as your Son, born of the Holy Spirit and of the virgin. He carried out your will and won for you a holy people. He stretched out his hands in suffering in order to deliver from suffering those who trust in you.
>
> When he was about to hand himself over to voluntary suffering, in order to destroy death and break the chains of the devil, to crush hell beneath his feet, to give light to the just, to establish the rule [of faith?], and to show forth the resurrection, he took bread, gave you thanks, saying, "Take, eat, this is my body which is broken for you." Likewise the cup, while saying, "This is my blood which is poured out for you. When you do this, you do it in memory of me."
>
> Recalling his death and his resurrection, we offer you this bread and this cup. We give you thanks for

having judged us worthy to stand before you and serve you.

We ask that you send your Holy Spirit upon the offering of your holy Church. Gather it together. Grant that all who share in your holy mysteries may be filled with the Holy Spirit so that their faith may be strengthened in truth. And so may we praise and glorify you through your Son Jesus Christ. Through him may glory and honor be to you in the Holy Spirit in your holy Church now and forever. Amen.

Of all the records from the early Church period, the *Apostolic Tradition* of "Hippolytus" is now considered to be one of the most instructive, especially for these Eucharistic words. Of first importance is the fact that these words really are a Eucharist, an expression of "thanksgiving." The gratitude centers upon "your beloved Son Jesus Christ," and sweeps from his pre-existence as the one "through whom you made all things" to his "voluntary suffering" as the one who "was made flesh" and through whose suffering deliverance has come, death has been destroyed, the chains of the devil broken, hell has been crushed, light has been given, and resurrection has been shown. There is a near-creedal cadence to these affirmations, each one marching in triumphal procession with its fellows, each one testifying to another dimension of the accomplishment of Christ. He is emphatically not depicted as a sacrificial victim—he "hand[s] himself over to voluntary suffering." Christ's work, as summarized in these phrases, is the many-splendored triumph of a victorious liberator. There is in this prayer no mournful blood-soaked remembering[16] of "an old rugged cross" as an "emblem of suffering and shame;" rather, there is a joyful recital of the mighty works of God wrought through Jesus in the Spirit. Here is a script for glad celebration and banqueting!

Indeed, this feast had been authorized (ordered!) by none other than Jesus and therefore he is rightly considered to be its truest host—and he is present among the banqueters! This is the significance of the prayer for the coming of the Holy Spirit ("We ask that you send your Holy Spirit upon the offering of your holy Church") within this act of worship, a prayer so central to all early Eucharistic rites that it was given a specific name, the *epiclesis* (Greek for "call upon"). These believers realized, as we do, that "all is vain unless the Spirit of the Holy One comes down,"[17] and thus—especially at the table—they "called upon" the presence of the Lord to be "made known to them in the breaking of the bread" (Luke 24:35). Considering the abundant references made to Eucharist in their writings, one may justifiably assume that the Lord faithfully came among them in power in these moments.

It is not puzzling therefore why they would refer to this meal as the Eucharist, the thanks. Here was where the "real presence" of Jesus was to be known and shared! If ever "experiencing God" was to occur in Christian worship, it would be as a grateful people gathered prayerfully around the fellowship table to remember God's deeds throughout history and supremely in Christ, and to eat and drink a bread and a wine that was ever so much more than the fruit of field and vine. This was not a long-faced, funereal ritual performed in memory of a fallen Martyr-Savior. This was Eucharist, a time of joy and thanksgiving, of remembrance and anticipation.

However, don't overlook that all of this is preserved for us by "Hippolytus" in a prayer of elegant expression and obvious concern for theology and proper sequence. This does not sound like an ad hoc, "anything-will-do" affair. (Indeed, scholars conclude that *Apostolic Tradition* was written as a rebuke to some who had become casual about these matters.) Perhaps even more important, however, is the fact that all this is couched in language that is Church-oriented, not individualistically referenced. The very first-sited accomplishment of Christ in this prayer is that "He carried out your will and won for you a holy people." Before anything else is mentioned, this gathering of a people is celebrated. Later, when the *epiclesis* is spoken, note that the Spirit presence of Christ is requested on behalf of "your holy Church" that it might be gathered together, filled with the Holy Spirit, strengthened in truth, and be a participant in the Spirit's and the Son's now-and-forever glorying and honoring of God. Thus, this prayer reaches far beyond the house-church walls where it is being spoken; it is not a selfish prayer asking that those within the room "experience" something electrifying. It is a prayer for the presence of God's Holy Spirit to be powerfully at work forever in the life of the far-flung Church—including, of course, this local expression of it! Fittingly, it is also a thanksgiving, a reveling that those inside these house-church walls have been included within this great work of God, "having [been] judged worthy to stand before you and serve you." In this prayer and through this act of worship, believers "stand amazed in the presence of Jesus the Nazarene,"[18] dumbfounded that they have been swept up into God's "holy mysteries" of eternal consequence. And they claim this astonishing identity and dignity in glad contradiction and repudiation of the stigma society attached to them as being "the rubbish of the world, the dregs of all things" (1 Corinthians 4:13).

It may be difficult for many of us twenty-first-century American evangelicals to identify with several aspects of this Lord's Supper act but, given these understandings, there can be little wonder why the Eucharist received the wondrous, extended written discussions it did. It must also be noted that these discussions carried the assumption and sometimes aggressively-asserted claim that the elements of bread and wine were the actual body and blood of Christ. A literal understanding of "this is my body" and "this is my blood" pervades this literature, creating another layer of potential fascination with the Eucharist. However, even if we today find ourselves incapable of granting a similar literal understanding to the elements, may we not find other riches within this meal that our immediate past has ignored? One need not assign literal significance to the elements *on* the table to sense the potency within worship *at* the table.

"Sing psalms and hymns and spiritual songs among yourselves"
Careful readers will surely have noted that in the preceding interpretation of the climaxing Eucharistic moment of early Christian worship two
songs were cited from evangelicalism's rich store of folk hymns and gospel
songs. This reveals another dimension of worship, namely that it is nearly
impossible for any of us to speak of worship without venturing into the
arena of poetry and song. Worshipful hearts have always found this to be
so. But scattered throughout the writings of the early Church there are
stern warnings about church music which are as informative as anything
Justin says about the order of worship or "Hippolytus" teaches us about
its Eucharist.[19]

One clearly curious fact discoverable from the early Christian
writings is how few and sparse are the references to music within worship. Even the scriptural phrase used as a heading for this section employs
terms that have proved to be devilishly difficult to define with specificity—e.g. what precisely was a "spiritual song"? And within our earliest
records of post-biblical Christian worship there is only one reference to
singing as a part of the worship gathering, and its meaning is not fully
understood. This reference appears in a letter written (111-112 C.E.)
by Pliny the Younger, the Roman governor of modern-day Turkey, to
the emperor Trajan for guidance regarding Christians. He states that his
interrogations of Christians had established that:

> . . . the substance of their guilt or error amounted to no
> more than this: they customarily gathered before dawn
> on a fixed day to sing in alternation a hymn to Christ
> as if to a god, and they bound themselves by an oath,
> not in a criminal conspiracy, but to refrain from rob-
> bery, theft, or adultery, from breaking their word, from
> reneging on a deposit. After this they usually dispersed,
> reassembling later on in order to take food of a common
> and harmless kind.

The precise meaning of Pliny's description of singing "in alternation" is argued among historians but it's probably a reference to some form of antiphonal chanting of a psalm (done however, as Pliny says, as a "hymn to Christ"), a practice not unlike what might have been learned or heard within synagogue worship. Thus, here is an early testimony to song within Christian worship. But there is no comparable testimony within Justin's reports, nor is music mentioned within the *Apostolic Tradition*, nor within the *Didache*, the previously mentioned church manual which is generally thought to have been issued somewhere around 100 C.E. Here and there one can find occasional references to praise and to song within worship, but these hardly explain why such a vital component of today's worship remains so sparsely documented and poorly described within the literature of the early Church.

A reason for this may begin to be found, however, in the fact that the Hebrew and Greek languages had no separate word for music. Thus "the frontier between singing and speaking was far less precise. As soon as speech turned to poetry, or when public and ceremonial speaking was involved, rhythmic and melodic features were incorporated which today would be classified as musical or at least pre-musical."[20] Paul Westermeyer concludes that "the whole of worship was musical" and consequently "it is difficult to distinguish music as a separate element of worship."[21] In effect this means that the "sound" of much of early worship was somewhat akin to the worship of today's Eastern Orthodox congregations, the priests singing (or chanting) much of the liturgy with "sung" congregational responses (e.g., "Alleluia," "Amen," or "Maranatha") interjected throughout.

It is, however, necessary to distinguish this practice from the use of song within the Agape Meal mentioned earlier. For instance, as a part of the Agape meal, Tertullian (ca. 170-225 C.E.) encouraged "each to come into the middle and sing to God, either from sacred scripture [Psalms] or from his own invention [perhaps a reference to "spiritual song"]." However, during the first four centuries "evidence of the congregational singing of hymns is either nonexistent or controversial."

In whatever manner congregational song was engaged, it's normally understood that it was to be done in unison—"harmonizing" was impermissible, even though men and women surely sang on the octave. This one-voice, one-note singing was lauded as aural evidence of the unity of the Church. Moreover, this singing must be done without instruments. The associations that musical instruments had with places and occasions of vice and pagan worship were enough to prompt rejection of any form of music-making other than that of the human voice raised in unaccompanied solo or unison song. Biblical references to the use of instruments in worship, such as those named in Psalm 150, were allegorized so that "harp" was said to mean "tongue," and "lyre" was said to mean "mouth," etc.

Clearly this is a much more regulated use of music in worship than anything evangelicals recognize. It is also a sobering reminder that the explosive years of the Church's growth were not what might today be called musically rich—and certainly not performance-oriented. Something other than the power of its music made this worship compelling. Music in some form(s) likely was an integral part of their worship, but it was used as a facilitator and expression of unity and offered in a manner distinct from the wider, secular culture.

Signs and Wonders?

A persistent myth circulated among evangelicals implies that the early Church era was marked by informal, electrifying worship services marked by powerful, evangelistically-oriented, Spirit-anointed preaching being divinely confirmed by miraculous signs and wonders. However, as this historical fly-over has been attempting to demonstrate, this construal is highly questionable, more myth than truth.

Of course, it is essential to confess that our knowledge of this period is incomplete. It is, in fact, a significant error to speak of *the* worship of the early Church, as though Christian worship across these years was uniform in all places and times. This is manifestly not so—a fact liturgical historians are emphatic in repeating. But, it is also manifestly

the case that the construal described above finds scant support within the
literature of the Church.

For instance, I trust that all that has been said will establish that
the preaching that was heard was scriptural exhortations to, as Justin put
it, "imitate all these excellent things," rather than the sermonic form and
content heard more commonly today. The earliest Christian "sermons"
we have are clearly more akin to devotional comments and pastoral exhortations than to evangelistic proclamations. Moreover, the gathering space
and the context of persecution made sermonic oratory impractical.[22]

The record concerning signs and wonders is less clear. Without
doubt, healings and exorcisms are certainly noted in early Christian
sources. In fact, exorcism—though not of the current Hollywood-
portrayed type—was even a part of Christian baptismal rites. But our
narratives of worship from this period give us sparse documentation of
exorcisms and healings as a recurring experience in worship gatherings.
It may be the case, of course, that these were so common that they went
unreported. But in light of such complete reportage of so much else, such
a silence seems odd. By the same token, it may be that the exercise of the
gift of glossolalia, or speaking in tongues, was so common an accompaniment of prayer and Eucharistic celebrations that it also went unreported.
Even so, a similar wonderment persists as to why such a silence prevails.
A foremost historian of the early Church concludes that the references
we do have concerning speaking in tongues "leave us in little doubt
about the apparent insignificance of tongues in their day," and concludes
that "we can safely assume that [glossolalia's] demise occurred between
ca. A.D. 250-350."[23] As much as some may want to construct an early
Church golden age of spine-tingling worship services as a hallmark for
later Christian worship, the records simply do not provide the materials
for such.

A concern about leadership

Finally, one can profitably note that within the literature of this period
there is a clear concern about the Church's leadership, not least of all

concerning those who would offer its prayers and lead its worship. Given the exponential growth and the increasingly pagan cultural background of Christianity's converts (that is, persons with no Jewish heritage but with probable great exposure to the rituals and ideologies of the era's many religions), there was concern to maintain the integrity of the faith, particularly in its corporate worship, and through this worship nurture the recently baptized in the ways of Christ.

This surfaces first in documents like the *Didache*, which provided guidance for ferreting out charlatans purporting to be prophets. One finds it more prominently in letters written by bishops. One of the earliest of these was authored by Clement, a bishop of Rome who (ca. 96 C.E.), scolded the church at Corinth for its dismissal of its bishop: "It is no small sin on our part if we eject from the episcopacy those who without blame and in holiness have presented [to God] the offerings."[24] Another bishop, Ignatius of Antioch (ca. 30-107 C.E.), wrote seven letters to various churches as he was being taken, under arrest, to Rome where he would be martyred (by the same emperor, Trajan, to whom Pliny the Younger wrote). In these his concern about leadership and especially worship leadership is clear. To the church in Smyrna (modern Izmir) he wrote: "Let no one do anything apart from the bishop which pertains to the Church," and admonished them "to follow the bishop just as Jesus Christ follows his Father."[25] He then says there is "only one legitimate Eucharist, namely, the one done under the bishop or whomever the bishop has committed it" and "without the bishop's permission it is not allowed to baptize or hold an agape, but whatever he approves is also pleasing to God."[26] In his letter to the Magnesians, Ignatius is even more restrictive, telling them that if any act apart from the bishop "their gatherings are neither legitimate nor in conformity with the Lord's commandment."[27] In the *Apostolic Tradition* of Hippolytus, as previously mentioned, a motivating concern was to correct theological and ritual errors that had intruded into worship. All of this is to say that the earliest Church showed great concern about those who would lead its worship. Novices, those unknown to and untutored by acknowledged Church

leaders, were said to be unacceptable leaders of worship, not yet competent to handle holy things or to voice its prayers well.

Clarifying Characteristics

Now, let us identify several characteristics of the worship of this period,
which I believe have much to say to our current confused understandings
of worship.

First, the worship of the Church of the first four centuries was
decidedly *a corporate vertical-dialogical occasion*. The gathering of the
community is obviously of great importance to them; assembling the
'body' a matter of high importance. Absentees were noted and the unifying elements of bread and wine taken to them immediately after the
meeting's conclusion. Faithful participation of all within this event (even
if by extension) was deemed essential. This was the occasion when the
Church, God's chosen, became a visible reality in the world. This was
the occasion when the local "kingdom of priests" gathered to offer the
"sacrifice of praise" (Hebrews 13:15), to intercede for the world's needs,
to listen to God's counsel, and to share "a meal with God," just as ancient
Hebrews did on special worship occasions. These meetings were being
played out to God and God alone, through Christ in the Spirit by a body
of believers. The determinative agenda at work seems to be the community's desire to draw near to the God of their salvation and in that
relationship be remade in the image of the Christ of this God. This is
worship that is seeking God's face, worship that is "about God."

A second characteristic is that this was decidedly *Trinitarian
worship*. Even though the term Trinity was not yet in use, the reality it
signifies is clearly in evidence. It is present as early as Justin's Offertory
prayer and as late as the communion prayer of "Hippolytus," each
member of the Trinity being named in clustered fashion. Christians
knew the God they worshiped was unique; there was no comparable god
within the pantheon of Greek, Roman, or other deities and thus they
were clear about their worship being offered to the God and Father of our
Lord Jesus Christ, whose presence and power was made known through

Holy Spirit.[28] Thus, the God being worshiped could not be confused
with any other. Moreover, this God had a long history, a record of self-
revelation, even a body of literature that provided authoritative guidance
in honoring and worshiping this God. Worship therefore, had content. It
had theological "meat" for the body's consideration as it assembled, and it
also knew an illumining Spirit whose work within the listening assembly
could "make gravy" of this good meat.

A significant but not immediately seen aspect of this emphatic
Trinitarian worship is its political implication. In its soon-to-be canonical
documents, this Church offered its praise "to the only wise God through
Jesus Christ to whom be glory for ever" (Romans 16:27), and declared
"You are worthy, our Lord and God, to receive glory and honor and
power, for you created all things, and by your will they existed and were
created" (Revelation 4:11). It also affirmed that "salvation belongs to our
God who is seated on the throne, and to the Lamb" (Revelation 7:10),
and in its worship times it doubtless had occasion to tell the story of
Peter and John defying earthly rulers with the response: "Whether it is
right in God's sight to listen to you rather than to God, you must judge;
for we cannot keep from speaking about what we have seen and heard"
(Acts 4:20). In these ways this Church voiced a singularity of focus and a
loyalty to the triune God that dethroned all other gods—even Caesar. "In
this sense, by the mere fact of its celebration, [Christian worship] is basi-
cally political action: it reminds the state of the limited and provisional
character of its power, and when the state claims for itself an absolute
trust and obedience, [Christian worship] protests against this preten-
sion to claim a kingdom, a power, and a glory which belongs of right to
God alone. This is why, in gathering together for Christian worship, men
compromise themselves politically."[29] Bill Wylie Kellerman underlines
and expands this by asserting that " . . . every act of worship, every occasion where the sovereignty of God is celebrated, every instance where the
realm of God is acknowledged, is always and everywhere expressly political."[30] The threat to the state posed by worshiping Christians was clearly
understood from the time of Trajan until Constantine's ascendance.

A third and parallel characteristic of this worship is that it was *not a public event, nor was it ever construed to be an occasion of outreach to unbelievers.* Even if weekday evangelistic conversations with unbelievers indicated a seeker's deep readiness to profess faith in Christ, seeking unbelievers were carefully investigated by Church leaders as to motive and sincerity before they were permitted even to begin the catechetical stage of Christian discipleship, which alone would permit them a seat within the worshiping assembly—and then only for the first portion of the service, the portion later called The Service of the Word. None but the fully confirmed, baptized, and faithful were permitted to participate in the latter half of the service, the portion later called the Service of the Table. Christian worship, therefore, was a distinctly Churchly act and none but Church people were within its intention.[31]

A fourth characteristic is *a discernible and apparently stable structure.* Although we don't have records from every congregation within the numerically exploding young Church, such records as we do have give no indication that church leaders in, say, Pergamum or Thessalonica or Alexandria or Rome were creating new orders of worship each week. It is a real stretch of imagination to think of them as crafting novel programs of worship weekly for each city and house church. Assuredly there were differences between regions and periods during these early years; liturgical scholars can document such variations. Even so, everything we know about this era suggests that those differences were minimal in comparison with the astounding commonality they shared. All devoted the first time period to scripture and the second time period to the Eucharist, bathing the whole in prayers of thanks and longing.

In this structure they were building upon memories and traditions stemming from scripture itself. The Emmaus-bound disciples of Luke 24 saw the risen Lord in the breaking of bread after he had opened the scripture to them; the Pentecost-struck disciples of Acts 2:42 devoted themselves to the apostles teaching and the breaking of bread. (See also Acts 20:7 for a possible allusion to this same pattern.) In developing this two-fold structure of word and table, they combined the historic tradition of the synagogue's word-centered worship with the newly Jesus-mandated "Do this in remembrance" meal (in itself a copying of Israel's many "meals with God"—the Sinai wilderness manna, the Passover, celebratory meals following certain temple sacrifices, and domestic *charuba* worship/fellowship meals), thereby creating "a new thing," though firmly rooting it in history and tradition. Though very much aware they were participants in God's new ("end of the ages") work, they also seem to have been gratefully mindful they were joining in the ages-long march of God's continuing work throughout history.

Fifth, this worship *found its climax in the Eucharist.* This was the summit toward which each service traveled. It was the holy of holies moment for the early Church. Admittedly, this may strike many of us as extremely odd. This is especially so among those who are theological descendants of the Swiss reformer Ulrich Zwingli (1484-1531). Zwingli championed the minimalist idea that the Lord's Supper elements have only symbolic value and that the meal itself is best understood as a solemn memorial. His views, though immensely influential within subsequent Protestantism, are in shocking contrast to the reverence and awe portrayed in the early Church's table talk. Further complicating our ability to understand the high voltage character of the early Church's estimate of the table is the 18th century intellectual revolution known as the Enlightenment. The Enlightenment stripped from the Western world a lively sense of mystery and wonder, replacing it with a straitjacket of scientific, evidential demands. Therefore, children of the Enlightenment experience intellectual hurdles when confronted by expressions like "This is my body." Nonetheless, the supremacy of the Table and its numinous attraction within earliest Christian worship is undeniable.

A sixth characteristic of early worship is the *predominance of prayer* within it—even more so than preaching! In our review this was seen in Justin's repeated reference to prayer and in the model prayer "Hippolytus" provided for the worship leader's use at the table. Their attention to prayer is but a fraction of the prayers and model prayers to be found within the literature of the early Church, literature that was written as guidance for church leaders' use in worship. Liberty was given to these leaders to offer prayers of their own composition, but liberty was not given to them to dispense with the prayers or to offer them thoughtlessly. The assembly was expected to make these prayers its own by speaking an "Amen" to them—meaning, of course, that the leader's prayers had enough substance to them that they merited a congregational amen. Nor were the leaders' prayers the only prayers offered. Justin's account suggests that the individuals within the assembly were expected to offer their own prayers at a specified time during the course of the service. The participative and dialogical dimension of worship is much in evidence here, but the greater issue is the abundant evidence of great time and passion being given to prayer in worship. No doubt their defenselessness against persecution, their experiences of shunning, and their lack of worldly status drove them to prayer. But the number of references to "others" being prayed for also indicates that here were believers who understood themselves to be a priesthood, an assembly convened by the Spirit to offer serious prayers to God through the Son for the good of all. Without unduly stretching the definition of prayer, it might be justifiably concluded that this service was essentially a prayer service, every act within it understandable as an expression of vertical-dialogical prayer.

A seventh characteristic of the worship of this period is its *intimacy*. The physical setting of it, within the homes of members, is a key factor here. This may have diminished some when out-of-doors worship in cemeteries was the case and when basilicas began to be claimed as worship venues. But, whether early or late in this period, indoors or outside, a sense of knowing and being known is communicated in these writings. Anonymity wasn't a live possibility when "church" was an extended family—names and needs were known, gifts and reluctances noted, admonition and affirmation were predictably individualized. Leaders knew their sheep and called them by name.

An eighth characteristic of the worship of this period is *the care given to the qualifications of worship leaders*. Though some may denigrate the bishops' outlawing of non-appointed worship leaders as evidence of

Spirit-quenching power-games played by ecclesiastical big-wigs, a fairer judgment is that these leaders understood, even before it was articulated, the principle of *lex orandi, lex credendi,* which was noted earlier. They knew how easily this infant faith could become something other than itself if those who formed the faith of its people through the prayers of worship and led its word and table moments were not thoroughly grounded in this faith. They wanted those who handled the body and blood of Christ, those who interpreted the scriptures, those who led the prayers and worship of the Church, to be theologically-mentored persons whose maturity in faith and life perspective had been tested and found worthy.

[A final note must be entered, even if only in brackets, that *the mood of these worship meetings is not a matter which the sources discuss.* There can be little doubt that joy, even ecstasy—though not in a shallow, giddy sense—was evident. Similarly, there can be little doubt that solemnity and reverence were also evident or that interpersonal concern (love) was palpable. But, like so much of the scriptural writings they read, these worship reports don't dwell on the affective, the psychological dimension of the assembly, a characteristic that's in stark contrast to our day when worship services are described primarily by their emotional "feel."]

When these worship characteristics are reviewed, it is most difficult to imagine that the worship of the earliest Church was anything other than a joyful work and a family reunion of a disciplined, minority faith movement engaged in "seeking the face of God." This was sacred "play" enacted in childlike awe, with great care ("rules") being given to certain particulars. Other descriptors may also be fitting, but surely these are sufficient to offer an historical critique and to evoke a serious wondering if our present worship conversations are nearly radical enough.

Radical enough?

Most evangelical churches, when discussing worship changes, imagine the flash-points to be about the soundtrack ("Should we change the kind of music we use?") and set design ("Should we do away with a robed

choir, dress the pastor in denim and shirttails, and install screens for song
lyrics, flood and strobe lights for the stage?"). These are important issues,
unquestionably. But this survey of early Christian worship puts those
questions into question. The better questions cluster about the fundamental issue of the purpose of the gathering itself, and to what degree
non-worship agendas have hijacked it. While we've been warring over
style and presentation, has anyone checked substance lately?

Rather than more conversations about retrofitting or defending
the worship gatherings we've most recently known, more conversations
need to discuss if these gatherings honestly deserve to be retrofitted. Put
most plainly: Is what we have called worship consistent with the understanding and practices given us by our own founders? The challenge
therefore isn't just one of retrofitting our worship, it is the challenge of
re-conceiving worship from the ground up.

Review, if you will, the characteristics of early Church worship
just identified and ask how evident those are in the worship of the church
you know best. Is this Christian DNA unmistakably evident on Sundays
today? If the family resemblance is not strong, there is work to be done.

Spiritual practices/spiritual formation once again

While you are conducting that self-assessment, do include a recurring
theme within this book: the formative power of worship. Our survey
of earliest Christian worship has shown that worship was not only the
"oven" in which so much of our Christian beliefs was baked, it was also
the "oven" in which the Christian Church itself was formed. As the first
Spirit-drawn, Christ-centered worshipers of God gathered, they became
not only a new sociological entity, they became a people with a perceiv-
ably different outlook and ethic. "In the second and third centuries,
Christians were known as the 'Third Race,'—neither Jew nor Greek—
and they claimed it with pride, picking up the biblical themes of having
their citizenship in heaven."[32] If we seek to explain their transformation
into such a discernibly-different group, the power of God through the
Spirit must surely be credited as of first importance. But it is impossible

to conceive of this transformation without also crediting the earthly vehicle of the worshiping community.

Corporate worship was most instrumental in shaping this early community (a "peculiar people" according to Hebrews 2:9 KJV) in a distinctly different way of valuing and of living.[33] Through their gatherings God made a distinct people, a Christian Church, out of a multi-national and economically-diverse aggregation of individuals. An identity as "Jesus People" was sculpted week by week; through their listening, their praying, and their communing they were weaned from the ways of the world and fashioned into Christ-people. "With unveiled faces [seeking the face of God]" they were "transformed into the same image from one degree of glory to another" (2 Corinthians 3:18). They became like the Lord they worshiped. Though this was not a stated purpose of their worship, it was an inevitable outcome, given the transforming nature of the God they worshiped and the God-centered focus of the meetings. As they sought God's face, God in Christ "rubbed off" on them.[34]

When the Apostle Paul pled with the Romans to "present your bodies as a living sacrifice, holy and acceptable to God, which is your spiritual worship," he employs liturgical terms even though a ceremonial program certainly isn't his goal. His goal was a transformation, a "renewing of [their] minds" (Romans 12:1-2). But Paul cannot conceive of such a transformation without using the vocabulary and categories of worship. Worship was associated with and understood to be a mind-destroying/renewing channel of God's power.

The issue here penetrates even to what we mean by salvation. As children of Finney's revivalism, we are accustomed to think of salvation as an event, as a gift of grace received upon our accepting Christ as our personal Lord and Savior. This is surely one way of approaching the matter, but the early Church saw salvation just as much or even more in terms of a process—indeed a process of becoming ever more like God—than of a datable transaction:

The early fathers believed that God's salvation through the life, death, and resurrection of Christ meant providing a believer with the means to perceive God and thereby share in his divine life. That is, salvation was supposed to culminate in divine *theosis* or deification— becoming transformed according to God—a seminal part of the teaching of early fathers such as Irenaeus, Athanasius, and Gregory of Nyssa. The point is that faith is a divine work of salvation "in us" as well as "for us" in order to change us, that we may behold God.[35]

This is in keeping with Paul's thought of presenting ourselves (continuously) as living sacrifices to God so that we might "discern the will of God." To think as God thinks, to value as God values, to act as God acts—this is to "be saved"—and this is a matter of being of transformed, not least of all by the day-by-day and week-by-week discipline of worshiping God.[36]

A desirable cult

Rodney Clapp is one of many current authors who has pled for today's Church to give more attention to this formative dimension of worship. Taking his cue from the Latin-French word *cultus*—a term used often among liturgical and biblical scholars for the practices of worship— Clapp speaks of worship as being a principal means of shaping a *culture* of distinctively-Christian identity.[37] He doesn't mean to suggest that the vertical-dialogical priority of worship be lessened or that an educational purpose now be introduced as an additional confusing factor in our worship thinking. But he does want us to understand that in our worship services spiritual formation is taking place, consciously or unconsciously, for better or for worse, and that it behooves us to evaluate all worship practices so as to maximize their potential as sculptors of a Christly cult-ure.

Examples of this careful scrutiny can be seen even within the period of the writing of the New Testament. James, for example, addresses the seemingly-innocuous matter of worship seating. He insists that the world's way of bowing and scraping to the rich must not be permitted within worship. So he condemns the practice of providing a chair for the rich while dismissively directing the poor to a seat on the floor. This, he says, is in effect a denial of their belief in Christ, and in such practices "you make distinctions among yourselves, and become judges with evil thoughts" (James 2:1-7). Something as necessary and as easily overlooked as who sits where during the worship service is for James a spiritually-significant matter; it teaches a way of valuing and honoring that is opposite to the world's way.

Paul displays a similar concern for the formative power of worship practices. His letters open with salutations we have reason to believe were also used as greeting words for worship ("Grace to you and peace from God our Father and the Lord Jesus Christ" Romans 1:5; 1 Corinthians 1:3; 2 Corinthians 1:2; Galatians 1:3, et al.), and within the letters (which would be read during the assembly time) he frequently includes phrases from worship songs he knew were being used in the very services where this letter would be read. By such tactics he deftly placed himself in their midst, at their elbow as they worshiped the Lord. But it appears he also "doctored" some of the songs he quoted. New Testament scholars have noticed that his citations sometimes fail to conform to the poetic meter of a hymn. Upon closer inspection some have come to believe Paul altered a word or a phrase here and there in order to correct a theological inadequacy in these songs. This seems to be especially so if the hymn tended to become too triumphalistic. He introduces a meter-destroying correction, thereby drawing attention to words that were misleading or untrue and in doing so drew the congregation back to the unwanted way of the cross and to the discipline of hope.[38] Thus Paul, the wise pastor and worship leader, recognized that shallow or "wrong" songs formed shallow or "wrong" disciples; he wanted Sunday's services to offer "renewal of mind," a worship that would shape the believing community into the image of Christ.

The unwelcome truth is that those who wish to become Christian in any age must be detoxified from the world's "mind" and methodically and persistently molded into a distinctively new, Christly culture. In this re-formation corporate worship plays a crucial role. To delete this understanding from our worship concepts would be a grievous error. It would mean endorsing worship that only applies a thin Christian veneer to a bone-deep pagan culture, granting continuing validity to Jim Wallis' stinging dictum: "The only thing left of Jesus in much American Christianity is his name."[39]

"You will know them by their fruits"

We "need to attend very closely to what is being said and believed and celebrated in corporate worship," says ethicist/pastor J. Phillip Wogaman. "The world is being put together or torn apart in the liturgy," he adds, and "we had better pay attention." He then cites a portion of a "Prayer for Enemies" found in *Book of Worship for United States Forces*.

> Have mercy, Father, upon those who live to enslave the world rather than let men live in freedom. Bring light to their darkened minds, peace to their warring hearts, and sanity to their warped designs. Hasten the day when international enemies are won to friendship by those who have the power of your love.[40]

Wogaman is understandably dismayed by the appalling self-righteousness reflected in this prayer, but similar patterns can be found in non-military settings. It is sad that we, who know our Master calls us to turn the other cheek and even forgive our enemies, still conduct worship services that glorify the use of violent and or militaristic response to wrongs. Surveys consistently document that evangelicals remain the staunchest proponents of being "armed and dangerous" in defense of our "stuff," a finding verified in Sunday's silence about our national gun culture and the video games, movies, and television shows that espouse a philosophy of "kill or be killed." Additionally, in countless worship services, the non-gospels of happiness and monetary gain are peddled as God's truth, and then buttressed with a promise that God is even going to provide a protective "hedge" about us and our "stuff" so we can keep it all! In short, the world's culture is so pervasive and toxic that its fatal fumes are inhaled unwittingly. From this we desperately need "saving;" only a radical renewal of mind is sufficient if salvation is to be anything more than a spiritual fiction. This change will not come in a moment, but surely the discipline of worship ought to have a role to play in sensitizing us to and weaning us from this culture of death and introducing us to a redemptive culture of Christ-life.

An encouraging example of just such formative worship was given to me as I attended a gathering of fifty or so male pastors (they are still wrestling with the issue of female pastors) of the Original Freewill Baptist denomination. I was their guest and had been informed that during the first night's worship service they would honor their worship tradition of observing the Lord's Supper and the washing of one another's feet. Having never participated in such a service, I asked if I might do so, and, upon receiving assurances that I would be welcome, I did. I'm most glad I did.

The Lord's Supper observance was not that different from many I have attended or even led, but I'd never participated in a foot-washing service. I was seated beside one of my divinity school students, and, when the moment came, he and I walked together to the front of the room, where basins of water and towels awaited us. As we removed our shoes, this twenty-something student asked, "Dr. Day, may I have the honor of washing your feet?" The question stunned me. I stammered "Yes" and sat down. He lifted one of my feet and placed it in the basin, washed, and then dried it. He repeated the process with the other foot and then looked up at me from his kneeling position and said, "Thank you for letting me do this." Then it was my turn. And I, step by step, and word for word duplicated my student's worship action. All about us, others were similarly engaged, washing each other's feet. A song I didn't recognize was quietly being sung by some of the men, its words having something to do with serving one another. Fathers and sons, young men and old, denominational brass and rookie pastor, professor and student—all were kneeling, washing, embracing, and encouraging one another. It was amazing.

Candidly, I doubt if this practice will ever become a worship norm for many of us. It's too great a stretch, either hermeneutically or aesthetically, to include it within our regular worship. I understand. I also know that this rite powerfully inculcated a culture of humility and service among these participants. Kneeling before one another, doing something so awkwardly old-fashioned and personal as washing another's feet—and asking for the honor and expressing thanks for the privilege!—puts a dagger into the heart of pride even as it incarnates relational bonds. In those moments, in that mountain chapel, among those men, I realized afresh how formative our worship actions and words can be. Regardless of one's opinion regarding this particular rite, that act was forming among those men a culture—a way of life and valuing—that is tuned to the Jesus frequency.

I believe the worship of earliest Christianity exemplified this, and this goes far toward an explanation of how an upstart faith centered around a crucified Jew turned the Roman world upside down.[41] Attempting to duplicate every worship particular of that long-ago "greatest generation" of Christians is both unnecessary and unwise. I'm confident Justin had his flaws and that "Hippolytus" and his fellow bishops were not always saintly and that there are more stories of early Church failures than I want to hear. Theirs was no more a sinless, superhero age than ours, and, therefore, discretion must be used in holding them up as models; however, maintaining the clarity of their worship purpose (to seek God's face) and emulating the worship wisdom within their practices (a God-centered order of scripture, prayer, word, table, offering, etc.) is one of the smartest things evangelicals might do.

RESOURCE: THE FORMATIVE POWER OF WORSHIP

One provocative description of the spiritual formation that can occur today through thoughtful worship is offered by Stanley Hauerwas and Samuel Wells:

> Through worship God trains his people to take the right things for granted. When Christians gather they learn to value every person God has made, big, small, bright, slow, not because they are each individuals with rights (which inevitably conflict) but because each one has been given gifts by God that the Church needs to receive if it is to be faithful. When Christians confess their sins they recall the passion and recklessness of God and realize that every saint has a past and every sinner has a future. When Christians listen to Scripture they remember that God's purposes can never be limited by the meanness of the human imagination. When Christians share bread together they rediscover that every person brings different things to the table but each receives back the same. When Christians are sent out they are reminded that each one has a vocation to witness and service and that ordinary discipleship can find an elixir in the words "for thy sake."
>
> Worship is the time when God trains his people to imitate him in habit, instinct, and reflex. The people who listen to children talking about God learn to listen to children talking about growth and sadness. The people who expect God to communicate with them in worship learn to discern his voice in the shopping queue or the news bulletin. The people who hear the story of the homeless young mother who became a refugee learn

to welcome such people whom they meet elsewhere. Together, God's people reform the descriptions they use to name the outcast, the sinner, and the unclean, and reshape the ways people are received, nurtured, respected, and empowered. Together they reflect on the patterns of life that build up the body. In discussing whether, how, and when it is appropriate to speak in tongues or dance or prophesy or use contemporary music or pray extempore, the body discovers when it is appropriate to campaign, denounce, protest, or be silent. In discussing who should lead, preach, preside, pray, and how much people should attend, pray, give money, be patient, the body discovers the gifts God gives the Church and the instincts of community.

Above all, worship trains God's people to be examples of what his love can do. Worshiping God invites him to make the life of the disciple the theater of his glory. Worshiping God together invites him to make the body of believers the stage of his splendor. Over and over, God's people see the way God's Son took, blessed, broke, and gave, so that this pattern might give life to the world. The next day he himself was taken, blessed, broken, and given, for the life of the world. Over and over, they ask God to take, bless, break, and give them, for the life of the world. The saints are those whose lives have been transformed in this way—those through whom God has given life to the world. Worship trains Christians to be saints.[42]

2. Landmarks from our Longer Worship Heritage

Distinctives Drawn from Two Millennia

If Christian worship is to be *Te Deum*—that is, to God and about God and for God in such fashion that it declares God's great goodness even as it transforms the church into a visible sign of that goodness—guidance is needed. Some of that guidance we have already sought from the example of our first ancestors. But more resources are available to us; indeed, the entire worship heritage of the Church has clarifying light to lend us. The great importance of seeking it has been put in parable form by New Testament scholar N.T. Wright, and, though his parable was given with reference to biblical interpretation, it is applicable to liturgical concerns, as well.

Wright imagines the discovery of an unknown play written by William Shakespeare, a discovery that sets the literary and theatrical worlds abuzz with excitement. The fly in the ointment, however, is that the manuscript is unfinished—only four acts are extant. Scholars debate what should be done. Ought a master playwright be authorized to write an appropriate and concluding fifth act? But where might one find a playwright comparable to Shakespeare? Wright suggests that rather than permit one individual to risk such a feat, the wiser path would be to enlist a team of sensitive, experienced Shakespearean actors and commission them to immerse themselves thoroughly in the first four acts as well as in the culture and language of Shakespeare's day—and then work out the fifth act themselves.

The assumptions of Wright's tactic are that the secret of the fifth act is lodged within the previous four acts and that an informed, thoughtful ensemble, listening carefully to what has come before, will have the greatest chance of reproducing Shakespeare's genius, flavor, and design. As he says, this tactic "would require of the actors a free and responsible entering into the story as it stood, in order first to understand how the threads could appropriately be drawn together and then put that understanding into effect by speaking and acting with innovation and consistency."[43]

Interpreting this parable for worship practices, one surely must note the inevitable improvisational nature of our assignment as worship planners. Because Jesus didn't leave a worship manual lying beside his grave cloths in the empty tomb, a degree of "innovation," as Wright terms it, is inescapably ours. But alongside this there is a required immersion in what has gone before so that there is "innovation and *consistency*." This is where the matter of "rules" surfaces once again, for freedom is surely ours as worship planners but not a liberty to create "whatever" and call it Christian worship. The parable also says that the best hope of coming up with something that displays innovation and consistency arises when the work is done collaboratively, not independently, and with contemporary sensitivities linked to historical fidelity. The drama will be best performed by those who learn with others what the longer, greater tradition is and then, out of its authenticity and in sympathetic conversation with the present, create the fitting prolongation. Lacking this kind of listening to one another and to the past, one can anticipate precisely the kind of confusing scene we currently have.

However, lest this assignment sound like an academic game of researching from here to eternity, one must note that the task is assigned to actors (read: worship leaders), the persons who are invested in doing rather than in theorizing. Naturally, the scholars, the historians, and theologians are integral to the discussion, but this is ultimately the work of those who stand each Sunday before an assembled congregation and say, "Let us worship the Lord."

Accordingly, the next pages identify some of the highlights or landmarks from within the longer worship heritage of the Church, from the witness of Church leaders who, across the past seventeen hundred years, have stood before congregations on the Lord's Day to lead them in worship. Immersing ourselves in their wisdom we gain the historical consistency we need if we are to be faithful innovators today.

The Priority of God

It is not for nothing that among the concluding words in the final book of our New Testament, The Revelation to John, there is a twice repeated imperative: worship *God* (19:10; 22:9). Idolatry, be it in the form of Israel's alluring Baal, Revelation's "beast," ecclesiastical forms, an inspired book, or a preferred worship style, is an ever-present alternative to worshiping the God revealed in Christ. Thus, it is no slight thing that we train ourselves to think and speak of worship as the worship *of God.* Just by doing the simple, yet significant thing of adding the prepositional phrase *of God* to the word worship—especially in our thinking!—we make a good beginning toward a better use of the word and a right use of the meetings we call worship.

When worship is thought of as an act with God as its Object and Subject, we place a defining focus around the purpose and content of this gathering. We remind ourselves that this meeting is to be about, for, and directed to this specific Holy One. Helpful boundaries are then established. Every proposed action and word must now be judged by its appropriateness as an act that expresses the worship *of God.* (It is not about us! It is not about our needs or hurts or cravings or anything else other than about God!) Every existing action and word must be justified by its value as an expression of the worship *of God.* Now the meeting has theological gravitas anchoring its spiritual flight; it can be understood as being a meeting that is God-centered and God-directed. This, of course, is because right worship always has God as its *initiator* as well as its recipient.

The revelation and response dynamic of worship

This is a concept clearly evident within the Church's master narrative, scripture itself. A review of the Bible's many worship scenes reveals that worship of God is consistently a response to revelation *from God.* This means worship begins with God's action in opening the eyes of our heart so that we perceive God's glory, holiness, mercy, generosity, or such. This self-disclosure has historically been called revelation.

In some manner God initiates all worship by showing us a portion of God's own self, a self-revelation. Then we respond in thanks or praise or song or offering or deed. Our response to what God has done or shown is our side of worship. Ours is always a response to God's previous gracious overtures, a reply to what has been "said" to us.

Perhaps it helps to think of this, somewhat crudely, as a tic-toc movement. God's self-revealing is the initiating tic, and our acknowledging response is the toc. There is therefore a back and forth dynamic within worship. From our vantage, worship is an outward-bound expression directed God-ward. From God's vantage, however, our act is only a reply to a preceding, initiating call or word from God directed to us. Worship always originates in God's kind self-giving that creates and enables our response. The action, therefore, begins and ends with God.

For several years I lived in Columbia, Missouri, and during that time I was introduced to the pageantry of the University of Missouri's football games on autumn Saturday afternoons at Faurot Field. Actually, I happened to reside there during a bleak stretch of Old Mizzou's football fortunes, so I was obliged to find most of the pageantry and excitement in something other than the games themselves. As a newcomer I was initially puzzled by a frequent antiphonal cheer enjoyed by the fans. As best I could tell, during this specific cheer, the University's cheerleaders would prompt the fans on the west side of the field to shout out three short words. Then the cheerleaders on the east side of the field prompted the fans to return the words. So, the cheer was thrown back and forth across the playing field in rousing fashion. Eventually I figured out (I am a slow learner!) that the fans weren't shouting words. They were shouting three letters. The westside fans were shouting M-I-Z and the eastside fans were responding with another three letters: Z-O-U. And, presumably, sweating MIZZOU players on the field took heart from the back and forth waves of audible support for the home team.

This is a rough illustration of the way worship works. God speaks the revealing words of cheer and of blessing; we, in return, voice the divinely-desired echo of thanks and praise. Thus the "playing field" of the entire creation is filled with the Church's worshipful reply. The call of God has been answered with an affirmative response, or alternatively, with the tragic scenario described by Isaiah: "when I called, no one answered, when I spoke, they did not listen" (66:4).

Once we grasp this dynamic we can hear it expressed in many hymns whose words we perhaps have sung uncomprehendingly. For instance, Edmund Sears' beloved Christmas carol "It Came Upon the Midnight Clear" concludes with the longing for "the whole world [to] give back the song which now the angels sing." That's a plea for the universal presence of the worship of God. Issac Watts' grand Christmas hymn "Joy to the World!" expresses a similar pattern. Watts states his joy that "the Lord is come" and then adds his longing for a worshipful response: "let men their songs employ" while "fields and floods, rocks, hills, and plains repeat the sounding joy." Joachim Neander's "Praise to the Lord, the Almighty" says: "Let the Amen sound from his people again." That's a plea for an earthly "So be it!" to be joyfully shouted back to what God has said; in other words, it's a prayer that worship might occur. Finally, "When Morning Gilds the Skies," written in litany form, declares that "in heaven's eternal bliss the loveliest strain is this" and then offers the response: "may Jesus Christ be praised!" This is followed by a plea for creation's response to heaven's song: "Let earth and sea and sky, from depth to height reply, may Jesus Christ be praised!" The Church's hymnody is filled with the understanding of worship as a pattern of revelation and response.

It may be briefly noted once more, however, that if worship is fundamentally a matter of revelation and response, all attempts to design worship services for unbelievers are rendered problematic. The reason, to put it most crudely, is that "corpses can't dance." Only those who've "heard the joyful sound" and have been raised to new life can dance. Of course, we can also thankfully add that the Church's worship can be a converting witness to unbelievers. The Apostle Paul wrote of this possibility (1 Corinthians 14:24-25) long ago; but the worship he had in mind was a gathering of and for the faithful to worship God—not an event to which outsiders were invited. However, the central point presently is to establish that the worship *of God* is a gift from God, a possibility only because God has spoken and allowed us to hear.

Orienting Landmarks

With this foundational concept that Christian worship is a glad, echoing "Yes!" spoken to God by those who have heard God's grace-filled "Yes!" spoken to us in Jesus, the journey of worship exploration is able to begin. In this trek we are in search of useable guidance from the Church through the ages. There are landmarks, "rules" if you will, which wise worshipers and worship planners may use for navigation. They may be likened to universal constants, truths whose truth we are foolish to ignore or downplay. In our several contexts they may be honored in various ways; but in every context their wisdom is essential if we desire worship that is truly about God. I name seven.

    Landmark One: *The Unique God of Christian Faith: The Trinity.* The Church of two millennia would insist that Christian worship must be about the unique God of Christian faith: Father, Son, and Holy Spirit. For us, God is not just "God," but is "God in three persons, blessed Trinity."

    The honoring of this distinct understanding within our worship is far more than just a theological nicety to satisfy the purists—you know, the academic-types or our high-church neighbors who've learned to conclude their prayers with impressive phrases like, "in the name of Christ, who lives and reigns with you and the Holy Spirit, one God, forever and ever. Amen." No, something is at stake here that's infinitely more important than simply crossing one's theological t's or displaying doctrinal orthodoxy for appearance's sake—this isn't a game of theological "gotcha's." It is a gift/task that requires thoughtful discernment—and particularly so as we live into an increasingly religiously pluralistic culture where the word God may be understood in numberless ways. Specificity matters!

For example, when I was first introduced to the fact that the word LORD (printed in all capital letters), when it appears in my English Bible, represents the Hebrew word *YHWH*, commonly pronounced *Yahweh*, it deepened my understanding and appreciation of many Old Testament texts. For *Yahweh* is the mysterious, too-sacred-to-be-spoken name of the covenanting God of Israel. It is the specific, self-declared name of Israel's God (see Exodus 3:13-15). This God was not to be confused with any other of the multiple deities worshiped by Israel's neighbors, and therefore this God had a distinct name. The Old Testament writers wrote the Hebrew letters for *Yahweh* into their manuscripts in order to be precise about this when precision was called for. But when later Hebrew readers of their writing came to those letters, they never vocalized them. For those letters were the written reference to the too-awesome-to-be-uttered God of Israel. The word *Yahweh* was too holy to be spoken—so they inserted a substitute word, *Adonai*, when they came upon the Hebrew letters for *Yahweh*.

Upon learning this, I changed my way of reading the word LORD whenever I came across it in the Old Testament. I realized this might be a clue for me to realize that the text was being very precise and definite in this reference to God, emphasizing that it was the very unique, distinctive God of the Israelite covenant who was being referenced. I began to feel the nuances and deeper significance of countless Old Testament texts. I began to see how often Israel was being called to a singular, discriminating focus of loyalty: "*This* One—and no other—is your God! *This* One—and no other—is the source and end of your life!"

A similar kind of clarifying, focusing specificity is given to Christians through our Trinitarian understanding of God. Because we believe God isn't "the big Guy upstairs," or just "the First Bang of the Big Bang Theory," or a benign sense of holiness pervading all creation, or even just another name for Jesus, but is "the God and Father of our Lord Jesus Christ" and also "the Holy Spirit, whom the Father will send in my [Jesus'] name," we are obliged to make this clear and constant within our worship of God. This is the uniquely Christian understanding of God, a particularity that must be honored in our worship.

In truth it already shapes our ways of worshiping (or should). For instance, in our worship we accept the words of Jesus as being words from God rather than just the teachings of a very wise, albeit solely human rabbi. Consequently we typically give earnest attention to the reading of the Gospels (the Jesus-books) in our worship—some traditions even stand for this particular reading—and we do not consider the words of any poet or the purported revelations of any latter-day prophet to be of comparable worth.

Also, we offer our worship to God through this Jesus, because we believe that he alone is our great High Priest—because of his perfect day-by-day lifestyle worship as well as his sacrificial death and perpetual intercession, we who are far from perfect are now able to come before a holy God as acceptable worshipers. Our grasp of the character and purposes of God come to us through this Jesus, never from the antics of mythological Greek or Roman deities or even from isolated Old Testament texts. God, we say, is like Jesus the Christ, for "he is the image of the invisible God" and "in him the fullness of God was pleased to dwell" (Colossians 1:15, 19). Hence, we deem this One the second person of the Trinity.

Moreover, we believe that this understanding is not one which we have gained by our own intelligence or searching; it has been shown to us by the God's own Spirit, by the unseen One who is present with us in all of life and especially as we worship. This One we have learned to call the Holy Spirit, recognizing this One as none other than the divine spirit of Jesus still lingering with us—a third person of the Godhead.

But as circumference and context for the second and third members of the Trinity, there is surely the all-encompassing One we call God the Father—not as a gender reference but in acknowledgement of originating significance. This is to say that Trinitarian worship has deeper foundations than just the Jesus story, for we recognize that before Christ's appearance the story of God's loving intentions became visible in the

gift of creation itself and was most surely secured in the thrilling saga of
Israel's story. Our Trinitarian faith doesn't suddenly begin with Joseph
and Mary and the Babe (the second member of the Trinity), or with the
Day of Pentecost (the day of the full appearance of the third member of
the Trinity). It reaches all the way back to the creation of the universe and
it winds through long ages as the work of the God of Abraham, Isaac, and
Jacob—and subsequently of Jesus and the Spirit. Therefore our worship
acknowledges the lavish nature of this revelation and includes assurances
of the multi-faceted, three-in-one God of all of holy scripture. Or, at least
it should. Otherwise our worship is offered to a less-than-God, and we
become a people who are less-than-complete, a people who myopically
worship only fragments of the God who is and offers so much more.
Indeed, if a Trinitarian understanding of God isn't within our worship,
we are in effect bearing false witness to the very God we profess to be
worshiping.

Nonetheless, this interest in Trinitarian distinctiveness is not
just a matter of theological nit-picking. As a principle of spiritual life it
may be said that the richness of anyone's worship is directly proportional
to the depth and scope of the god being worshiped. One dimensional
gods and tangible deities are incapable of offering richness of worship.
The God of Christian faith, however, is incomparably multi-faceted and
all-encompassing, a treasure safeguarded for us through the concept of
Trinity. When this treasure is honored the profundity of worship truly
mushrooms in significance.

For instance, there are immense worship riches lodged within
the Trinitarian construct of the high priesthood of Christ, a wealth seen
most clearly when we reflect upon our Sunday practices. Typically we
think of Sunday worship as what *we* do in church: *we* sing songs, *we* voice
prayers, *we* listen to sermons, *we* offer our monies, etc. All well and good,
but questions arise if one dares to ask how high all our efforts rise. Is
there nothing more to our worship than what *we* do? If worship is just us
doing-our-thing with the help of the minister-in-charge, then it is fair to
label it as being functional unitarianism rather than Trinitarian worship,

for it is worship that is offered as though God were some distant deity with no apparent participation in this activity.

However, according to the New Testament and Christian teaching, true worship is much more than just what *we* do. In the scriptural understanding the second member of the Trinity is the One who has made possible our worship of God through his own priestly ministry on earth; through the perfect worship he offered on earth through his daily life and supremely through his obedient death on the cross he offered for us and for our salvation the once-for-all sacrifice for our sins and thus made possible our worship of God through him. But he has not relinquished this priestly role; "we *have* a great high priest" is the present tense statement of Hebrews 10:21. As the second member of the Trinity he continues to intercede for and to usher worshipers into the very life of God. He comes to us, in the person of the Holy Spirit, and stands with us now in our times of seeking, praying, longing, and rejoicing. God, in other words, is not distant—One to whom *we* must reach out across the ethereal reaches of time and eternity—but One who is with us as a very present teacher, ally, and intercessor as we worship.

This is to say that the three-in-one God has not only acted in mercy-filled grace to elicit and to enable our worship, but is very much in the room with us as our attending all-sufficient High Priest, laboring for and with us even as we offer that worship. And thus, to worship is really to be caught up into the dynamic inner working of the Trinity itself! As James B. Torrance puts it, "the real agent in all true worship is Jesus Christ. He is our great high priest and ascended Lord, the one true worshiper who unites us to himself by the Spirit . . . , as he lifts us up by word and sacrament into the very triune life of God." Therefore, worship "is our participation through the Spirit in the Son's communion with the Father, in his vicarious life of worship and intercession. It means participating in union with Christ, in what he has done for us once and for all, in his self-offering to the Father, in his life and death on the cross. It also means participating in what he is continuing to do for us in the presence of the Father and in his mission from the Father to the world."[44]

This stunning image of worship—of being lifted up by grace into participation within the life and harmony of the triune God!—is but a hint of the many large rooms of wonder which are opened to us when worship reverently acknowledges the fullness of God as Trinity.

To be sure, the concept of the Trinity exceeds our "explaining" powers; it is more of a mystery to be hymned than a riddle to be solved. We are swamped by fathomless and wondrous Otherness when we approach the courts of this Triune God. Even so, there is the need to use words, to speak to and of God in our worship and to do so in ways that honor this inexplicable mystery. In the days of his flesh Jesus taught us to speak to God as "Our father," and this is certainly baseline speech for all Christian worship. But the fuller revelation of God that came in the later gift of the Holy Spirit surely permits us to speak to and of God in more ways than that of fatherhood and to address our prayers to more than just this one person of the Trinity. No worshiper's ears, therefore, should be so habituated to prayers to "Father God" or "heavenly Father," that they would be disappointed or surprised to hear "Lord Jesus, our reigning Savior," or "Spirit of God, present with us always" as the address of a public prayer. Similarly, songs to and about all three persons of the Godhead give indication of whether or not only one person of the Trinity is actually being worshiped.[45]

A mostly-Jesus church is as spiritually misshapen as is a mostly-Holy Spirit church or a mostly-Almighty God church. Admittedly, these terms are inelegant, but regular visits in many non-liturgical and non-creedal evangelical churches convince me of the existence of such churches and the off-kilter spirituality within them. In such places, Michael Quicke says, "we are witnesses to the incredible shrinking God."[46]

The challenge is to achieve a balanced spirituality by a proper recognition of the full presence of God, a fitting response to each member of the Trinity. Even a Trinitarian greeting or benediction would be a helpful move toward the desired balance: "The grace of our Lord Jesus Christ and the love of God and the fellowship of the Holy Spirit be with you all" (2 Corinthians 13:14).[47] And to be sure, offering prayers in the name of

Christ "who lives and reigns with you and the Holy Spirit, one God forever and ever" is not a practice to be snickered at—it is a valid means of striving for a deeper honoring of the fathomless God to whom we pray.

The experiential fact is we Christians need the fullness of this revelation if we are to be fully Christian. The multi-layered richness provided to us within worship of the Triune God must be cherished as inexhaustible treasure, for there can be no satisfying or acceptable worship except that which is *Te Deum*—to God!—Father, Son, and Holy Spirit. Thomas Torrance sums it up well: "In our worship the Holy Spirit comes forth from God, uniting us to the response and obedience and faith and prayer of Jesus, and returns to God, raising us up in Jesus to participate in the worship of heaven and in the eternal communication of the Holy Trinity."[48] To settle for less is to worship on a landscape too barren.

Landmark Two: *A God of mystery.* Another and somewhat parallel truth about God which the Church's worship has prized is God's impenetrable, inscrutable, otherness. The God we worship conforms to no human category, is vaster than our comprehending apparatus, and eludes all our puny word nets—this God is Other! From the earliest days of Christian thinking, the Church has realized we can often speak more satisfactorily about what God is *not* than about what God is: God is *not* selfish, God is *not* erratic, God is *not* uncaring. The conviction that drives this strain of thought (apophatic theology) is that the depths of who God really *is* remains far more difficult to comprehend and express that do the characteristics we can name. There is, in other words, a vastness to the true nature of God that defies mapping and precise labeling.[49]

Now most certainly, Christians believe we have received the definitive revelation of God in the person and work of Jesus of Nazareth. Even so, repentance is required whenever we imagine our sinful eyes are capable of seeing all there is to see—even when the object of our vision is Jesus. In the language of the Gospel of John (1:18), the only Son has "made [the invisible Father] known"—but John does not say that this Son disrobed the Father or told all the family secrets! Or, perhaps more to the point, John does not assert that our comprehension of what we have seen is infallible. His unique method of telling the story of Jesus through dialogues filled with misunderstanding and double entendres indicates that our understanding is always incomplete. Again, the same New Testament passage which rhapsodizes upon "the household of God . . . the church of the living God, [as] the pillar and bulwark of the truth" also admits that "without any doubt, the mystery of our religion is great" (1 Timothy 3:15-16). "The truth," in other words, is still a mysterious truth. As Paul confesses, "now we see in a mirror, dimly . . . [and] know only in part" (1 Corinthians 13:12). Wisdom unites in urging worshipers to acknowledge "the depth of the riches and wisdom and knowledge of God" and to confess "How unsearchable are his judgments and how inscrutable his ways!" (Roman 9:33). Even with all we claim to know, it still remains in the very nature of God to "dwell in thick darkness."

This fascinating Old Testament expression appears first in the terrifying Mt. Sinai appearance of God. In that story the recently-rescued Israelites are awakened at dawn with a theophany—with ear-shattering trumpet blasts, with flashes of lightning and peals of thunder, with rain and fire and smoke. In speechless awe they see before them "the mount of God," swathed in clouds and swirling smoke, convulsing in earthquake tremors as the mighty God of Exodus, the Holy Other, descends to its summit. Fearing for their lives, they plead for Moses to deal on their behalf with this terrifying deity—so Moses alone "drew near to the thick darkness where God was" (Exodus 20:21). Centuries later the same expression appears on the lips of King Solomon when the Jerusalem temple was being dedicated. There Solomon again speaks of this God who dwells in thick darkness (1 Kings 8:12, *passim*) and, though his historical reference is likely to Sinai, perhaps this refers to the dark and secluded residential cubicle of Yahweh, the Holy of Holies, in the temple's darkest recesses. It was an area to be entered only once a year and then only by the High Priest—its holiness would kill all other intruders. Thus, in Israel there was a trembling, life-and-death respect for this One who dwells in thick darkness, this indescribable Other (cf. Psalm 18:6-15).

But "thick darkness" is too rich an expression to confine it to a wilderness event or a hallowed cubicle. As the foregoing discussion of the Trinity must surely remind us, the unknown and the unknowable within the reality we call God is immense. For all our gains since the days of the Old Testament, we are still, like Moses (Exodus 33:23), dealing with the backside of God.[50] The light shines in our darkness, but the darkness remains thick. Ponder the immensity of the star-filled heavens, the intricacy of the human body, the archaeological history of this planet. Who can contemplate these things without admitting wonder and mystery at the center of all? Or, on an opposite front, who can confront the events of life without awakening to how little we truly understand God? The death of a child. The savagery of war. The persistence of injustice. If God is truly like Jesus, as we Christians claim, how can these things continue century after century? Our best answer, and our only honest answer, is that the God we worship "dwells in thick darkness." There is so very much we do not know! There is so very much that must be taken by and lived in wondering faith.

This means that reverence, humility, and modesty befit our worship. The Church at its best hours of worship has never spoken of God as though we were equals, "slapping him on the back and calling him by his first name."[51] No, humble reverence has been the historic Church's worship mode, even if it must be admitted that in some worship services, the word reverence sounds almost quaint, if not wholly foreign! But it has not always been so. Humble reverence has been the historic Church's worship mode—an infinite respect that can be detected in the voice when addressing God in prayer (certainly not the "Hey, God!" mentioned earlier), in the awe with which we recount the mercies of God, and even in our posture and worship gestures. To be clear, reverence does not mean servility or timidity—Christ's ministry does, after all, grants us boldness, but reverence always leans noticeably in the direction of respectful awe and humility.

Right worship, therefore, will have about it the awe and eagerness a freshman from a "one-stop-sign city" would appropriately display upon entering Oxford University's Bodleian Library—and her shock of being assisted by a most cordial librarian. If we are truly standing on holy ground in the presence of the thrice-holy God of time and eternity—even though we cannot pretend to fathom even one word of this description!—then surely something about our demeanor must indicate it. Conversely, if our worship demeanor is not different from our demeanor in any other setting, the historic Church of the Triune God has good reason to ask why. It's not a matter of us "acting natural" in worship, it's a matter of remembering in whose presence we are assembled.

Our scriptures speak of a God who hides (Isaiah 45:15) as well as a God who reveals, of a God who is a dreaded warrior as well as a good shepherd, of a God whose power is strangely made perfect in weakness. On page after page of our Bible the Spirit has placed expressions, images, and stories that call us to nuanced, holy ground in our thinking about God, that invite us to lift the low ceiling of our limited experience and enter wider worlds of love and praise. All these literary doors left ajar are in effect the voice of *lex orandi, lex credendi* pleading with the Church in all ages to reverence "the God who dwells in thick darkness" in its worship. For in deepest truth, a god we are able to comprehend as effortlessly as an algebraic equation is not worth worshiping. Certainly, "easy" gods are available—even in church!—but those who worship them are damned to disappointment. Only the God of Overwhelming Otherness, the One who dwells in thick darkness, merits our worship.[52]

Landmark Three: *A God of time and place.* It is also essential to remember that the God of Christian faith has chosen to be known to us through actual events which happened at specific places to named people. Therefore, we speak of what happened at Mt. Sinai and Jerusalem, of deeds done in Capernaum and on the Sea of Galilee, of Gethsemane and Golgotha; our creeds recall names like Pontius Pilate and use verbs like conceived, born, suffered, crucified, buried, raised. Ours is a faith built around real people in real history on real earth encountering datable revelation. Such is not the case with all other faiths. Some consider time to be illusory if not insignificant and some treat place (the material world) as merely accidental. The Moralistic Therapeutic Deism of American teenagers referenced in the first chapter and the individualistic "Sheilahism" reported by sociologist Robert Bellah[53] decades ago—a mélange of snippets from various world religions, psychotherapy, philosophy, and mythology concocted by various "Sheilahs" into their own do-it-yourself religion—may be the most recognizable and popular form of this avoidance of religious specificity in North America. In all such religious expressions, however, God is essentially a matter of universal and timeless ideas divined by spiritual gurus—not the living Lord of history whose this-worldly acts reveal a dynamic Person of perceivable character and historical purpose.

This historical and materialistic dimension of our faith is honored in part by our appreciation for the physical creation, for nature, for soil, for earthliness and for all that contributes to the wellbeing of God's creation. Therefore, God's graciousness in daily bread grown from seeds and fertile soil and timely rain is not extraneous to our worship. Christians do not worship nature but neither do we overlook its essential role as a gift from God, a theater of God's deeds and our God-given habitat. Thus, right worship includes thanks to the Creator of all this, and sorrow for its misuse, and commitment to its thriving. It also includes thanks for our bodily existence, for touch, hearing, sight, sex—with prayers that we might enjoy and use these gifts wisely, to God's glory.

But Christianity also clearly "speaks of climactic events and of a finale to time . . . In the fullness of time, God invades human history, assumes our flesh, and heals, teaches, and eats with sinners. There are specific temporal and spatial settings to it all."[54] Therefore, through the centuries Christian worship has reflected this. Our Hebrew ancestors honored this historically-revealed God and faith with their cycle of festivals recalling the great acts of God on their behalf: the Passover, the giving of the Law (Pentecost), and their preservation in the wilderness (Tabernacles). The early Church followed suit and began teaching the faithful to worship the God of Christian faith through the means of days and seasons that remember and rehearse our founding stories and thereby calibrate believers' swiftly-passing lives to God's enduring story and its rehearsal of God's saving acts.

Our Christian worship calendar is appropriately built around the life of our Lord and begins with a month long season (Advent) of preparation for his birth. In this season the Church listens to the prophecies of his Messianic coming (and return). His birth (Christmas) is then celebrated for a brief twelve days in preparation for his manifestation (Epiphany) to the seeking Magi, whose coming symbolizes Christ's universal significance. In the following weeks of this season, the Church, through its Scripture readings, traces his career from his ministry-inaugurating baptism until he begins his life-ending trek to Jerusalem and Calvary. That fatal turn is remembered by one day (Ash Wednesday) in which his mortality and ours is solemnized. Thus begins the forty-day season (Lent) in which the all-important final weeks of his life are the focus of attention, culminating in the day-by-day observance of Holy Week (Palm Sunday, Maundy Thursday, Good Friday, Holy Saturday/ Easter Eve). The Sunday of his resurrection (Easter) ushers in a fifty-day season celebrating this greatest of all miracles: the conquest of sin, death, and hell itself. Its joy is crowned by Christ's ascension and the coming of the Holy Spirit (Pentecost) as the birth of the Church. Observance of this entire cycle requires six months of the year and is therefore sometimes referred to as "the Lord's Half Year," the remaining months of the year being designated as "the Church's Half Year." In this portion of the year other scriptures, events, and themes nourish the Church's life and, fittingly, this half-year concludes with a remembrance of all who have preceded us in the way of Jesus (All Saints Day), an occasion to recall God's care for the Church throughout all ages.[55]

Churches that follow this calendar have a Bible-based template for week-by-week worship that grounds believers' faith and hope in the God of this ongoing redemptive story. For it is an ongoing story, and the effort invested in recalling past deeds is also a goad to expect God's acting in this day and hour. Rootage in history is encouragement for today and hope for tomorrow. The lectionary texts for the Lord's Half

Year, while anchoring us in times past, also point us toward promises still to be fulfilled by our redeeming God. Past, present, and future are thus held within the spectrum of this annual round of worship. Such a worship orientation tethers us to a God who is both beyond and near, a God who was and is and is to come, a Trinitarian God. It also anchors us in a real-time, this-worldly discipleship and in lively hope for the time when time shall be no more and God will grant a new heaven and a new earth. Supremely, by means of this calendar, the Church forms a people whose life and valuing is being shaped by Christ's life and word rather than by the holidays and calendars of school and government. The purpose of the Christian calendar therefore isn't to bog down the Church in righteous rigmarole but to form a distinct people who understand and plan their life around God's deeds—past, present, and future.

And, surely, this also serves as a wonderful magnification of the significance of our "three score years and ten" (Psalm 90:10). For worship that rehearses and renews us in the ongoing story of a God of time and place sweeps our broken lives and little stories into the greater, eternal story of God. Living into this story, Sunday by Sunday and year after year, the smallness of our mortal lives begins more and more to be understood as a part of God's grand and eternal life and story. Thus, we are freed from our own insignificance by being included as grateful participants within the Great Story. There is, in other words, a strong pastoral care dividend to be discovered within the observance of the Christian year.

Landmark Four: *A People for God's Use.* Although the opening chapters of our Bible tell of the worship of several individuals (e.g. Cain and Abel, Noah, Abraham, Jacob), the definitive history of worship begins only with the story of Moses and the liberation of the Hebrews from Egyptian bondage. Pharaoh is told: "Let my people go, so that they may celebrate a festival to me in the wilderness" (Exodus 5:1), and at Mount Sinai Israel is told that the LORD has rescued the Hebrews "and brought [them] to myself" that they "shall be for me a priestly kingdom and a holy nation" (Exodus 19:5-6).

These words indicate that worship is basic to this peoples' identity. She was to be creation's worship leader and teacher, giving witness to the nations through her lifestyle, especially through her Sabbath worship. This was inherent within her founding. A distinct Hebrew word, *qahal*, is even used to refer to Israel as this chosen assembly or congregation. Instructively, when the Hebrew Old Testament was translated into Greek (3rd century B.C.E.), in the translation now called the Septuagint, the translators used the Greek word *ekklesia* (*ek*, out of + *kaleo*, call = the called out) to translate *qahal*. This is the same word later used for the Church by the authors of the New Testament. We find this in passages such as 1 Peter 2:9 wherein the Church (the *ekklesia*) is said to be, like Israel, "a royal priesthood, a holy nation, God's own people."

Thus, worship was seen as inherent within the Church's self-understanding just as surely as it was for Israel. We, like Israel, have been called out from the larger mass of persons in order to be worshipers of the Triune God.

But do note this—in both cases there is a specificity. "You" are to worship and serve me. There is in this both a summons and a distinctiveness. Not all people, not everyone is so chosen. We are a select body, chosen to be God's priests among the peoples of the world. Our responsibility is therefore immense and has not been assigned to all peoples. To be sure, the Psalmists often express a longing for "all the earth" and "all nations" to praise God, but these are compassionate expressions of longing, not declarations of fact. A respectful "Court of the Gentiles" was provided within the Jerusalem temple grounds, but no accommodated rituals were instituted in order for these on-lookers to participate. It was through Israel's faithful integrity as a distinct, *Yahweh*-worshiping people that her destiny was to be met. And this is also true for the Church. We are called as a people to be the world's priests, offering on its behalf the worship that is due God by all—but we are the ones upon whom the assignment rests to offer worthy worship for all.

Thus, whatever we may say about the joy and privilege of worship, this must always be coupled with the solemn responsibility of it.

Sunday's service is not just for our profit or enjoyment. It is also our assignment from God on behalf of all creation. We are the creation's priests! The burdens and brokenness of the world are ours to lift to God. The groans of creation are ours to remember before God. This is what good priests do. This is what it means to be chosen, called of God to be a part of the worshiping community.

It also means that we take very seriously the corporate nature of this calling. The center of gravity in both biblical testaments is always the congregation, the assembly, the people, the group. Certainly, the individual Hebrew is not forgotten or irrelevant to the aggregate body, but the focus is certainly not upon the singular person. The focus is upon the *ekklesia*, the "we" rather than upon the "I." The desire is for a chorus of praise, not an assortment of soloists; for a holy nation, not a collection of independent citizens. Students of the grand worship songs of the Old Testament will recognize that though these psalms are very mindful of the individual and often voice the individual's experience, their context and priority is always the assembled people of Israel, not just the singular Israelite. Psalm 122:1 summarizes this priority well: "*I* was glad when they said unto me, 'Let *us* go to the house of the LORD.' *Our* feet are standing within your gates, O Jerusalem."

For today's evangelical worshiper this corporate priority becomes a stern rebuke to our individualistic desire for worship that speaks to or moves "me." Not only is this extraneous to our calling to be priests, engaging in the work of worship on behalf of others, it is also contrary to the biblical emphasis upon the corporate nature of God's people. Our Bible understands worship to be a corporate-focused and group-forming event, not an event convened to meet "my" needs. Recall the critique offered earlier of inspiration as a confusing purpose for worship. In that critique "individualism" was cited as a characteristic of that model of worship. Even though the Enlightenment has schooled us to prize persons as individual entities (so that we now speak of "my" rights, "my" freedom, "my" pursuit of happiness), the Bible repeatedly moves in a different direction. Biblical thought portrays persons as "father," "mother," "husband," "wife," "brother," or "sister,"—all terms that understand persons as being persons in relationship. Moreover, the documents of the New Testament, even when addressed to individuals (such as Timothy or Titus), are all written either to churches or in concern for the well-being of the leaders of the group, the Church.

Even the dominant metaphors for Christian existence are corporate metaphors: body, family, colony, kingdom, temple, etc. "We" is the overriding pronoun and context of the New Testament. The same holds true among ancient Israel's worshipers; the dominant yearning was to be among the great congregation and to find oneself among the faithful assembly. Worship to them was a means of fulfilling *God's* desire to have a priestly nation among the earth's many nations. Worship was a means of responding to *God's* calling and of answering *God's* dreams. Most emphatically, it was not construed as a means of having God meet "my" needs. John Witvliet states the Bible's greater expectation clearly and elegantly when he writes: "God's Spirit works through public worship to lead us from the claustrophobia of our own narcissism into the spacious, luminous reality of the Triune God—a place so expansive that we find ourselves in communion with God's people across centuries and continents and in transformative encounter with the Holy Spirit."[56]

An instructive sidelight of this is visible in Rodney Clapp's helpful—even if indicting—insight when he bemoans the me-centeredness of those who say, "I go to church so I can be fed." Clapp observes that "being fed" is something done for infants and therefore those who go to worship desiring "to be fed" are inadvertently saying, "I go to church so I can act like a baby."[57] Whatever one may say to this charge, it is true to the biblical portrait of worship that what transpires among and within and through the people, the "we" of God's calling, is of far greater import than the "me" of an insatiable appetite.

The spiritual assignment for the individual within congregational worship is clear. That assignment is for individuals, in the time of worship, to take their place humbly among the greatly sinning and greatly forgiven people, to consider others' needs as important as their own, and gladly join God's family in grateful chorus and confession—especially on those days when their individual needs aren't met! True worship, in other words, is a call to relinquish the "me first" pattern that has bedeviled our race since the Garden of Eden. Worship is a call to self-forgetfulness—a call to "get over my self" and to blend my voice with others, lifting my heart with theirs to God. It is a beckoning to enter into the holy place in order to speak the hurts and hopes of others! It is a summons to seek the unity and harmony that is at the center of God's own Trinitarian being, as well as at the heart of God's mission among humankind.[58]

Anglican Archbishop William Temple once provided a classic description of Christian worship. Unfortunately, his words are seldom quoted in full and therefore Temple's emphasis upon self-forgetfulness usually goes unheard. Read him, therefore, in entirety:

> For worship is the submission of all our nature to God. It is the quickening of conscience by His holiness; the nourishment of mind with His truth; the purifying of imagination by His beauty; the opening of the heart to His love; the surrender of will to His purpose—and all of this gathered up in adoration, the most selfless emotion of which our nature is capable and therefore the chief remedy for that self-centeredness which is our original sin and the source of all actual sin. Yes—worship in spirit and truth is the way to the solution of perplexity and to the liberation from sin.[59]

Corporate worship, rightly conceived and practiced, transforms us from acquisitive, self-seeking religionists into other—and Other—oriented members of God's priestly people.

Landmark Five: *Content, Structure, and Style.* Another landmark of Christian worship has been helpfully clarified by Robert Webber, the twentieth-century evangelical theologian whose lifework is most closely identified with the renewal of Christian worship. From his extensive studies in the history, theology, and practice of worship, Webber identified three always-present issues. All worship, he said, has content, structure, and style.[60] This short list is most helpful as both summary and guide.

In Webber's opinion the least important of these three is the style of one's worship. This is because he understood that style is ultimately a reflection of the host culture. For example, worship conducted in a remote, third-world village ought to be in a style that is appropriate to that setting. It should be conducted in a manner that allows those believers to express their faith in ways indigenous to that culture and in ways that form them into a counter-cultural people in that setting. To impose upon them a highly literate, Euro-centric style of worship would be foolish, as was tragically illustrated too often in the history of the modern missionary movement. Webber, who was a child of the mission field, easily understood that decisions regarding style had to be left to context-specific readings of the local culture. For this reason he saw that matters such as musical patterns and instruments were not inherent to worship's integrity. These were facets of a style of worship, not expressions of its essence. Therefore, new musical styles and more participative engagement in worship were among the stylistic alterations of worship he affirmed. If certain stylistic changes fit the culture, Webber saw no reason to oppose them. His only concern was that the chosen style be a fitting conduit of worship's content and structure.

These two issues of content and structure, however, he did consider to be of importance. This is because he believed that the content and structure of worship transcend cultural norms and speak to the heart of worship. They have a theological and historical core that is important.

In this basic orientation I am a disciple of Webber, not wanting to engage in unwinnable "worship wars" over style, wars that most often come down to clashes about musical preference. I have my preferences in these matters, of course, just as everybody else. But only when style overwhelms or disregards content or structure do I have a reasoned basis for entering the wars. Otherwise, the issue of style is best left to the sensitive discernment of those who are attempting to provide spiritual guidance to a specific people in a particular locale and time.

Still, the other two matters on Webber's list, content and structure (or order), remain for consideration. Unquestionably, the more problematic of the two, at least among evangelicals, would surely be order. The content of worship we can more easily see as basic, and content has been the burden of this book thus far, and will continue to be. But why should anyone consider the order of worship to be important?

Landmark Six: *"All things decently and in order."* A survey of the New Testament reveals no mandated order of worship within it, so how can it be said that order is in any way an important factor to consider? Especially if the pursuit of such might lead to suggestions that we must follow a fixed order of worship! Our freedom, the freedom granted us by the Spirit, releases us from all expressions of liturgical rigidity, does it not? Why, then, would Webber or anyone else suggest that the order of worship is a matter for serious thought?

The problem here is not a fiction. There are many who are troubled by an emphasis upon ordering worship because they perceive such efforts as an interference with the Spirit's work. In their view, the worship planner who is concerned about good order is attempting to exert human control upon the workings of God. We ought, they say, "leave it to the Spirit" rather than impose human structures and plans upon worship.

In response to this objection to good order, one may quickly agree that "man [sic] proposes but God disposes." Any order we devise needs to be viewed as open to the Spirit's interruption or redirection and therefore one need not interpret a concern for order to be proof of a desire to control or thwart God's work. (Of course, there are surely cases where this has been and is the case; but this unfortunate fact does not merit a dismissal of the practice of ordering worship as in itself a carnal quenching of the Spirit.)

Perhaps more to the point, however, is the biblical teaching concerning stewardship. God has committed much to the care of humankind and has committed very much indeed to the Church. The Church, empowered and guided by the Spirit, is accountable as a steward of the gospel before the world. By its very nature, stewardship requires us to "take charge" and to manage God's gifts. With regard to worship, this suggests that "leaving it to the Spirit," though appealing in theory, may, in fact, be a failure in stewardship and all abdication of responsibility. Jesus' command to the Apostle Peter to "Feed my sheep" may, by extension, be understood as our Lord's command to the Church to provide nourishing meals for His sheep, including worship that is as well-balanced and healthful as any nutrition-minded home-maker might plan for his or her family. This is a homemaker's responsibility, not an evidence of a control mania. The same might be said for those who are responsible for the Church's worship.

In any event, let's realize that order is already a fact within our churches. Every congregation has an order for its worship even if that order is the principle of "Thou shalt have no fixed order of worship other than what the Spirit dictates for the occasion." The presence of some expression of order is a functional reality in every church. This is so whether it is printed on several pages of a prayer book or is an agenda printed in a weekly bulletin or is the worship-set song list shared among the praise band members or just the predictable routine of Sunday's meeting—all of us follow some kind of structure that becomes our template for worship. The question is why we follow that particular order and if that order has good theological rationale.

Consider, then, some reasons why order rises to the level of being a landmark for worthy Christian worship. First, although it is true that the New Testament doesn't prescribe a specific order for Christian worship, the Bible does speak to the importance of order in worship. One example of this is found in Deuteronomy 26:1-11 in a step-by-step procedure for Israel's harvest festival. Consider how complete and detailed this order of worship is.

> When you have come into the land that the LORD your
> God is giving you as an inheritance to possess and you

possess it, and settle in it, you shall take some of the first of all the fruit of the ground, which you harvest from the land that the LORD your God is giving you, and you shall put it in a basket and go to the place that the LORD your God will choose as a dwelling for his name. You shall go to the priest who is in office at that time, and say to him, "Today I declare to the LORD your God that I have come into the land that the LORD swore to our ancestors to give us." When the priest takes the basket from your hand and sets it down before the altar of the LORD your God, you shall make this response before the LORD your God: "A wandering Aramean was my ancestor; he went down into Egypt and lived there as an alien, few in number, and there he became a great nation, mighty and populous. When the Egyptians treated us harshly and afflicted us by impos- ing hard labor on us, we cried to the LORD, the God of our ancestors; the LORD brought us out of Egypt with a mighty hand and an outstretched arm, with a terrifying display of power, and with signs and wonders; and he brought us into this place and gave us this land, a land flowing with milk and honey. So now I bring the first of the fruit of the ground that you, O LORD, have given me." You shall set it down before the LORD your God and bow down before the LORD your God. Then you together with the Levites, and the aliens who reside among you, shall celebrate with all the bounty that the LORD your God has given to you and to your house.

In this passage "the LORD your God" is mentioned no fewer than thirteen times—this is worship that is about God! But notice that in this worship there is an obvious concern for procedure—for ritual and ceremony, if you will—for proper order. A specific offering is to be brought at a certain time to a certain place within a specified container. It is to be taken to the on-duty priest and a verbatim speech-explanation is to be spoken to the priest who will accordingly receive the offering and place it before the altar. Next, a proto-creed rich in historical detail is to recited ("A wandering Aramean was my ancestor . . . " One might profitably note how this "creed" moves from telling about what happened to "my *ancestor*" to a personal appropriation of the story—"When the Egyptians treated *us* harshly," and the final declaration: "So now *I* bring this."). All this is followed by a proper bowing down before the altar. Finally, a celebration is to conclude this worship service.

One cannot imagine any God-fearing Hebrew tampering with, let alone dispensing with, the protocol or speeches prescribed in this worship commandment. It was given by Yahweh as a matter of prescribed worship. Granted, Christians today recognize no mandate from God to replicate the speech or protocol prescribed in this ancient scene, but are we wise to discount the apparent concern of God for proper order which finds expression in this and other Old Testament texts?[61]

To this Old Testament example of concern for procedural order one might also add the Apostle Paul's New Testament directive to the Corinthians that worship be conducted "decently and in order." His precise meaning, of course, is debated but Paul apparently assumed there was both an appropriate demeanor ("decently") and a proper sequencing ("in order") for the activities of worship. With regard to decency he likely wanted to avoid associations with indecent pagan worship rituals, while with regard to order it may be that he wanted Corinthian worship to comply at least with the human need for order—if not with the rabbinic-synagogue order of worship he would likely have personally commended.

A careful reading of the Bible teaches us that the *way* things are done is often of as much concern as *what* is done. Order is important within scripture. So it is puzzling when some dismiss concern about worship order as evidence of a hang-up with Old Testament "ceremonialism." One might profitably note that when it comes to matters of judicial, national, and/or military significance, we still consider protocol and right order to be sacrosanct. The flags must be raised and lowered at a precise time and flown or posted just so; the military funeral must include this prescribed ritual; the court must convene and proceed in just this manner. And remarkably, observers and participants will often later say that these very ceremonial actions were the most powerful of the activities. When words fail us, ceremony sustains us; when chaos descends, known routines stabilize.

Is it not odd, therefore, that objections of "ceremonialism" are raised when the need for good order in worship is mentioned? Why is this so? It is a reaction that needs to be reassessed. Certainly we're not obliged to replicate ancient Israel's worship order, or any other for that matter. There is a demonstrable concern for order in Israel's liturgy. There is a comparable concern for order in the worship of the one New Testament era church most open to our view. Finally, there is a clear and continuing concern for order in significant moments of our social-national life. How, then, can *dis*regard or *un*concern about meaningful order in worship be defensible?

Another "answer" as to why good order in worship is significant is that the longer history of Christian worship shows an obvious concern for it. Here we encounter the historical fact that a minimalist worship order of scripture and communion, or Word and Table, of sermon and supper, has been the Church's preferred pattern of worship—in both Catholic and Protestant traditions—until the emergence of present-day evangelicalism. The two acts—feasting on the Word and then on the Sacrament—done in that sequence, have characterized the Church's worship through the better part of two thousand years. Also, though in a less definitive and consistent way, acts of entrance and of departure have been a part of this historic schema. To jettison this precedent is a departure from the historic Church's practice.

I would not argue for a moment for a present-day order of worship that repeats item-per-item the services conducted by medieval Catholics or by eighteenth-century Calvinists—or any other group or age of the Church. Such slavishness to details would be both silly and bordering on historical idolatry. But the cumulative weight of a continuous pattern of Word and Table, with accompanying rites of assembly and dismissal, does rise to a level of a historical identity-marker of Christian worship that can't be dismissed with a wave of the hand. This is a benchmark of historic Christian worship. If we choose to discontinue or to minimize these acts or the order in which they have been handed down to us, we need to realize we are spurning the spiritual wisdom of most of the Church through the ages.

A third reason to consider worship order as an important factor in worship flows from what was just said about the spiritual wisdom latent within historic order. Recall, if you will, what was earlier said about the spiritually-formative character of worship. If there is any merit at all in the idea of worship having formative significance and power, then order's importance is quickly evident.

In multiple areas of our life we recognize that regularized, repetitive actions are essential to the forming of new habits and thought patterns. Physical therapists work with this truth as an unassailable part of their rehabilitation regimen with patients. Drug and alcohol addicts must submit themselves to regular and similarly-formatted meetings and disciplines to achieve and maintain sobriety and liberation. Athletes in training don't have the option of omitting a daily regimen of exercises—exercises done in a methodical, step-by-step progression, training muscles to recognize and repeat certain movements reflexively. Surely training of the spirit is no less dependent upon repetitious acts done in a considered manner over an extended period of time. A pattern of helter-skelter improvisation is a sure sign of an undisciplined life. Similarly, a church's worship order can be an expression of "doing our own thing"—what Michael Quicke calls COW worship (Church our Way)[62]—or it can provide the congregation with a historic and proven regimen for its transformation into the likeness of Christ. The choice is always ours, but those who know themselves best may be the first to confess that being "put through the paces" in worship is a helpful and powerful aid in our re-patterning.

Consider this matter from a slightly different angle. As true as it is that worship must be offered in a style that is compatible with its host culture, it is also true that it must be offered in a way that challenges that culture. For if worship is to possess any true transformative power it must be in some fundamental ways unlike the culture in which it is conducted. It must possess a dissonance, an oddness that stands in contrast to that culture. Worship that sounds and feels and acts too much like its host culture cannot call its participants to a discipleship that is counter-cultural. It will have lost its saltiness and will "no longer be good for anything except to the thrown out and trodden under foot" (Matthew 5:13). In our present culture of flitting images, sound-bytes, multi-tasking, frenetic distraction, and pervasive me-ness, the worship that calls for sustained attention, ordered discipline, and we-ness will be the worship that forms long-term disciples. Order alone is not the magic bullet in this regard, but it does play a crucial role.

No less a spiritual guide than C.S. Lewis pled for a consistent and sensible order in worship, saying that it was essential to his worship. Novelties and innovations he considered a distraction from the known order that helped him reflect and pray in a methodical, measured manner. Regardless of the good intentions of the innovating priest, the net effect upon Lewis was that he was always wondering, "What's he up to now?" rather than being mindful of his prayers. Just as a dancer dances best when the steps are known and therefore doesn't need to fret about the movement of his feet, so Lewis felt the dance of worship required a well-ordered and known liturgy to be beneficial. To all worship innovators he offered the famous line: "The charge to Peter was 'Feed my sheep,' not 'Try experiments on my rats, or even, teach my performing dogs new tricks.'"[63]

I conclude from all of the above that good order in worship, with its constituent acts, is about our respect for historic Spirit-taught grooves of grace and about our need for spiritual discipline. Good order in worship confesses that worship's value is not just in what we may express to God through it, but also in what God may form in us as we submit our bodies and spirits to a sustained regimen that is not based on our *ala carte* whims. Surely, a thoughtful sequence of God-directed acts, whose specific order has been tested and found worthy across centuries, and that enables a community to access the fountainheads of spiritual vitality every week, cannot be considered irrelevant to serious contemporary Christians.

Landmark Seven: *Ardor.* A final landmark that must infuse every other one is ardor, passion—emotion! Without it, worship is nothing. Thankfully, not one of the preceding landmarks denigrates this—every landmark previously mentioned can be honored with feeling, with rapture, with hilarity, with shouts of hallelujah, as well as with solemn wonder, intense thought, or quiet tears. It is a tragedy that we who are body/soul creatures, persons of feelings as well as intellect should ever have imagined that any dimension of our created nature must be left in the church foyer. Is it really possible for one to enter the presence of God and to recall the mercies of God and not be "got" by the experience? It must be stressed once more, the problem is not with experiencing or with emotion. The problem arises only when these are sought and valued as being of equal value with the revelation that rightly awakens them.

For myself, I want nothing to do with a worship style that will not let the soul "play" in the Father's good pleasure as well as hold it accountable to do God's bidding. Does not life itself teach us that "play" is always at its best when we truly lose ourselves in the game, when caution and decorum are cast aside in the sheer delight of the moment? Rules we must have—if the game is not to be nonsensical—but rules are meant to facilitate the game, not to smother it! It may well be that the explosion of Pentecostal exuberance in the twentieth century was the inevitable eruption of suppressed energy and "playful" emotion bottled up in the overly-regimented strictures of other worship forms. A lightness of being, a heart-felt gulp of astonishment, a shudder of amazement, a bent knee, an open hand, a swaying body—all this and more rightly find a home within the courts of the Lord we worship.

William Tyndale, the first translator of the New Testament into English, is stereotypically presented as a stern-faced, frosty scholar who lived in an age when emotional religion wasn't in vogue. But in the prologue of his 1525 New Testament translation he explains the word "evangel" (gospel) in these quite remarkable words:

> *Euangelio* (that we cal gospel) is a greke worde, and signyfyth good, merry, glad, and joyful tydings that makes a mannes hert glad, and maketh him syng, daunce, and leepe for ioy.

And John Wesley, the founder of Methodism, who believed there was no liturgy in all the world comparable to the sequencing and elegant language of the 1662 Anglican *Book of Common Prayer*, did not insist his followers confine themselves to its expressions. In his "Directions for Singing" he ordered his followers to "sing lustily and with a good courage," being wary of singing "as if you were half dead or half asleep." For him it was important that they should participate in the Church's worship and praise with heart as well as mind; he clearly wanted them to sing as heartily in church as they had previously "sung the songs of Satan." This is not a counsel of timidity or of one who was afraid of whole-body worship. This, to use a phrase fashioned by Methodist theologian Don Saliers, this is worship that is "humanity at full stretch."

In sum, ardor is as much an abiding landmark of God-pleasing worship as is order (or any other landmark of Christian worship).

∾

I believe these seven landmarks, drawn from the Church's worship history and theological reflection, provide valuable "rules" for Christian worship. These seven are not offered imperially, as though they are the only and final words to be said on the subject. Better minds and more reverent spirits could surely offer better. Nonetheless, these get us started. They are foundational for anything else that may be rightly added. They provide the characteristics that qualitatively differentiate corporate Christian worship from any other gathering known to mortals. They make our gatherings a seeking of God's face.

For clarity's sake, here is a restatement of them in declarative form (and a worship-planning correlate for each):

1. *Christian worship will be about God, offering praise to the triune God of Christian faith as both Object and Subject of its worship.* Therefore, services of Christian worship must not permit our gatherings to become about "us"—be it our feelings, our politics, our ministry, our traditions, etc.

2. *Christian worship, while honoring the specificity of God as Trinity, will also confess the continuing mystery and incomprehensibility of God.* Therefore, services of Christian worship must not present God either as fully known or as unknown, but as transcendent, saving Mystery wondrously immanent among us.

3. *Christian worship will utilize as its norm the historical revelation of God recorded in Christian scripture, rehearsed in annual seasons and holy days, and testified to in our ancient confessions of faith.* Therefore, services of Christian worship must not minimize the importance of scripture being read and interpreted within the assembly or the guidance of the Spirit through the Church's Great Tradition and calendar year.

4. *Christian worship will assist Christ's Church in fulfilling her corporate priestly calling.* Therefore, services of Christian worship must not neglect their task of glorifying God through weekly acts of praise, intercession, attentiveness, and communion in order that the Church engage and be renewed in grateful participation in God's mission.

5. *Christian worship will be theologically responsible in its content, its structure, and its style.* Therefore, services of Christian worship must not ignore the formative significance of any one of these as a means of glorifying God and sanctifying the Church.

6. *Christian worship will be concerned that all things are done decently and in order.* Therefore, services of Christian worship, while expressed in modes that will be culturally compatible with the worshipers, must not be so congruent with the culture that they do not stand apart from it or fail to form believers in an alternate culture.

7. *Christian worship will be holistic, giving legitimacy to mental, physical, and emotional responses to God's revelation in Christ.* Therefore, services of Christian worship must not countenance lethargic participation nor frown upon varied responses to the Lord's gospel.

There is a rich heritage here, a heritage that is to be appreciatively honored, but there is also a notable lack of specificity as to how it is to be honored. How these "rules" might be worked out in the practicalities of planning a worship service is the subject of the next chapter.

RESOURCE: WESLEY'S "DIRECTIONS FOR SINGING"

John Wesley's "Directions for Singing" provides an interesting study of a balancing of the individual and corporate as well as the blending of rational and emotional elements within worship. That he recognized the goodness within congregational singing is obvious by the document itself. That he also recognized the need to make singing a formative as well as an expressive occasion can be clearly seen in his counsel to be mindful of one another (V and VI) and also in his direction (VII) to give most attention to the text rather than to the "sound" (or today, perhaps to the rhythm?) of the song. With good reason his "Directions" are still printed as a frontispiece in the hymnals of the United Methodists.

I.   Learn these tunes before you learn any others; afterwards learn as many as you please.

II. Sing them exactly as they are printed here, without altering or mending them at all; and if you have learned to sing them otherwise, unlearn it as soon as you can.

III. Sing all. See that you join with the congregation as frequently as you can. Let not a slight degree of weakness or weariness hinder you. If it is a cross to you, take it up, and you will find it a blessing.

IV. Sing lustily and with a good courage. Beware of singing as if you were half dead, or half asleep; but lift up you voice with strength. Be no more afraid of your voice now, nor more ashamed of its being heard, than when you sung the songs of Satan.

V.   Sing modestly. Do not bawl, so as to be heard above or distinct from the rest of the congregation, that you may not destroy the harmony; but strive to unite your voices together, so as to make one clear melodious sound.

VI. Sing in time. Whatever time is sung be sure to keep with it. Do not run before nor stay behind it; but attend close to the leading voices, and move therewith as exactly as you can; and take care not to sing too slow. This drawling way naturally steals on all who are lazy; and it is high time to drive it out from us, and sing all our tunes just as quick as we did at first.

VII. Above all sing spiritually. Have an eye to God in every word you sing. Aim at pleasing him more than yourself, or any other creature. In order to do this attend strictly to the sense of what you sing, and see that your heart is not carried away with the sound, but offered to God continually; so shall your singing be such as the Lord will approve here, and reward you when he cometh in the clouds of heaven.

From John Wesley's *Select Hymns*, 1761

QUESTIONS FOR DISCUSSION

1. How many of the characteristics of earliest Christian worship are evident in the worship services in which you participate?

2. If a visitor from another culture visited the worship service you attend, what characteristics do you imagine she might identify as being most prominent? Which are most prominent to you?

3. Review the named Landmarks. How might you determine if these are truly functional in your worship? Are there other Landmarks you wish had been named?

4. Are the seven "rules" helpful, or unduly constricting? In what way(s)? If you personally were to translate the Landmarks into "rules," how would your "rules" differ from those given?

Notes

[1]The most wide-ranging, one volume survey is Geoffrey Wainwright & Karen Westerfield Tucker, eds. *The Oxford History of Christian Worship* (New York: Oxford University Press, 2006). However, two shorter, helpful and more popularly written surveys are: James F. White, *A Brief History of Christian Worship* (Nashville: Abingdon Press, 1993) and William H. Willimon, *Word, Water, Wine, and Bread: How Worship Has Changed Across the Years* (Valley Forge, PA: Judson Press, 1980). Another invaluable resource is Robert Webber's seven- volume *The Complete Library of Christian Worship* (Nashville, TN: Star Song Publishing Group, 1993), especially volumes Two and Six.

[2]Although his concerns are broader than those developed in this work, D.H.Williams' *Evangelicals and Tradition: The Formative Influence of the Early Church* (Grand Rapids, MI: Baker Academic, 2005) presents a fully developed plea for evangelical retrieval of the wisdom of the ancient Church.

[3]Samuel H. Miller, *The Life of the Church* (New York & Evanston: Harper & Row, Publishers, 1953), 69.

⁴With regard to "hundred-year-old hymns" it must be readily admitted there is always need for fresh musical expressions of the faith. But the appeal to "sing a new song," often cited by some as scripture's mandate to marginalize old songs, is questionable. "Sing a new song" occurs seven times in the Old Testament. Two of these (Psalm 33, 40) are psalms of lament in which the "new song" likely refers to a different kind of song, that is, a change from lament to thanksgiving. A third (Psalm 144) is similar, expressing a vow to sing a new kind of song (i.e. not a plea for help) when the psalmist is rescued. Two other Psalms (96, 98) speak of a new song in the context of other nations joining in Israel's ancient, enduring song of praise for God's mighty acts. These psalms rejoice in the widening circle of praise to Yahweh; they are not necessarily pleas for freshly composed songs. Isaiah 42 has a similar ambience to it, leaving only Psalm 149 as being a plea for musical creativity, per se. Obviously, every song was new at some time and musical and lyric preferences change; thus "new songs" are to be encouraged and welcomed. But it is unwarranted to invoke these passages as biblical insistence upon musical innovation.

It is a curiosity that evangelicals demand sermons that mine ancient texts for contemporary relevance (that is, biblically-based sermons), but have been characteristically slow to believe that any (even remotely) comparable value might be gained from subsequent historical texts or songs or practices.

⁵Our shifts have traditionally involved methods and have been defended by saying "the message remains, but methods change." Unacknowledged has been the fact that methodologies do eventually alter the message.

⁶Lesslie Newbigin, longtime bishop of the Church of South India, defines history as being "a conversation between the present and the past about the future," adding that this conversation "is not just an academic one; it is a practical one. We have to go on questioning the past because we want to know what is the way forward into the real future." He also adds wise advice as one considers the old and the new in worship: "It is very easy, and it is quite futile, to get into a state of mind in which things and ideas are valued because they are modern or because they are ancient, instead of being valued according to whether they are true and faithful. A sense of history is a great help here" [*The Good Shepherd: Meditations on Christian Ministry in Today's World* (Grand Rapids, MI: Eerdmans, 1977), 129].

⁷This phrase is taken from the dedication of James F. White's *Christian Worship In North America*, to his grandchildren "and those yet to be."

[8]James F. White, *Introduction to Christian Worship*, third edition, revised and expanded (Nashville: Abingdon Press, 2000), 67. White's inclusion of the fourth century permitted him to show the important shifts in worship that came as a result of Constantine's legitimization of Christianity in 312 C.E.; however, our study does not need to examine those shifts and may confine itself to the worship practices prior to the Constantinian legitimization.

[9]A brief, helpful treatment of this is in Hurtado's *At the Origins of Christian Worship*, but an expansive source for more detailed study is found in the text and copious footnoted sources within Everett Ferguson, *Backgrounds of Early Christianity* (Grand Rapids, MI: Eerdmans, 1987), chapters 3 and 4.

[10]Cemeteries, typically located outside the cities, also eventually became a worship venue; they offered a relative degree of privacy and a greater amount of space. See Ramsay MacMullen, *The Second Church: Popular Christianity A.D. 200-400* (Atlanta: Society of Biblical Literature, 2009), 9 *et passim*.

[11]A recent and thorough discussion of this is in Paul Post, "Dura Europos Revisited: Rediscovering the Sacred Space," *Worship*, Vol. 86, Number 3, May 2012, 222-244.

[12]Unless otherwise noted, all quotations from early Church sources are from the translations provided in the four volumes of Lawrence J. Johnson, *Worship in the Early Church: An Anthology of Historical Sources* (Collegeville, MN: Liturgical Press, 2009).

[13]It is believed that, at this point in the service, believers who were still undergoing catechetical instruction, but not yet baptized, were excused; only the baptized were permitted to remain for participation in the Eucharist. This practice led to an eventual designation of the two portions of the service being called the Service of the Word (or of the Catechumenate) and the Service of the Table (or of the Faithful).

[14]The masculine term is in the original and for purposes of historical/literary integrity is retained in this translation; however, the presence of "sisters" in the assembly is certain.

[15]The *Didache*, a manual of instructions for churches, written earlier than Justin's *Apology*, told [8:2] Christians to pray the Lord's Prayer three times daily; thus Sunday's prayers were augmented by an ardently encouraged life of daily prayer.

[16]"Remembering" is a key word in all discussions of the Eucharist. The Greek word *anamnesis* has become the scholar's way of referring to it. In "Hippolytus" this

anamnesis is clearly present, but is remarkably expressed in categories of accomplishments rather than sufferings.

[17]George Askins, "Brethren, We Have Met to Worship."

[18]Charles Gabriel, "I Stand Amazed in the Presence."

[19]James McKinnon, ed. *Music in Early Christian Literature* (Cambridge: Cambridge University Press, 1987) surveys musical references from the New Testament through Augustine, providing over 400 passages with commentary.

[20]J. Gelineau, "Music and Singing in the Liturgy," in Jones, Wainwright, Yarnold, eds. *The Study of Liturgy* (New York: Oxford University Press, 1978), 444.

[21]Westermeyer, *Te Deum: The Church and Music* (Minneapolis: Fortress Press, 1998), 60.

[22]The exponential growth of the Church in these centuries can't be attributed to preaching per se. As church historian Ronald E. Osborn notes, "the leading edge of witness" was the personal testimony of one individual to another" adding that this was "the dominant form of speech to outsiders" (Osborn, *The Folly of God: The Rise of Christian Preaching*, vol.1, *A History of Christian Preaching* (St. Louis: Chalice Press, 1999), 413, 414. Also see O.C. Edwards, Jr., *A History of Preaching* (Nashville: Abingdon Press, 2004) for samples and discussion of the earliest extant sermons. E. Glenn Hinson, *The Evangelization of the Roman Empire: Identity and Adaptability* (Macon, GA: Mercer University Press, 1981) provides an overview of the broader subject; Rodney E. Stark, *The Rise of Christianity: How the Obscure Marginal Jesus Movement Became the Dominant Religious Force in the Western World in a Few Centuries* (New York: HarperSanFranciso, 1997) is a sociologist's well-received interpretation of the subject.

[23]E. Glenn Hinson, "A Brief History of Glossolalia," in Frank Stagg, E. Glenn Hinson, Wayne E. Oates, *Glossolalia: Tongue-Speaking in Biblical, Historical and Psychological Perspective* (Nashville: Abingdon Press, 1967), 45, 53. The anomaly in this is the non-conforming and short-lived Montanist movement. A good summary of patristic references to the "signs and wonders" at work in the early Church is found in Charles H. Talbert, *Reading Corinthians: A Literary and Theological Commentary*, rev. ed. (Macon, GA: Smyth & Helwys, 2002), 103-119.

[24]Johnson, op cit., 44. Clement to Corinth.

[25]Ibid., 51. Ignatius to Smyrna, VIII.

[26]Ibid.

[27]Ibid., 49. Ignatius to Magnesia, IV.

[28]The nuances of this may be traced in James D.G. Dunn's *Did the First Christians Worship Jesus? The New Testament Evidence* (Westminster John Knox, 2010), and in Dunn's primary dialogue partners, Larry Hurtado and Richard Bauckham.

[29]J-J von Allmen, *Worship: Its Theology and Practice* (New York: Oxford University Press, 1965), 64. See also Mark Labberton, *The Dangerous Act of Worship: Living God's Call to Justice* (Downer's Grove: IVP Books, 2007).

[30]Bill Wylie Kellerman, *Seasons of Faith and Conscience: Kairos, Confession, Liturgy* (Maryknoll, NY: Orbis Books, 1991), xxvi.

[31]Our cultural situation has changed dramatically since those days of necessary hiddenness. Many argue that this demands a more public purpose in our services. However, an altered cultural context doesn't necessarily authorize an altered purpose for the meeting itself; the purpose of worship remains steadfast regardless of the setting.

[32]Frances M. Young, *Brokenness & Blessing: Towards a Biblical Spirituality* (Grand Rapids, MI: Baker Academic, 2007), 100.

[33]Evangelical predisposition to attribute "sanctification" to solo efforts fail to account for the centrality of the Church within God's redemptive purposes. There is point to the saying: "Outside the Church there is no salvation."

[34]Not to be downplayed is the extensive catechetical instruction (sometimes up to three years in length) that was given to "seekers" prior to their baptism. Such educational programs are as essential today as they were then for the spiritual formation of the Church. While affirming the urgency of such efforts I write principally to stress the crucial role corporate worship plays as a component in the total process.

[35]D. H. Williams, *Evangelicals and Tradition*, 140.

[36]This is not to present worship as a work done to earn salvation; it is to understand salvation as inclusion within a body called Church whose life and worship is essential to our growth in Christ.

[37]Clapp, *A Peculiar People: The Church as Culture in a Post-Christian Society* (Downers Grove, IL: IVP Academic Press, 1996). See especially Chapter 6, "The Church as Worshiping Community." Daniel T. Benedict, Jr. *Patterned by Grace: How Liturgy Shapes Us* (Nashville: Upper Room Books, 2007) and E Byron Anderson, *Worship and Christian Identity: Practicing Ourselves* (Collegeville, Minnesota: Liturgical Press, 2003)

and Kendra Holtz and Matthew Matthews, *Shaping the Christian Life: Worship and the Religious Affections* (Louisville: Westminster John Knox Press, 2006) are similarly focused.

[38]See Ralph Martin, "Worship," in *Dictionary of Paul and His Letters*, Hawthorne, Gerald F., Ralph P. Martin, and Daniel G. Reid, eds. (Downers Grove, IL: InterVarsity Press, 1993), 988.

[39]Jim Wallis, *The Call to Conversion* (New York: Harper & Row, 1982), 20.

[40]Wogaman, *Faith and Fragmentation: Reflections on the Future of Christianity* (Louisville: Westminster John Knox Press, 2004), 149-150. The prayer is found in *Book of Worship for United States Forces* (Washington, D.C., 1974).

[41]That a comparable and precedent-setting formative dynamic was also operative in Israel's worship can be demonstrated. Reviewing all the Old Testament tells us about Israel's worship it is possible to discern that in and through it she was sculpted as a people who: 1) perceived the created world as Yahweh's gift and care; 2) ordered their temporal life in weekly and seasonal Yahwistic cycles; 3) re-membered their self-understanding as Yahweh's covenant people repetitiously; 4) practiced a life of honesty and celebration before Yahweh, and a life of generosity and justice with others; 5) preserved holy mystery at the heart of their faith and found Yahweh to be gracious; 6) found in worship a womb for Godly hope, "the steadfast love of the Lord endures forever."

[42]Hauerwas & Wells, *Blackwell's Companion to Christian Ethics*, 25-26.

[43]N.T. Wright, *The New Testament and the People of God* (Minneapolis: Fortress Press, 1992), 140.

[44]James B. Torrance, *Worship, Community & the Triune God of Grace* (Downers Grove, IL: Intervarsity Press, 1996), 17, 20-21. Torrance, from whom I draw the Unitarian/Trinitarian contrast, illustrates how the first (Unitarian) yields a discipleship grounded in "religious experiences" while the second (Trinitarian) yields a discipleship grounded in grace.

[45]It is regrettable, for instance, that Matt Redman's good song "The Heart of Worship" repeatedly declares "it's all about you, Jesus." One understands his meaning, but in a song that purports to be about the heart of worship, one must protest. Worship is really all about God: Father, Son, and Holy Spirit.

[46]Michael Quicke, *Preaching as Worship: An Integrative Approach to Formation in Your Church* (Grand Rapids, MI: Baker Books, 2011), 43.

47Such "formulaic" greetings are not meaningless. To say the assembly gathers in the name of the Trinity means we are assembled in response to and to participate in the story of God's age-long self-revelation. It says this meeting is about God, and that in this meeting God' story, rather than our own, is primary.

48Thomas Torrance, *Theology in Reconstruction* (Grand Rapids, MI: Eerdmans, 1965), 250.

49The apophatic theologian, St. John of the Cross, warned in *The Spiritual Canticle*, that "however much it seems to thee that thou findest and feelest and understandest him, thou must ever hold him hidden...the less clearly they understand him [God], the nearer they are in approaching him." Alan Jones [*Soul Making: The Desert Way of Spirituality* (New York: HarperSanFrancisco, 1989), 25-26], citing St. John of the Cross, observes, however, that "It is hard to imagine many who call themselves Christians in our culture being able to accept the advice of St. John of the Cross. Feeling, not understanding, is very much a part of popular North American religion. To suggest that there might be something beyond thought and feeling sounds very strange and is very threatening. Religion in our culture has become something of a commodity. We want to possess as much 'religion' as we can in order to enjoy the emotional satisfaction it brings."

50John Killinger, *The Thickness of Glory* (Nashville: Abingdon Press, 1963) develops this image. Consider that the doxology of 1 Timothy 6:16: "He alone who has immortality and dwells in unapproachable light, who no one has ever seen or can see" actually converts the "thick darkness" image into one of "unapproachable light." But In both figures, the import is the same.

51The phrase comes from Samuel Miller, but its location remains elusive.

52There is also an abiding relationship between this mystery and the beauty that characterizes good worship. I cannot explore it here, but the beautiful always contains mystery.

53Robert N. Bellah, *Habits of the Heart: Individualism and Commitment in America* (Berkeley: University of California Press, 1985), 221. Sheilah's precise words: "I believe in God. I am not a fanatic. I can't remember the last time I went to church. My faith has carried me a long way. It's Sheilahism. Just my own little voice . . . My own Sheilahism . . . is just try to love yourself and be gentle with yourself. You know, I guess, take care of each other."

[54]James F. White, *Introduction to Christian Worship*, third edition, revised and expanded (Nashville: Abingdon Press, 2000), 47-48.

[55]Worship planners will find in this cycle such an abundance of interpretative possibilities that the need for weekly novelty is minimized. Sticking with the story gives us all we can possibly appropriate.

[56]Witvliet, cited on introductory end-paper endorsement within Edith M. Humphreys, *Grand Entrance: Worship on Earth as in Heaven* (Grand Rapids, MI: Brazos Press, 2011).

[57]Clapp, *A Peculiar People: The Church as Culture in a Post-Christian Society*, 95.

[58]It may well be that it is within the practice of worship as an act of prayer-closet piety, rather than in worship as corporate event, that the individual's yearning for "experience" is most appropriate.

[59]William Temple, *Readings in St. John's Gospel: First and Second Series* (London: Macmillan & Co, Ltd., 1963), 67.

[60]Webber highlighted these three in many writings, but an excellent summary statement is found in his *Worship Old and New*, rev. edition (Grand Rapids, MI: Zondervan Publishing, 1994), ch 13.

[61]Many interpreters understand the creation story of Genesis 1 to be a liturgical celebration of creation. If so, can one imagine there not being any significance to the order in which things are said to be created—and celebrated?

[62]Michael Quicke, *Preaching as Worship*, 111.

[63]C.S. Lewis, *Letters to Malcolm: Chiefly on Prayer* (New York: Harcourt, 1964), 5.

IV

PLANNING WORSHIP THAT SEEKS GOD'S FACE

"My little children . . . , I am in the pain of childbirth until Christ is formed in you."

Galatians 4:19

≈

The remainder of this book offers an order for Christian worship that is both new and ancient. Such novelty as it may have is found principally in its geographical place names for the journey of worship. Such antiquity as it has will be evident momentarily. In truth, however, this particular order with its New Testament place names points to a profound but sometimes overlooked truth concerning worship.

Our worship is made possible only because of the ministry of Christ. His life, death, resurrection, ascension, and intercession on our behalf authorize and enable our worship. We have no other standing or access other than that which Christ has and continues to provide. It is because of our Lord's daily worship, that is, his moment-by-moment glorification of the Father throughout the days of his flesh as well as on Golgotha's cross, that our worship was and is made possible. To worship "in Jesus' name" means our worship is in Him and because of Him and through Him. He is the "be all" and "end all" for Christian worship of the triune God![1]

But please note that this emphasis upon the second person of the Trinity does not now mean an abandonment of worship that's "about" God. The Christological focus that is now being offered for the structuring of our worship of God should in no way be understood as a "Jesus-ology" now being sneaked in, a move that minimizes either the Father or the Spirit. Not at all. The Christological focus is a grateful acknowledgement that our understanding of God is a gift to us through the earthly presence of Christ and the Spirit. God has spoken to us through the Son and our only access to the Father is through this Son. Therefore our worship (our response to God) may rightly be shaped in the same form through whom God has spoken to us: Jesus.

Theologians come to our aid here with their classic distinction between the "immanent" Trinity and the "economic" Trinity. They use the term "immanent" Trinity to speak of the fullness of God's being—the inscrutable mystery within God's Trinitarian unity. This is God as God is within God's own self. This "immanent" Trinity we can and do affirm by faith, but because it is so far beyond us little else can be said about it other than to affirm it. In fact, the only reason we can and do speak of it is because of the "economic" Trinity. The word "economic" is an awkward inheritance from the history of theology, since "economic" today refers to monetary matters. However, in the history of theology, "economic" refers to the historical, this-worldly manner in which God chose to reveal the fact of God's fullness. The "economic" Trinity means we know the fact of the mysterious "immanent" Trinity of God only through the earthly appearance of God's Son and the continuing work of the Spirit who opens our understanding that we may perceive the truth that is in Jesus. Thus, the Spirit and the Son are our access points, our openings to the infinite mystery. Jesus, then, is in truth our avenue for the worship of God, the divinely-designated flesh and blood portal into the courts of the Lord. And his pilgrimage among us can therefore be appropriately used as a template for our times of worship.

This being said, it is surprising how little influence this Christological base seems to have had in the ordering of our worship. Studying orders of worship garnered from hundreds of churches, one might conclude that our collective response to the centrality of Christ has been: "That's nice, but what's Jesus got to do with it? Let's get on with planning next Sunday's worship service." It is indeed puzzling why we have so easily walked away from this, the greatest story ever told and the greatest deed ever accomplished.

We can do better. We can actually order our worship services in the shape of his life. We can recapitulate his story, actually walk through it every time we gather "in his name," and thus order our worship upon a foundation that is not based on human psychology or cleverness, nor on churchly agendas or anything less than the foundation that was laid for us in the life of Christ himself. He is our doorway into worship. His life also provides our holy pathway through that worship. The narrative "shape" of the four Gospels shows us the way to do this.

Worship in the Shape of Jesus' Life

As unique as each of the four Gospels is in its own right, there is a shared storyline, a literary "shape" that is common to all four of them.

In one manner or another each of the Gospels begin with the news of God's grace appearing in human form in the person of Jesus of Nazareth. Whether this is announced through the nativity vignettes of Matthew and Luke, the baptismal scene of Mark, or in John's elegant "the Word became flesh" prologue (1:1-18), this astounding proclamation is the gist of the opening pages of each Gospel. In theological terms, this is an assertion of the incarnation of God and its celebratory truth is that the God of Abraham, Isaac, and Jacob is with us in the flesh and blood reality of Jesus of Nazareth. This common starting-point of all four Gospels also provides a valid first "moment" for those who assemble to worship God through this Jesus. I call this the *Bethlehem Moment.*

Each of the Gospels then continues with a more extensive reporting of the activities and speech of this Jesus. Though each Gospel fashions this material in distinctive ways, all of them quickly fasten all attention on the words and deeds of this Jesus. The suggestion here is that we use this same progression and let worship's second vantage point be one of inquiry into the words and deeds of this Jesus and his significance within the grand story of the God he reveals. Thus, a theological term appropriate for this second moment is "revelation." The principal assignment within this portion is to be students of the revelation of God, which reached its zenith in the person of Jesus. We listen to and learn from the same scrolls that nourished Jesus, and also to the witness of those who found in him the One promised in those scrolls. Because the Gospels depict the majority of Jesus' ministry of revelation being given within the region of the Galilee, I call this the *Galilee Moment.*

With dramatic intensity, however, all the Gospels make their way to the climactic scenes in and about Jerusalem. Here the upper room, the garden, the trial, the crucifixion, and the burial-resurrection transpire. The cruciality of this segment within the story is to be remembered in our worship through a third moment that I call the *Jerusalem Moment.* In this time of worship a key theological term is reconciliation—that is, the communion effected between God and humankind through the sacrificial ministry of Christ as well as the communion to be entered and maintained within the human community created through his passion.

Finally, the Gospel narratives concerning Jesus conclude with a commissioning farewell. Matthew's Great Commission most easily comes to mind here, but each of the other Gospels leaves us in little doubt that Jesus authorized his story and significance to be extended into the coming ages by faithful witnesses. Matthew locates this on an unnamed mountain in Galilee (28:16). Mark's two "endings" supply no place name for this commissioning, while John situates it within the farewell teachings of the upper room. Luke, in his second volume, says the site was "the mount called Olivet" (Acts 1:12) and for some reason his geographical statement has been best remembered. Hence this fourth vantage point or moment I call the *Olivet Moment*—a time for worship to focus on continuing mission. By any name the task is to conclude worship with renewed awareness of and glad fidelity to the ongoing mission of God—and God's promise to be with the Church on mission "to the end of the age."

The Gains of a Gospel-shaped Order of Worship

Consider the value that the use of this order might add to our worship. First, this order firmly grounds worship within the familiar story of Jesus' life. If the divisions of this order are placed before the worshiper, he or she will be given an opportunity to "walk where Jesus walked" every week. By locating the service within this frame the worshiper will understand that this meeting is, in the best possible sense, a "come to Jesus meeting." And certainly, by arranging the progression of our worship in a Christ-life form, we are declaring that in this, the Church's highest hour, the focus is patently upon the highest form of the knowledge of God that we have received. Hence, a Christological focus for worship is evident every Sunday of the year, not just during the Advent through Trinity Sunday period of the Christian calendar.

Second, this order has the potential to pattern us in the image of Christ. Here reference must be made to the earlier discussion of the power of repetitive acts to train and re-program our waywardness. If those who walked with him long ago were transformed by his company, is it inappropriate for us to entertain the same hope as we join their company two thousand years later? Might not worshipers enter more thoughtfully into each step of the weekly journey if they understood that with each step they are following the path of their Savior? Remembering that Jesus never said, "Worship me," but often said, "Follow me," we cannot discount the potential that is latent within Christ-shaped worship. This worship order, based on "following" him liturgically, effectively expresses a prayer to follow him in all ways. This order is a self-conscious corporate following of Christ as one part of the congregation's shared desire to be molded into a more Christ-like people.

Third, this order reflects a deep respect for holy scripture. Yes, it gives supreme honor to the apex of God's revelation in Jesus, but it also confesses that our doorway to this Lord is through the Spirit-inspired texts that tell us of Bethlehem, Galilee, Jerusalem, and Olivet. The biblical narrative is placed in a primary, shaping role for the Church's worship. And because the Bible's subject matter reaches from creation to consummation this worship order implicitly calls worshipers to affirm the importance of history and of hope, of linkage to times past and to challenges present and to a promised not-yet. It roots them in an ancient and still unfolding story. No one can rightly accuse this order, therefore, of being a moldy crust of questionable church history or tradition. No, not when scripture itself provides the divisions and categories for the service. This order is captive to the word and invites worshipers to be the same.

It might also be added that this order is biblical in another important way; it repeats the story form of biblical revelation itself. If God has revealed God's own self through the vehicle of history, particularly through the one extended narrative of the Bible, then a fitting response to that revelation will also operate narratively. It will not ignore the way in which God has spoken, but will build upon it and duplicate it, providing an acknowledging echo to the Speaker and Author of the story. A Gospel-shaped order of worship does this.[2]

Fourth, this Gospel-shaped order places a theological frame about each moment of worship. There is a meaty theme that permeates each step of the journey. In succession, incarnation, revelation, reconciliation, and mission are rehearsed Sunday after Sunday. Most certainly, there are multiple other theological themes that surface within the context of worship, but the foundation provided in these four is capable of hosting all other appropriate themes. The greatest gain in this respect, therefore, is that this order asks worship planners to work theologically rather than psychologically or pragmatically. Their challenge becomes one of restating and interpreting saving, foundational facts rather than a charge to create "experiences," save souls, or be inspiring.[3]

Fifth, an order based upon the shape of the Gospels, has movement within it. A frequent criticism of much worship is that it displays a lack of flow or movement, having little sense of drama to sustain the worshiper's attention. Thus, the service simply plods willy-nilly from one thing to another without any sense of progression other than a slow march toward the longed-for benediction. The alternative proposed here has inherent movement, narrating the greatest story known by mortals, a story that has the additional plus, at least for worship planners, of unfolding in various places and moods. It walks through this story and actually casts worshipers as characters within the story—if they will play their part.

This very characteristic suggests a sixth gain. Because this order is oriented to a real-life story, it subliminally says that this story is connected to the real-life story of every worshiper. He or she isn't being led through a slate of allegedly sacred rites, but is being led to re-live the hand of God at work in the Great Story and is being invited to trust her or his little story to this same Guiding Hand. This order encourages worshipers to see their own fragile life stories within this epic story. What is done in worship on Sunday, therefore, isn't unrelated to Monday; it is of a piece within the saga that is playing itself out as my life.

Finally, and very significantly, this Gospel-shaped order has the benefit of being the ancient Order of Christian worship throughout past ages. It is even latent within Justin's description of worship in Rome in 155 C.E. Thus, this is simply a restatement of the Church's historic four-fold order of worship: Gathering, Word, Table, Sending. This sequencing of actions was introduced earlier, and reasons given for its use, so no more needs to be said to commend it now. What was not said earlier, but is now forefront, is that the "coincidence" between that ancient sequence and this reformulation of it only demonstrates once again the deep instincts and habits of the earliest Church. Their order for public worship was in truth Gospel-shaped even if that term was not in their vocabulary. They knew what we must also preserve, that worship that is about God must arise from God's word to us in Christ.

There is therefore nothing actually new in this Gospel-shaped order other than the use of a new image and set of terms for these four ancient moments of worship. More than likely this geographical schema was suggested long ago by someone whose work is not yet known to me, but whose thought is now being poorly imitated. My only conscious debt, however, is to the Swiss theologian J-J von Allmen who wrote of Galilean and Jerusalemite "phases" in worship[4] and thereby primed my curiosity about expanding his cited "phases." This again illustrates a fact commended throughout this book, that Christian worship is a gift handed down from generation to generation. We may and must mold it "to serve the present age," but in this endeavor we also serve a Great Tradition. We are children of a great heritage who are charged to honor the wisdom within that heritage respectfully, even if at times this may mean a perplexed but reverent searching for its non-obvious wisdom. To wait patiently in its presence is a profound sign of humility and hope.

With this, however, the most important signposts and markers for the journey of Christian worship have been noted. Keeping them in view, let's now turn our full attention to a worship journey that honors our Lord even in its step-by-step progression.[5]

1. THE BETHLEHEM MOMENT: THE INCARNATION OF GOD

"The grace of God that brings salvation . . . has appeared"
(Titus 2:11 KJV)

Long before there was a Bethlehem event there was a Bethlehem promise. The prophet Micah said, "But you, O Bethlehem Ephrathah, who are little to be among the clans of Judah, from you shall come forth for me one who is to be ruler in Israel, whose origin is from of old, from ancient days" (Micah 5:2). This historic prophecy reminds us that the work of God is in process long before it becomes visible.

Just so, Sunday's visible worship begins long before a worshiper hears the first word or note of Sunday's service. The meaning here is not the admirable preparatory work done by worship leaders, pastors, singers, teachers, typists, techies, sound engineers, custodians, and the like—

as essential and beautiful as their work is. Rather, what is in mind is the fact that the day's worship began when worshipers choose to attend. Within that initial yes or no there is the believer's first response of the day to the revelation he or she has received—an expression of lifestyle worship, if you will. In truth, that moment of decision represents a working of the Spirit: to draw the Church together for its weekly appointment with her Lord for her priestly duties and spiritual renewal. The actual congregating of a people in Jesus' name to worship God is a Spirit-worked phenomenon; it is the Triune God at work for the benefit of the whole creation. Although this assembly will do several things before it dismisses, the most essential thing it will do is simply to be! Its very existence is a fresh creation of the Triune God—done not for self-aggrandizement, but for God and for the world's sake!

Consider the wonder of it by returning to that imagined helicopter ride. Regardless of the glum prophecies of the end of Christendom, the fact is that on any given Sunday that higher perch will still reveal a queue of millions of believers who've been awakened by grace and faith to be in attendance and on duty Sunday. The child of Bethlehem has drawn them. Wherever even two or three gather in his name, a God-wrought miracle is occurring; a newborn testimony to the present-tense reign of God is before our eyes. For this gathering of souls isn't really a result of our work, it is ultimately a trophy of God's grace and by that same grace can become for worshipers a foretaste of the promised reign of God for which we pray. The best expression for the amazement and thanks appropriate for this easily overlooked gift may still be Charles Wesley's hymnic words:

> And are we yet alive, and see each other's face?
> Glory and thanks to Jesus give for his almighty grace.
> Preserved by power divine to full salvation here
> Again in Jesus' praise we join and in his sight appear.

The traditional term for this first portion of the worship service is the Gathering. It is a term that recalls God's gathering into existence a people called Israel as well as calling together a people in and through Jesus Christ. Gathering also fits our Bethlehem Moment schema, for one of the first deeds of Jesus was to gather twelve disciples through whom his work for the world was to be carried out. It's not inappropriate therefore to think of ourselves as being gathered to "fill their shoes" today, as part of God's continuing work. A future dimension is also evident in this moment, for our faith promises a last-times gathering of all the called to the marriage supper of the Lamb. The Sunday gathering may rightly be thought of as a dress rehearsal for that consummation, an occasion for a tantalizing taste of "more to come."

"Here's the church, here's the steeple, open the doors...and see all the people!"

Push this idea of the miracle of the assembly farther back in time. Push it past Micah's prophecy—push it all the way back to Moses' time. You see, we are not the first to engage in such weekly gatherings. At least since the giving of the Ten Commandments and its fourth item, "Remember the Sabbath Day to keep it holy," persons of faith have been assembling weekly to worship the God and Father of our Lord, Jesus Christ, even if not yet in Trinitarian understanding. So, we are far more than just twentieth century "stand-ins" for the twelve disciples; in this assembly we actually enter into an ongoing worship story that began millennia ago. "The hopes and fears of all the years are met in" this Bethlehem, and thus this moment becomes essentially our entrance into the panorama of worshipers from all ages past. It's a part of what the New Testament's most liturgical book, the letter to the Hebrews, calls being "surrounded by so great a cloud of witnesses" (12:1). In truth, our roots, our history, is deep, even if amid our Sunday morning scurrying, they are too seldom remembered.

Consequently our numbers are huge, even if too seldom correctly tallied. J-J von Allmen helps us recalculate Sunday's attendance by reminding us it is shortsighted to be mindful only of those whose physical bodies we can count on any given Sunday. The full measure of the gathered assembly must also include the spirits of all the departed faithful, the angels and archangels of heaven, the world and its sighs (seeking our intercessions on their behalf), and especially the reigning Son of Man![6] When rightly tallied, the room is quite full; it is indeed a standing-room-only crowd! The French tell a story about the priest of a woebegone village parish who was often teased about his paltry flock by a cynical military veteran. Passing the church one Sunday as the service was concluding, the veteran noted the handful emerging from the building. "Not too many at church today, eh, Padre?" he hollered. But the faithful priest truthfully called back: "To the contrary, sir. Thousands upon thousands!"

"On the first day of the week"

This awesome, more-than-meets-the-eye nature of our gathering extends to the day of its occurrence. Our Jewish ancestors worshiped on the Sabbath, the seventh day, the day on which God rested from God's creating labors. However, the earliest followers of Jesus boldly decided to worship not on the seventh day but on the first day of the week—the day of Christ's resurrection—and, as Justin explained to emperor Antoninus, it was also the day on which God began his creating work. For this reason Christians also chose to speak of this first day as being "the eighth day" of creation—the day on which God re-creates all things. Thus our gatherings aren't held on a day selected randomly and without significance—this assembly transpires on the day of resurrection and re-creation. The day itself points to miracle—the miracles of origins and of new birth, to a past event, and to a promise for the present and the future. With only a small amount of imagination one can see that more—so much more than is usually credited—is being assembled as the sun rises on this day. It is as though, "when morning gilds the skies," the eyes of the heart can see that elaborate preparations have been made for this hour. Something momentous is about to transpire.

"My Father is still working, and I also am working"

Another clue that this is so is found in the terms the early Church used to speak of this hour. As earlier said, they called this hour the "Eucharist," a term referring to the climactic event of the shared meal of bread (body) and wine (blood) as thanksgiving. But another term that surfaced during this era is the Greek word *leitourgia*. This word literally means "work of the people" (*laos*, people + *ergon*, work = work of the people). So, in addition to the expectation that the weekly gathering was to be an occasion for glad thanksgiving (Eucharist), there was a parallel understanding that it was also an occasion for the people to engage in a distinctive kind of "work" (not a Sabbath "rest"). The hour had a dual agenda, one of delight and also one of duty. Divine work was anticipated and was eagerly expected.

Unquestionably, our entertainment-oriented culture and our long-established pattern of couch-potato worship are repulsed by the introduction of any expectation of labor as a component of worship. Our revulsion doesn't negate its truth, however. Sunday's worship arrives as the hour of the great "work" of the redeemed of all ages. In these moments the earthly assembly of priests will offer sacrifices of praise and prayer, will incline its ear to hear and open its mouth to receive the Word, and will join with the Spirit in interceding for a groaning world with sighs too deep for words (Romans 8). They will seek God's face and enter the Holy of Holies on behalf of the world. They will do the work of a kingdom of priests.[7]

And, as is always the case when God's expectations are met with integrity, the obedient discover that "my yoke is easy, and my burden in light" (Matthew 11:30). The work inherent within worship actually becomes in time, as Guardini expressed it, joyful work and even restorative and formative "play."

Thus, the people, the day, and the agenda are assembled. All things are now ready—for Bethlehem's moment.

"Do not be afraid . . . I am bringing you good news of great joy"
To worship rightly in this moment is to be aware of two moods named
by Bethlehem's announcing angel: fear and joy. Fear, because it is none
other than the God of fearsome holiness and majesty being approached;
joy, because this approachable One has come to us as "a child wrapped
up in bands of cloth and lying in a manger" (Luke 2:12). Even within the
first moment of worship there is a solemn recognition of God's transcendence and of God's immanence, of God's mind-numbing otherness, and
of God's astounding humility. In this moment there ought be a trembling
remembrance that we draw near to the God of far-flung galaxies and
of an eternity beyond time—and One who is also in this very moment
"closer than breathing, and nearer than hands and feet." Even though we
are mortal creatures of dust and time, this inexplicable One-in-three has
enlightened our darkness and given us the privilege of being participants
in eternal purpose.

Once again we face the reality that this assembly is of God's
convening. This gathering is not a creation of human imagination; it
is of divine origin. "For a child has been born for us, a son given to us"
(Isaiah 9:6), and to this site we have been called. We are standing on holy
ground. In the words of the Letter to the Hebrews, we "have come to
Mount Zion and to the city of the living God, the heavenly Jerusalem,
and to innumerable angels in festal gathering, and to the assembly of the
firstborn who are enrolled in heaven, and to God the judge of all, and to
the spirits of the righteous made perfect, and to Jesus, the mediator of a
new covenant, and to the sprinkled blood that speaks a better word than
the blood of Abel" (12:22-24). And our proper response to such a placement, such a moment? This same section of Hebrews continues: "Do not
refuse the one who is speaking . . . [and] give thanks, by which we offer to
God an acceptable worship with reverence and awe; for indeed our God
is a consuming fire" (v. 25, 28). Our proper response is reverence and
awe, as well as glad thanksgiving. This is a moment of fear and of joy, of
infinite respect and astonished delight.

What it is not is a casual sauntering into commonplace territory. Annie Dillard's famous counsel comes to mind; she said that if we rightly understood this moment we would issue crash helmets to all in attendance and lash one another into our seats. Such is the dangerous, life-threatening zone we enter as worship begins. Here is where the razing and resurrection of the eighth day of creation is to happen once again. No wonder John Calvin ordered that the first words of the worship service should be: "Our help is in the name of the Lord"—for Calvin realized how greatly we needed help to sustain this awesome encounter. But Calvin did not quit there. He completed the verse by saying that this Lord is the One "who made heaven and earth"—and therefore we present ourselves in hope and in readiness to be made anew as the Lord's people.

Although we've grown accustomed to the idea that we need prelude music to "get us in the mood" for worship, if we thought of worship as this kind of divine encounter we might be equally or even more desirous of silence, silence in which to "prepare to meet thy God" (Amos 4:12). I once worshiped in a small evangelical church in the Swiss Alps. The silence as the congregation assembled felt almost funereal to my American evangelical sensibilities. But as I gave my spirit permission to enter it rather than to resist it, I began to experience the silence as calming and clarifying. This became all the more so as I observed the manner in which local residents entered the room. They did not simply walk down an aisle and slip into a pew. Rather, they walked down the aisle and then stopped beside their selected pew, standing in silence with bowed head. Only after a moment of standing (in silent prayer?) did they then enter their pew and sit down. I didn't sense that this was a Protestant knock-off of the Roman Catholic practice of genuflecting toward the altar before sitting, but what if it was? My German was too rusty to ask later if this was a widespread custom or only a local one. Regardless, I remain impressed that in some places, worship begins not with music to "get us in the mood," but with calling the mind and the body to attention, with recognition that a wonderful and divinely dangerous zone of encounter is being entered as worship begins.[8]

Just inside the front doors of one Roman Catholic church in Kentucky, worshipers encounter a life-size marble statue of an angel holding in its extended arms a basin filled with water. In the tradition of that church this is holy water, water in which to dip one's fingers as a reminder of one's baptism and then to cross one's self as a re-signification of Whose one is. Of course, in our Protestant heritage statuary has a problematic history, and holy water is a non-starter. But dare any evangelical imagine how our services of worship might be transformed if we were to remember that in our very gathering we truly are being welcomed by angels and being called to remember whose we are and to re-signify ourselves as children of the Father, Son, and Holy Spirit? Such an entrance reminder is a worthy goal.[9]

Garments (of praise) fit for a King

Within this Bethlehem beginning there is no hidden commandment that a certain kind of clothing must be worn. Presumably the shepherds arrived at the manger in work clothes! "Sunday best" clothing was deemed the only appropriate dress by worshipers in past generations, understanding that they were dressing for an audience with the King of kings. One hopes we can still appreciate their reasoning even if we are aware of the shameful "Easter parade" distortions that sometimes marred it—and also aware of the overreaction to this in today's informal "come as you are" obsession, which sometimes seems to bless a slovenliness that suggests ignorance of the occasion. Dress, however, is not the real issue here. The issue is attitude. The issue is reverent respect for the magnitude of this moment.

In convening the assembly, therefore, the wise worship leader will avoid both prune-faced solemnity and an "aw, shucks" informality. This will be done in recognition of the One in whose majestic presence the Spirit-drawn assembly has gathered. The task is for the worship leader to point immediately to the One who has come near, and to do so "with reverence and awe." John Calvin's pattern, as just noted, was to use a well-chosen scripture for the opening words. In other places and times throughout Christian history the Church found another gracious way to do this through the minister's greeting of "The Lord be with you" and the congregational response of "And with your spirit." These, too, are good words. They acknowledge the presence of Another in their midst, and they create an immediate bond of mutual support between leader and people, making a prayerful community out of separate persons and doing so "in the Lord."

Music, of course, is a favored way of accomplishing the same goal. In remembrance of Bethlehem's double mood of fear and joy and being in the presence of Bethlehem's Child, one of two kinds of song seems best: either quiet reverie (the response of the shepherds) or full-throated alleluias (the response of the angels). Continuing to use the Bethlehem motif, an example of the first category is "Let All Mortal Flesh Keep Silence," and an example of the second is, "Joy to the World." Whatever be the selections, whether historic hymns or more recent praise songs, let them declare the good news of the continuing wonder: God is with us! Let them be songs that all who are present can sing, the blending of all voices a testimony to the unity of the Church—just as the early Church taught. Let even those who "can't carry a tune in a bucket" or whose spirits are low join the song, for "sometimes a light surprises the Christian as he sings; it is the Lord who rises with healing in his wings."[10] Let the songs, therefore, be songs that proclaim that in this world and especially in this place and among this people we are in the presence of the prophecy-fulfilling, promise-keeping God of creation and history. Let the songs profess, as the opening and closing lines of the New Creed of the United Church of Canada professes: "We are not alone."[11] Gracious Presence fills the house.

This counsel seems to be all the more urgent in light of a present misunderstanding that it is through our praise that God is awakened to join us. I do not believe that informed leaders within the Praise & Worship tradition actually espouse this view, but I do suspect that many who worship in this tradition imagine it. To the degree anyone buys into it, they have bought into a gross distortion of grace and of the power of praise.

Our praise, however sincere or loud or fervent, does not summon God's presence. God's omnipresence—even in Hell (Psalm 139:7-12)—is a truth taught by scripture. This presence is a gift of grace, not a reward for meritorious work. Praise must not become a new form of works righteousness. Our Lord's presence has been promised to the community whether gathered (Matthew 18:20) or deployed (Matthew 28:20)—with no praise requirements attached. To be sure, our praise may awaken within us a greater awareness of God's presence, but our praise does not awaken God or create gateways for God to come to us. God's presence among us has already been effected supremely in the Bethlehem-born Jesus and through the Holy Spirit "who proceeds from the Father and the Son." So our praise, as welcome and supremely beneficial as it may be, is certainly not at the control switch. We gather in and even as God's "house" as those with whom he is pleased to dwell, and thus we may be assured that the Master isn't waiting for a coaxing of praise to drop in for a visit.

Praise is certainly befitting these opening minutes of worship; it has been so at least from biblical times. But it is essential not to equate biblical praise solely with happy songs. Marva Dawn observes that "some worship planners and participants think that to praise God is simply to sing upbeat music; consequently many songs that are called 'praise' actually describe the feelings of the believer rather than the character of God." In this regard she cites a lecturer who opined, "sometimes these days it is hard to distinguish praise from schmooze," and urged a praise of God that's more than a statement of our appreciation or our joy but is a declaration of what is everlastingly true about God, regardless of our present feelings about it.[12]

Exteriorizing our rottenness

The spiritually-formative subplot at work in this assembling portion of our worship is the miracle of grace. Focusing this grace within the Bethlehem metaphor, we might say that through Bethlehem the greatest Gift has been given—given without our knowledge or labor—and

though we are but rough shepherds, redolent with the odors of the ani-
mals we live with and are, we nonetheless dare believe that angels have
drawn us to this Bethlehem, to "see this thing that has happened, which
the Lord has made known to us" (Luke 2:15).

So this coming and this moment are a gift from above and
beyond. These we cannot claim to have earned. But it is most prudent to
remember that "God's kindness is [actually] meant to lead to repentance"
(Romans 2:4). This Pauline sentence states the always true and counter-
intuitive gospel sequence. It is not that we, out of need or desire, initiate
the relationship. To the contrary, God first moves toward us in mercy—
but in this very grace-filled drawing near, our need and spiritual sickness
are revealed. Thus, the hymn line is true when it says, "'twas grace that
taught my heart to fear." God's approaching beauty brings judgment
upon our disfigurement. Grace, though wearing a smiling face, reveals
our open wound. The measure of our guilt, whatever its dimensions,
in truth remains unknown to us until grace exposes it, its shameful-
ness appearing only when seen alongside the holiness of the One who
"became flesh and lived among us" (John 1:14).

In this very humbling revelation, another corollary fact also
appears. If it is true that "grace . . . taught my heart to fear," it is also
true that "grace my fears relieved!" The exposing One is also the covering
One. God's drawing near is both judgment and mercy. To be shown the
Child is to see oneself in an embarrassing, more honest way. But the very
fact that the Child has been given makes possible a vision of who we may
yet become, because he comes "not to condemn the world but that the
world through him might be saved" (John 3:17). This Child has come
and is present to help us ascend. So it is that Bethlehem creates dis-ease
as well as delight; it leads us to repentance, to a turn-around.

Thus, it is fitting for the Bethlehem moment of worship to
include opportunities for worshipers to "exteriorize their rottenness," as
William James once graphically put it. Stated more liturgically, confessions of sin have a place within Christian worship. Contrary to some
detractors, this act is not a moralistic, rub-your-nose-in-it perpetuation

of guilt. Indeed, it is as far removed from manipulative, revivalist guilt inducements as possible; it is an every Sunday re-encounter with the truth of the human condition, of our individual and our societal dilemma. Contrary to the cultural norm of finger pointing and self-excusing, here is a practice that insists on self-reflection and truth speaking. While some worship planners may see in this act only an opportunity for a moment of congregational participation, there is a theological wisdom and urgency latent within it. This act of worship is a counter-cultural call for the Church in weekly assembly to speak the truth and to face it personally. Evasions and projections of personal responsibility are impermissible here.

This is not solely an individualized confession, though. For if we understand ourselves rightly, Isaiah's confession must also be ours: "Woe is me! I am lost, for I am a man of unclean lips, and I live among a people of unclean lips" (Isaiah 6:5). In our confession we acknowledge that we are participants in a society whose ways are not God's ways; that willingly or not we are players in the world system of national, racial, and economic power games that bring oppression and death to us all. Any pretense of exempting oneself from this complicity would be the height of dishonesty. So here we speak truth and we own it before God, the God of the nations as well as of each one of us.[13]

When such confessions are paired with sincerely-spoken declarations of pardon and shared signs of peace, as such confessions must always be (otherwise they are devilish moments of paralyzing moralism, not the gospel of God), they are also a weekly participation within the continuing miracle of God's grace as our common hope. In this act of worship we repeat the evangelical experience of God's judgment and mercy and own it once again as our story and our hope. Therefore, through such confession we are formed as a people who remember and know who we are, sinners saved by grace and also, though pardoning words and acts of reconciliation, sinners included with the fellowship of the gratefully forgiven.

This good theological and spiritually-formative purpose, however, is forfeited if the act is done thoughtlessly or frivolously. Participants must be led to appreciate the dynamics just mentioned and therefore approach this rite as more than religious mumbo-jumbo, a self-flagellation for tradition's sake. And, the concluding signs of peace shared between worshipers must be explained so that their significance is prized as a high moment of worship. After all, it is the Calvary-wrought "peace of *Christ*" that they exchange, not the drugged-out "peace" of 1960s hippies or a friendly handshake of cordial etiquette.

One indication of the lofty significance these minutes may bear becomes clearer when an often-cited worship text is actually listened to rather than recited as a mantra: "For where two or three are gathered in my name, I am there among them" (Matthew 18:20). Usually ignored is that this promise is the capstone of a paragraph of instruction concerning reconciliation among alienated church members. Its primary focus is a reassurance of Jesus' presence—not just in every meet-up among believers, but in those fragile moments when the wounds of sin are being addressed and healed. Therefore, when in worship we confess aloud our sin to God (and are overheard by our neighbor), and then turn to one another to "pass the peace of Christ," a potent act is being shared. Here Christ's "two or three together" is encountered in the brother or sister before us. In effect "the real presence of Christ" emerges within the fellowship as it "gets honest" with God and with one another. With eye-to-eye contact, handshakes, and hugs the peace *of Christ* may be known in this reconciling moment.

Through the ritual of confession and forgiveness of sin, a theology of grace-filled incarnation, of God becoming flesh among us is released. For this reason it is approaching sacrilege to let this act of worship descend to just a moment of coerced friendliness, a meet-and-greet exercise of chatty fellowship with those around you. Here is an enactment of the gospel, a tangible actualization of Christ at work among his people effecting new life. Moreover, in keeping with the formative influence of worship, the inclusion of this act of confession and forgiveness within Sunday's worship trains us to value the necessity of humility and forgiveness in our Monday through Saturday interactions with others.

A review of the orders of worship used within Protestantism reveals that though such confessions of sin have a long history, they have no fixed location. The orders of worship issued by the early Reformers (Luther, Zwingli, Calvin) all had some "penitential" component as a first act of worship—an obvious vestige of the Roman Mass' opening *Kyrie Eleison* ("Lord, have mercy") prayer. Later orders of worship gave various homes to this act. Frequently it has been situated as a prelude to the observance of communion, in apparent compliance with Paul's instruction to "examine yourselves, and only then eat of the bread and drink of the cup" (1 Corinthians 11:28). Within the Gospel-shaped order advocated here, a confession of sin finds a legitimate place within the Bethlehem moment: it arises as a response to the opening vision of God's grace and thus will be met with gracious words and signs of Christ's peace.

This suggested placement goes a long way toward generating early and palpable bonds of fellowship within the assembly. Thus the body is reconstituted not only through praise of God, but also through the self-knowledge that such praise awakens, and the assurances of grace that are mutually shared. Peacock feathers of pride are challenged at the same time that isolating self-despising is penetrated. From the many individuals present, the Spirit creates a community, a cadre of forgiven and forgiving priests.

How, then, might confessions of sin actually be done? There are multiple forms they might take. They may be effected by a unison reading of a printed prayer of confession or they may be offered as responsorial pleas to petitions offered by a prayer leader, or they may even be prayers offered individually, in silence, at the prompting of the worship leader. This last option, however, may tend to isolate the individual within the very self-punishing cycle which forgiveness is meant to break or, conversely (and perversely), to provide only moments for arrogant congratulation within the self-impressed. So, silent confession times are best when offered as a momentary opportunity within the guidance provided by a well-considered, introductory corporate prayer of confession.

The first option, a unison reading of a prayer of confession, can be heard in churches which use historic prayers such as the following:

> Most merciful God, we confess that we have sinned against you in thought, word, and deed, in what we have done, and by what we have left undone. We have not loved you with our whole heart; we have not loved our neighbor as ourselves. We are truly sorry and we humbly repent. For the sake of your Son Jesus Christ, have mercy on us and forgive us; that we may delight in your will, and walk in your ways, to the glory of your Name. Amen.

A more contemporary unison prayer of confession that is also of merit says:

> Merciful God, in your presence we confess our sin and the sin of this world.
>
> Although Christ is among us as our peace, we are a people divided against ourselves as we cling to the values of a broken world.
>
> The profits and pleasures we pursue lay waste the land and pollute the seas.
>
> The fears and jealousies that we harbor set neighbor against neighbor and nation against nation.
>
> We abuse your good gifts of imagination and freedom, of intellect and reason, and have turned them into bonds of oppression.
>
> Lord, have mercy upon us; heal and forgive us.
>
> Set us free to serve you in the world as agents of your reconciling love in Jesus Christ.[14]

Again, a responsorial prayer led by the worship leader may not use a printed text for the worshipers to read. Rather, it will utter sentences prayerfully composed by the worship leader, each of which describes one expression of our sinfulness for which we seek forgiveness and long to be freed. In this form of prayer each petition concludes with leader and people saying, "Lord, have mercy," and "Christ, have mercy."

Another example of a responsorial prayer of confession—this one a litany that likely isn't feasible for weekly use, but which is memorable both for its beauty and its truth, would surely prove beneficial for occasional congregational use—is the following prayer:

> Almighty God: you alone are good and holy. Purify our lives and make us brave disciples.
> We do not ask that you keep us safe, but to keep us loyal, so that we may serve Jesus Christ,
> Who, tempted in every way as we are, was faithful to you.
> **Amen.**
> From lack of reverence for truth and beauty; from a calculating or sentimental mind; from going along with mean and ugly things;
> **O God, deliver us.**
> From cowardice that dares not face truth; laziness content with half-truth; or arrogance that thinks we know it all;
> **O God, deliver us.**
> From artificial life and worship; from all that is hollow or insincere;
> **O God, deliver us.**
> From trite ideals and cheap pleasures; from mistaking hard vulgarity for humor;
> **O God, deliver us.**

From being dull, pompous, or rude; from putting down
our neighbors;
O God, deliver us.
From cynicism about others; from intolerance or cruel
indifference;
O God, deliver us.
From being satisfied with things as they are, in the
church or in the world; from failing to share your indig-
nation about injustice;
O God, deliver us.
From selfishness, self-indulgence, or self-pity;
O God, deliver us.
From token concern for the poor, for lonely or loveless
people; from confusing faith with good feeling, or love
with wanting to be loved;
O God, deliver us.
From everything in us that may hide your light;
O God, light of life, forgive us.[15]

These are only examples of the innumerable ways in which this
act of worship may be done. If confession/pardon is left undone, however, a valid opportunity for soul-care is forfeited; and self-deception and
self-loathing are given carte blanche to flourish. Such outcomes are avoidable, however, if a congregation is taught to understand and participate
in this historic act of worship. Even this supposed "downer" can prove
to be a restorative, spiritually-formative component of the congregation's
vertical-dialogical experience.

Still, on a very personal and confessional level, I must admit
that when words such as these are "put in my mouth" in worship, I have
often mouthed them without depth of honesty. I say to myself that these
are simply pious sentiments someone imagined would "do me good."
And being a compliant fellow, I have usually played along and mouthed
the words without much sincerity. This is precisely the reason why my

ancestors tossed out all Prayer Books as being detrimental to true worship. I understand and appreciate their objection and sadly admit that often enough my behavior is Exhibit One of the error they wished to avoid.

Even so, I also have discovered another response to the charge of "vain repetition." If the words themselves are worthy words and if the statements they make are true and thoughtfully expressed, they have their effect. Sooner or later they wiggle into my thought world. I can mouth them only so long before their power begins to be felt. The Spirit eventually uses them to reveal areas where attention is needed, to direct me to amend what I can. This doesn't happen every Sunday; it is a cumulative dividend of participating in worship that is well conceived and gracefully led. It is a process that occurs too often for me to deny its reality or its benefits.

The discovery of this "coming clean" dynamic occurring within me has underlined for me the care worship planners must give to the words they put in worshipers' mouths—to make them words of truth, gracefully crafted. And to keep them in place long enough that the souls of those who speak or read them have ample opportunity to hear them not just as novel Sunday pieties, but also as enduring spiritual guides. In this respect, my hunch is that most worship planners are wisest to rely upon the words provided in historic confessions and in denominational handbooks—words that therefore carry more wisdom and art than most of us possess singly. Regardless of the origin, history, truth, or value of the words used, some worshipers will still dash through them flippantly— no tactic assures total success. However, the disrespect shown by some doesn't diminish our obligation to offer to all such means of grace as we can.

"Is that all there is?"

Within the Bethlehem Moment other acts of worship may certainly be included. The few discussed here are meant to be illustrative rather than exhaustive. It is quite fitting, for example, for baptisms to be performed during this portion of the service. Jesus' baptism was an initiating act of his ministry and therefore our baptisms might follow the same chronology, being observed in the first segment of worship. Baptism, after all, is a very palpable avenue of celebrating both the incarnate, fleshly nature of our faith—bodies washed with water—and the miracle of God's continuing presence with us in the converting, covenanting power of the Holy Spirit. Thus, the theological frame of incarnation can be given still another means of expression through baptism.[16]

Testimonies of God's gracious work in person's lives or through the ministry of the church also find a natural and fitting placement in this segment of worship, for these also give joyful witness and praise for the presence of God with us. There is no profit in being rigid about what does or does not belong within this time of worship, but it is legitimate to ask that anything that is done within it express as glad thanksgiving and testimony that "we are not alone." Let the majesty of gracious holy presence be the unmistakable focus during the opening minutes of our worship.

2. THE GALILEE MOMENT: THE REVELATION OF GOD

"The grace of God that brings salvation...has appeared, teaching us...."
(Titus 2:11-12 KJV)

In the Gospel of Matthew the first words Jesus speaks to us (i.e., words not addressed either to John the Baptizer or to the wilderness tempter) are the startling words: "Repent, for the kingdom of heaven has come near" and "Follow me and I will make you fish for people" (3:17, 19). For a first time reader, as well as for many longtime churchgoers, both commands cry out for an explanation. This need is ever-present. Even in the days of his flesh, Jesus' listeners "were astounded at his teaching" (Mark 1:22) and, observing his deeds, they "were all amazed, and kept asking one another, 'What is this? A new teaching—with authority!'" (Mark 1:27). Mystification, offense, intrigue—and delight—were and continue to be the responses of those who consider Jesus. Therefore, if the focus of God's self-revelation is this Jesus, and if our worship is offered through him, a necessary component of our worship must be an attempt to listen to this Jesus and to learn what his words and accompanying actions have to teach us about the One we worship. (And, of course, no attempt to understand Jesus can be successful without reference to the scriptures that formed him, the Old Testament. Hence, a focus upon Jesus does not dismiss the study of this first testament; it necessitates it.)

This leads us to the Galilee Moment within worship, the portion of the service when we are given opportunity to join his chosen twelve and the great crowds who observed and listened to him in Galilee long ago. In this portion of worship we ponder the meaning of the same ancient Hebrew scrolls Jesus studied and we sit at his feet to learn of the God he called "my Father." The theological frame for this portion of the service is therefore God's revelation.

Given this assignment, our immediate assumption is that this will be the educational portion of the service, the period when we will be taught by an expert. This, at least, is the way it seems to present itself. And it is this—but with a significant difference from familiar classroom protocol.

Educational or Educative?

Good worship does indeed teach, but it does so in a manner designed primarily to form character rather than to transmit information.[17] This difference may be expressed as a difference between worship as educative and as educational. The idea within this contrast has everything to do with the previously-discussed concept of worship as formative of individual and corporate spirituality.

If worship is conceived as being educational, the purpose of the gathering becomes the goal of teachers through the ages: to instruct. That goal is laudable and necessary, but when that purpose is enacted in a worship setting, the sanctuary's "feel" becomes that of a lecture hall; the preacher becomes the professor and worshipers become pupils whose worship assignment is to listen and learn. Sometimes these pupils are even given fill-in-the-blank outlines for the day's teaching. "A lecture with hymns" is the way this kind of service was characterized in earlier days, and early Protestantism provides us with classic expressions of it. Multi-pointed, didactic sermons on complex theological matters and lengthy word-by-word expositions of scripture were an expected feature of the worship services of that era. In the context of the sixteenth and seventeenth centuries this model of "worship as education" made some sense. The Protestant break from the Catholic culture required an accompanying heavy dose of instruction. Although printing was available in this period, with a lively market for religious literature, this was not yet the era of Sunday School curricula and small group Bible study-guides. So the Sunday services—particularly the sermon—became the primary vehicle for this instruction. However, as earlier noted, this manner of worship, with its overly-cerebral nature, was mostly supplanted by the revivalist tradition of Finney and his successors. Though this classroom ethos can still be found in many evangelical worship venues, the stance taken here is that the best channel for overt instruction in faith is through instructional classes rather than in the restoration of early Protestantism's model of "worship as education." In contrast, however, worship that is rich in *educative* quality is very much to be encouraged.

In educative worship, care is always being given to what is being nonverbally communicated or subliminally taught in worship. The various actions of worship are appreciated as multivalent acts, that is, they are appreciated not only for what they are and do in themselves but also for what they "say" on multiple levels. Consider, for instance, something so mundane as how the Bible, as a bound book, is handled in a worship service. "Educationally" we claim the most elevated things about this book. But "educatively" this is modeled by the care given to this physical book. Is it respectfully opened and read or is it wadded up like a rolled newspaper in the preacher's fist? Are its words read from a hand-held electronic device (thus treating it as an everyday app) or from the leaves of a book that is handled respectfully? Do worshipers stand when it is read or give other indications that this is *the* book for our faith? These are educative concerns. As another example, consider something as basic as the gender of those who lead our worship. If they are all male, something is being "taught" about sexual distinctions even though that subject never comes up as the day's sermon or lesson. Or consider the way visitors are welcomed. The most sincere and thoughtful words of welcome may be spoken by a worship leader, but these are negated if the actions of fellow worshipers speak the languages of indifference or rejection.

Educative worship understands that in every act there is teaching and learning going on even when instruction, per se, isn't the goal; it's mindful of what's being picked up "around the edges." As one dimension of the principle of *lex orandi, lex credendi*, this calls us to consider worship at a level beneath the surface and to use every act, gesture, and word to carry meaning beyond just its utterance or performance. Educative worship is concerned for consistency in word and deed, for creating an ethos that is a reinforcing, interpretively complementary companion to the orally uttered teaching. It is one of formative worship's greatest allies.

A little child shall lead them

The importance of this kind of thinking was awakened within me at the conclusion of a worship service I had judged as excellent in most every way. There had been hearty praise lifted in song and speech, the offering of sincere prayers, scriptures heard and interpreted through the sermon, baptism, and a communion observance. Evidence of the Spirit's presence had been visible. It had been, indeed, a very good occasion of worship—so far as I could determine. But an "Oh, no!" moment came after the benediction, as I chatted with a nine-year-old who had been baptized that morning's service.

Now, within my theological tradition we practice believer's baptism by immersion, and in this particular church it was customary to place a pinch of salt on the lips of each candidate as they are lifted from the baptismal water—a literal taste of being "the salt of the earth"—and to give them a small lighted candle to carry with them as they exit the baptistery pool, a symbol of being "the light of the world."

However, as I chatted with this freshly-baptized child after that day's service I noticed she wasn't nearly as bubbly as I. "Is something wrong, Marilee?" I asked. With trembling lip, she replied, "They took my candle." I was puzzled.

They took my candle? What does that mean?

Then I remembered that, as an intended help to drenched, newly-baptized believers, a caring deacon always was on duty, offering a warm towel and an open hand to retrieve the lit candle. So it was that Marilee had come out of the baptismal waters—her ears having just heard her name pronounced aloud as a child of God and her lips and hands being filled with symbols of that status—when a dutiful, well-meaning adult met her. Just as she was tasting the salt and seeing the dancing flame of a God-given identity, an interrupting voice said, "Here, I'll take that." Her candle had been taken, its flame blown out, and casually pitched into a waiting receptacle.

Our educative error was obvious. We changed our procedure. We decided we'd risk an accidental fire in the dressing room rather than have a new Christian have their "light" taken, blown out and dumped, all within three paces of the starting blocks! From that day forward, everybody kept their candle—and did with it whatever they desired.

Now, this slice of worship life arises from the Church's ancient practice of baptism, an initiation rite of great historic and theological significance that's voluminously addressed in textbooks and catechisms. So its meaning is very much an "educational" matter. But it is also important to note its "educative" dimensions. For instance, the fact that this particular baptism was done within the context of a worshiping community rather than during a private ceremony "said" something nonverbally about this church's understanding of the faith life as being a communal endeavor. The fact that this baptism was done in response to personal belief and in an immersionist manner added another non-spoken but powerful word about this act's significance within this community—

it "spoke" of death, burial, and resurrection; it preached Christ and offered testimony to personal experience to all present. Of course, those gifts of salt and candle offered still other layers of meaning. However, in the moment of enactment I, as pastor, made little effort to explain or educate those present; the acts and the symbols themselves were trusted to convey much of the meaning educatively. Sadly, in Marilee's experience, the "doing" of the act completely overwhelmed everything we thought we were "saying," because the educative message given to Marilee was that this "light of the world" stuff was just for show. We didn't really mean it, nor should she take it seriously, either.

Just so, much of the learning within worship occurs, as it were, in a subliminal fashion. This in no way eliminates the need for straightforward instruction, but it does acknowledge that educative learning forms persons, shapes character and identity just as surely—and arguably as effectively—as many overtly-educational programs.

The opportunities for positive, educative faith formation are abundant within our worship services. Through thoughtful use of them, our rituals become channels of powerful meaning and not just meaningless rituals. Once again, how we do whatever we do becomes formative. Seizing the educative dimension of worship means understanding the multiple levels of meaning and power within good worship practices and maximizing each one of them. It also means having the sense to let go of shallow or meaningless practices—especially destructive ones like snatching the "light of the world" from little Marilee.

Given this distinction between the educational and the educative, it becomes clearer that the Galilee Moment of worship is most important—and tricky. For this is when the textual dimension of God's revelation dominates the agenda and a teaching-learning assignment is rightly ours. Even so, a primary challenge during this segment of worship is to keep it from becoming just an educational experience, a sanctified study hall. In worship, even our learning ought to have a doxological dimension to it.

Consequently, although the preacher is often obliged by text and context to enter the role of congregational teacher—and this is a frequent necessity—the manner in which this is done is all-important. This teaching ought not to be overloaded with "noodle-nuggets," that is, ideas offered to amuse the intellect or simply to fatten the listener's information store. The sermonic "meat" ought always to be such as to yield soul "gravy." The teaching must have heart truth as well as head facts and inculcate yearning as well as instruct in clear thinking. In sum, if the sermon becomes a Sunday lecture, scholars may proliferate, but congregational worship will languish as a consequence.

More will be said about the sermon and the preacher in a moment, but as an introduction to those comments it's needful to state that all good preaching arises from biblical texts—texts that should be established in the congregation's mind by their being carefully read aloud.

"Give attention to the public reading of scripture . . . "
(1 Timothy 4:13)

From the survey of the worship of the early Church, we learned that even before there was an established canon of scripture, "the prophets and the memoirs of the apostles [were] read as long as time permits." In every subsequent age this has been the Church's pattern. She looks to this collection of documents as her written charter, compass, and mentor. She accepts these writings as unique, as God-inspired, as literature that speaks to the Church on levels incomparable even to the finest of other literature. Through these pages our family story is rehearsed, our heroes and heroines, our rogues and our closeted skeletons are "outed." Above all, through these pages the God of this family is glimpsed in revelatory ways. For good reason, then, young pastor Timothy was told to "give attention to the public reading of scripture." If these scriptures and the story they tell are omitted from the community's life, amnesia ensues and an internal dynamic of worship is omitted.

If worship is fundamentally a conversation initiated by God, an antiphonal process of revelation and response, then we must remember that the normative means of God's self-revelation is the witness of scripture. As Augustine counseled his flock, "Consider the scriptures to be the face of God for now."[18] Those who would seek God's face are to listen to God's scriptures. No scripture, no revelation!

Protestant reformer John Calvin, believing so strongly in the importance of hearing this Word as the baseline of worship, began and ordered the continuance of the practice of offering a Prayer for Illumination before the scriptures were publicly read. This prayer asked the Holy Spirit to carry the words into the souls of the listeners as a living word. Certainly, God may and does speak through countless means (especially within worship's many rich textures and moods), but the clarifying, benchmark word still comes to us through the witness of scripture. From its pages alone do we learn of God's creative acts and redemptive agonies through the centuries, culminating in the gift of Christ and the Holy-Spirit-born Church which is kept in vibrant hope by the promises of God's summation of all in final glory. Consequently, if the words of this word become strangers in our worship, we banish the very story that awakens us to worship; we hear no startling voice that reaches out of eternity and calls us to stammer our Amen. If the words of this book are few—or, excised!—from worship, God's voice is muzzled.

How ironic it is, then, that in countless evangelical worship services one will hear so little public reading of the scriptures. This seems to be the case even in churches that profess fierce loyalty to the Bible, in the very congregations that want most to be known as "people of the Book." If one gauged only from the number of minutes given to the sustained reading and listening to the scriptures in our worship, the strange silence of the Bible in the Church would be indefensible. It is not improbable that in the vast majority of evangelical churches less than one minute of the entire time of worship is given to actually listening to a portion of God's written Word. This reveals an appalling negligence, if not worse. Giving attention to the public reading of scripture is mandatory—*if* we want worship that is actually a dynamic response to the living, self-revealing God, and *if* we want a people who have any idea who they are and what they are about.[19]

Let it then be gratefully remembered, first of all, that scriptures can be heard through its use in prayers of confession, in responsive readings, and certainly through song. The power of choral settings of great passages of scripture is incalculable; believers from many centuries of the Christian past could attest to how indelibly many passages of scripture have been inscribed in their memory because they were paired with melodies that made them unforgettable. The singing of Psalms, for example, has a hallowed history within Christian worship and the practice continues to have great potential as a word-bearer to today's worshipers.[20] Indeed, some of the best of today's contemporary Christian music is found in melodic expressions of the ancient psalter; the same may be said for the haunting psalm settings coming from the European ecumenical center of Taize. Nonetheless, for evangelical worship, the spoken word, the scripture voiced in clear and confident speech, has a primary role that shouldn't be minimized.

Justin Martyr's church in Rome set a worthy standard for us by listening both to the Old Testament's "prophets" as well as to the New Testament's "memoirs of the apostles." Though the labels of Old Testament and New Testament weren't yet assigned, nor a canon of sixty-six writings yet established, this early church was profiting from the full range of the Bible's message. Good faith formation in every age needs the nourishment of both testaments, of Jeremiah's raging against God and of Mary's Magnificat submission to God, of Elijah's exploits and of Corinthian confusion, of Abraham's march to Moriah and of Silas' nights in jail. The surprising unity of the Bible's disparate writings becomes evident and even empowering to those who year after year hear these stories paired and read well. Even if the pastor's sermon for the day doesn't interpret and apply all of the passages that may be read (so that one or more remains as our ancestors dubbed them, "dumb" readings, that is, readings without speech interpretation), the ancient words have nonetheless been lifted from obscurity and spoken in our hearing for our profit—and perhaps the Spirit may apply them in more powerful ways than if they had been preached upon!

Of course, the pairing of texts from Old and New testaments is made easier if the worship planner utilizes a lectionary devised by biblical scholars whose knowledge of the Bible is far greater than that of most of us. Lectionaries provide complementing texts from the various strata of the Bible for each Sunday of the year. When consistently followed, lectionaries lead a listening Church through the grand sweep of revelation history every year and steer them away from backwaters. They also offer a potential corrective to preachers who tend to speak only from favorite texts and to congregations who prefer to hear only the strand of the gospel they already know.

In whatever manner a church worship planner accomplishes it, the goal in the public reading of scripture is to help worshipers develop an expansive room for faith, a big-picture view of God's revelation that narrates the astonishing story into which we are called. Christ's Church needs such panoramic views of God's mighty acts if it is to grow over time in the ability to discriminate between the trivial and the enduring. Hearing the whole counsel of God enables this accomplishment.

All of us know, however, that simply including more Bible verses within a worship service isn't a magical cure for spiritual anemia or for biblical ignorance. Like it or not, the benefit of the public reading of the scriptures is unavoidably harnessed to a great degree to the skill of the reader. Poorly-trained or inadequately-prepared readers can make this act of worship an agony. In pursuit of broader congregational participation, even children are sometimes asked to read—a laudable intent within itself—but if no training is given to them the focus of attention will inevitably be on the child's reading skills rather than upon the message contained within the scriptures being read. The same result befalls adult readers whose halting speech, disregard of punctuation signs, inappropriate vocal emphases, poor voice projection, use of "holy tones," or other errors in oral interpretation render the readings meaningless. Consequently, those who read the scriptures in worship ought to receive guidance and training for this most important form of ministry.[21] A skilled reader can make the moments of listening to the day's Bible passages as fascinating as hearing the tale of a master storyteller—or more interesting than the reading of the last will and testament of one's rich uncle. When this occurs, those who then stand to preach from one or more of those passages discover that the fruitful seed has already been well sown.

"In the presence of God and of Christ Jesus . . . proclaim the message" (2 Timothy 4:1-2)

Preaching has an honored place within the Christian faith. Jesus himself "came to Galilee proclaiming the good news of God" (Mark 1:14), and understood such preaching to be a crucial component of his mission, "for I was sent for this purpose" (Luke 4:43). He also sent his disciples out to proclaim the reign of God (Luke 9:2) and promised to be with them always as they continued to go and make disciples of all nations (Matthew 28:19-20). From the Acts of the Apostles we receive abundant documentation that these disciples obeyed this command with fervency, and in letters written to young leaders during those decades (such as the one to Timothy cited above), the imperative of preaching remained clear. Justin's description of Christian worship in Rome a full century later is only one of many references to verbal instruction and exhortation being a central part of the early Church's worship.

Preaching has, therefore, an indelible place within Christian faith and within Christian worship. This is not to say that sermons as we know them today have always been present or that they have been valued as an essential act of worship. The history of preaching within worship is a story of highs and lows, of periods of great emphasis and periods of almost total neglect—there are years within the Church's worship history when sermons were marginalized. The importance of preaching as an essential component of worship is unquestionably due to the Protestant Reformation, and it has now gained such prominence among evangelicals that one can scarcely imagine an evangelical worship service without some form of sermon—and often it receives the lion's share of the minutes of the service.

However, if worship is understood in the manner advocated in these pages, the role of preaching merits closer thought. If worship is understood as evangelism, the role of preaching is to effect the conversion of sinners. If worship is understood as inspiration, the role of preaching is to enthuse. If worship is understood as "experiencing," the role of preaching is to generate an experience. In each of these settings the sermon is a servant of the perceived larger purpose of the gathering. So, if the meeting is assembled for a purpose that is other or greater than these purposes, that is, if the meeting is assembled for the purpose of engaging in the Church's glad work of seeking God's face, what then is the role of preaching? Stated differently, what might it mean to see preaching as itself an act of God-focused worship, as an instrument of worship rather than an instrument of evangelism or inspiration or experiencing?[22]

Preaching as an act of worship

In search of an answer,[23] let's return once again to the basic dynamic of worship as revelation and response. If this is done, then the fact of an assembled congregation is itself, as earlier noted, a witness to the power of the revelation, to the Word's ability to speak and draw a people together. But now, within the context of the assembly, this summoning Word will also surround and speak in ways and forms too numerous to be tallied. The revelation will be brought before our eyes, our ears, our minds, and our imaginations in multiple ways—and the sermon will be but one of them. This means that preaching within the context of true worship will be one of the many voices within a great choir, but it will not be imagined to be the only voice.

To be in worship is to be engulfed in a swirl of astonishing truth, subjected to an onslaught of pounding, drowning, resurrecting Life. Through and in all of this, opportunities for response are opened to us—even of "tasting" the Kingdom come and coming through a tantalizing morsel of bread and a sip of wine. A cornucopia, an astonishing spectrum of revelation is given us in worship for our response. The Word is "coming at us" like some Hound of Heaven, offering God's own self in amazing patience and on many channels through this event of corporate worship.

It will not do, therefore, to imagine that the Word arrives only through the preached word. God's Word is being preached to us in the totality of the synergy of worship's several acts and moments. The sermon is surely one of those means, but if it is overweighted as the only channel of the Word—as is so often the case in many models of worship—these other overtures of God are undervalued. That this overweighting is commonplace among us is evident in the question most often asked of those who've just returned from an evangelical service: "What did the preacher preach about?" It's as though the service of worship were only an exercise in sermon listening—a misperception that is as understandable as it is regrettable.

This overweighting inevitably opens the door to the cult of the super-preacher or, if one is a preacher, the desire or pressure to become a super-preacher.[24] This overweighting also tends to create a culture of passive worshipers, of sermon gourmands, as it were. However, if the preacher and people can value the sermon as one of several cherished apogees within multi-faceted worship, then the sermon finds its proper place as an essential component, but not the only one. Moreover, so far as the preacher is concerned, he or she is thereby released from the unbearable burden of being "the whole show." When the synergy of worship is understood and practiced, even the preacher can actually become a worshiper.

This must not be heard as a suggestion that preaching is unimportant or that preaching the gospel doesn't require the best preparation and delivery a preacher can offer. These remain always urgent. Nonetheless, the fact that the Word isn't restricted just to what the preacher says is a healthy reminder that worship is more than the sermon. The proclamation is a most-important component, to be sure, but within a thoughtfully-planned service of worship, the Word will be offered in multiple ways and on many wavelengths.

"Remember, I am with you always . . . " (Matthew 28:20)

Moreover, if there is any truth at all in this concept of the prodigal self-giving of God within worship, this reminds the preacher that the sermon is given "in the presence of God and of Christ Jesus." In the preaching moment God is a very present participant, not a distant eavesdropper. But is not all preaching—all of life, actually—done in God's presence? Of course it is. But, it is astonishing how easily this Presence is forgotten during the act of preaching. Preachers become so aware of the listeners before them—of their observable interest (or disinterest) in the preacher's words, of the sound of the preacher's own voice or the quality of the sound system, of the temperature in the room, and a thousand other distracting things—that the Invisible Royalty in whose presence they speak is forgotten. Preachers are reticent to admit this forgetfulness, of course, for fear that it reveals a lack of spirituality (which it surely does), but the problem is multi-faceted. This sense of aloneness that often overtakes a preacher while preaching also reveals a lack of worship awareness. Preachers simply haven't been taught to see themselves, during the act of preaching, as being God's spokesperson, voicing God's word on God's behalf "in the [actual] presence of God and of Christ Jesus." Yet this fact of the real presence of a passionately-persistent and encouraging God within our times of worship and in our preaching is gloriously true—and it is a gladdening truth for all worship leaders.

How might it affect the pulpit if preaching were done as "in the presence of God and of Christ Jesus"? It has the potential to create both a more serious and a more lighthearted pulpit. More serious, in that preachers would find it insufficient to offer chirpy little talks about "How to Have a Super Marriage" when sermons that open artesian wells of living water are sought.[25] On the other hand, a lively sense that the sermon is being preached "in the presence of God and of Christ Jesus," enables a certain lightness of manner because the preacher may confidently trust that the preacher's Great Ally is both present and on duty to apply the prayer-wrought words of the sermon. Rather than fretting about being impressive or effective, and thereby working up a lather of anxiety, the preacher trusts the words and their Authorizer to accomplish more than pulpit theatrics, personal charisma, or oratorical skills ever can.

Another implication for preaching within this mindset is that the sermon itself becomes one of the preacher's acts of worship. A sermon in deepest truth is actually prayer, a cluster of words shaped from the depths of a human heart and uttered before God. It is offered not only "in the presence of God and of Christ Jesus," but also to God as an act of adoration, a token of the stewardship of the hours and events and thoughts of the preceding week (and years). To be sure this gift of words is spoken to an assembled congregation, but at its truest it is offered to God. One might think of such a sermon as similar to the monetary gift given to a charity in honor of a friend. The friend doesn't really need any gift I might buy, but through a monetary gift to a needy other I can honor my friend and express my love for him or her. So it is with the sermon—it is preached or given to needy humans, but is itself an offering of love given to God. In this way the sermon is a response to the revelation and the life the preacher has received; it is a portion of the preacher's worship.

One might also note, having deposited the weekly sermonic sacrifice on the altar of God, the preacher can leave it there!—without fretful post-Sunday hours worrying about its reception, adequacy, depth, clarity, etc., etc., etc.

Preaching as a verbal sacrament

This also means that preaching within the context of worship may be understood as a sacramental act, as a deed that does more than it says, as a deed that's meant to accomplish so much more than the verbal transmission of information. This line of thought returns us to the earlier distinction between educational and educative worship. If the preacher's assignment is fulfilled by offering a commentary about ancient texts within earshot of a congregation, the sermon falls within the boundaries of educational worship. This, unfortunately, is what some have called "preaching the Bible," meaning the re-hashing of texts. But if the preacher's assignment is to "preach the gospel" by means of the ancient texts, that is, to proclaim a present-tense gospel using historic texts as the conduit, then the sermon becomes an expression of educative worship. For this kind of preaching isn't satisfied with filling listener's notebooks; its purpose is to fill hearts. It is, as Fred Craddock has said, "making present and appropriate to the hearers the revelation of God."[26] Thus, this kind of preaching is devoted to transforming life and forming the character and community of worshipers. It's not so much an educational ministry of imparting information as it is a sacramental ministry of life touching life.[27]

One means of doing this is for the preacher to ponder long enough over the deep and complex themes of the Book so as to be able to translate and give these themes a soul force our abstract doctrines lack. Sermons on God's sovereignty, omnipotence, omniscience, aseity, and uncreatedness, for example, are needed—but not if the preacher can't clothe these big words in street talk. African-American homiletician Cleophus LaRue provides an example of this kind of preaching as he dresses such doctrines in artful, poetic, on-the-street words.

> Long after centuries of civilization shall lie closed and completed, God shall reign supreme. Long after empires and nations lay buried in the graveyards of history, God shall reign supreme. Long after time runs out exhausted and collapses at the feet of eternity, God shall reign supreme. There is not when he was not, and there cannot be when he shall not be. He's back behind yesterday and he's up in front of tomorrow. Waves from two eternities dash upon his throne and yet he remains the same. He's older than time and senior to eternity. He was before was was. Back before the purple hills of eternity, before there was a who or a where or a when or a there, God was.[28]

Admittedly, few of us can approximate this kind of verbal artistry—and its use in some pulpits would likely even be counter-productive—but LaRue's words do illustrate that the loftiest of ideas can be cast in cadences and metaphors that are vivid and in a sense sacramental. They are speaking life and conviction, as well as pointing to concepts and truth that can and should be doctrinally labeled and explained in another and different forum. Even the most pedestrian preacher can pursue this educative, sacramental goal.

Regardless of the presence or absence of a preacher's artful speech, the most important goal is a sermon in which "deep calls to deep" (Psalms 42:7). Presbyterian homiletician, Anna Carter Florence, understands this well and points a way toward it in her call for "preaching as testimony." By means of what she terms "testimony sermons," Florence calls upon preachers to "tell what we have seen and heard, and . . . confess what we believe about it." She does not mean sermons are therefore to be mostly autobiography; to the contrary, in a "testimony sermon," the "preacher tells what she has seen and heard *in the biblical text and in life*, and then confesses what she believes about it."[29]

This kind of preaching in essence exposes the preacher; it strips away any hiding place among the biblical bulrushes and the philosophical footnotes to the day's text. It demands that the person and discipleship of the proclaimer come out of seclusion and become a vulnerable part of the sermon. The preaching moment thus takes on the flesh and blood of real life as today's extension of the once-for-all flesh and blood Word that is its proper subject. Most important for this discussion of worship, sermons offered in this manner become the preacher's living "sacrifice," a public releasing of the preacher's life and faith-witness to God in the listening presence of others.[30] The sermon itself is one of the preacher's acts of worship. It transcends any secondary educational agenda, it becomes a sacramental act, a visible (and audible) re-presentation of God's invisible grace.

The "work" of listening to sermons

A final word might be added for those who listen to preaching. To do so returns us to the Greek word *leitourgia* ("the work of the people"), because listening to sermons can be real work! I wish every preacher and every sermon were a scintillating delight, but that's never been nor will it ever be the case. Even excellent sermons, perhaps as an inherent aspect of their excellence, will require listeners to work diligently to "hear" them!

But in every sermonic instance sermon listeners can improve the quality of the preaching by improving their listening labors. This enhanced listening begins long before the preaching moment actually arrives as congregants engage in their own sermon preparation. Just as surely as preachers ought prayerfully prepare their sermons, listeners are called to pray for the preacher and the preparation of the sermon. They might also then prepare themselves prayerfully to receive the prayed-for sermon. Otherwise the preaching moment in worship degenerates into that dreaded solo clergy performance offered to grading consumers rather than rising to a high purpose of an act of the whole people of God. Preaching, after all, is the Church's act, not just the preacher's task. It's probably too much to expect that congregations will ever be "drooling in anticipation"[31] as the sermon moment nears, but they would surely come nearer doing so, without disappointment, if their appetites were whetted by this kind of weekday sermon preparation work.

There are other ways listeners can heighten the effectiveness of preaching. They can ramp up their attention rather than tune out when the preacher stands to preach. They can "work" with him or her as the sermon is being preached by displaying on-duty body language: eye contact, leaning forward occasionally, nodding the head in agreement (not in sleep, please!), smiling, or chuckling when it's appropriate. They can pray with their eyes wide open: "Lord, help the preacher!" They can say "Amen"—yes, right out loud if the Spirit so moves! If they hear no grand idea reaching out to them through the sermon, they can listen for an occasional pearl of truth to which they can whisper, "Yes, Lord!" And when the sermon is concluded they can comment on it to the preacher in encouraging ways. Be specific about what helped. Ask questions. Be as affirming as honesty permits, realizing that while flattery is not helpful, withheld affirmation is murderous. "Work" with the preacher to make the sermon a "work of the people" and not just a solo performance. Worship gains in power in such cooperative labor—especially so if we dare to believe that the work of listening to the preached word is one expression of our desire to listen to and respond to God.

"I believe in God the Father, almighty . . . "

The use of creeds within worship, and even their value in Christian life, has been a source of frequent discussion and even division within the Free Church wing of evangelicalism. Creeds, it's been said, serve no purpose other than as informative, historic statements of faith. They were issued at a certain time by a certain group; in no case should they be imposed upon God's people as a boundary for the thought or expression of a later time or group, which, according to some dissenters, is a punitive use to which creeds have always eventually been put. When these same dissenters have been pressed to state what they believe, they've often pointed to the Bible, saying: "I believe *that*," a declaration that is as bold as it is frustrating to those who witness it. Of course, other Christians who use the creeds in their worship and as a base for doctrinal instruction find the objectors' objections puzzling. The debate is not likely to end.

Nonetheless, if the Galilee Moment of worship is to interpret the theological claim of revelation, there is one creed, the Apostles' Creed, which does provide a concise, accessible, and time-honored way of succinctly summarizing the Christian revelation.

> *I believe in God the Father almighty, maker of heaven and*
> *earth;*
> *And in Jesus Christ his only Son our Lord;*
> *who was conceived by the Holy Spirit,*
> *born of the virgin Mary,*
> *suffered under Pontius Pilate,*

was crucified, dead, and buried.
He descended into hell.
The third day he rose again from the dead.
He ascended into heaven,
and sits on the right hand of God the Father almighty.
From there he shall come to judge the living and the dead.

I believe in the Holy Spirit,
the holy catholic Church,
the communion of saints,
the forgiveness of sins,
the resurrection of the body,
and the life everlasting. Amen.
(*Book of Common Prayer*, language updated)

Though this creed wasn't composed by the Apostles, as its name implies, it does have roots in the earliest Church's baptismal rites. It comes from our founders. It is, as all worship should be, about God, the triune God of Christian faith. Its three paragraphs speak sequentially of the three persons of the Trinity and of certain aspects of Christian faith related to each. Its phrases rehearse the story of God's deeds from creation to consummation. In only two particulars (the frequently omitted phrase about Jesus' descent into hell, and the word "catholic" used in its historic sense of "universal") does it express affirmations that might draw rejection from evangelical worshipers. Thoughtful education (and deleting the "descent," as many do for justifiable reasons) can minimize these concerns. Therefore, it is difficult to see why this particular creed should not be included within our worship—at least on occasion. It is a succinct summary of the faith of the non-creedal church, just as much as of those traditions that use creeds freely. It predates and supersedes all our tribal lines and factions. It is not a Protestant creed or a Roman Catholic creed or an Orthodox creed; it is a Christian creed, and it is admirably brief.

Any local church can beneficially use this creed as an evidence of solidarity with the wider, global Church and as a means of uniting this local church to the Church of past centuries.[32] There is even a potential form of pastoral care latent within the use of the creed. In those seasons when an individual worshiper's personal theological clarity is befogged by tragedy or intellectual hurdles, the use of an historic creed can lend a steadying witness. The Church's *profession* can become a "default faith" for the worshiper while he or she struggles to regain a personal *confession*. Through this ancient "rule of faith," pastoral care is thus offered, the body upholds the individual member during times of confusion. Additionally, this creed can provide an elegant complement to the reading and the preaching of the scriptures, a corporately-expressed capstone for the revelation that addresses us in the Galilee Moment of worship. When sung or recited or read in unison it wraps up in one sweeping utterance the distinctive Christian revelation. Through it the congregation has one more means of saying a worshipful "Amen" to what God has said and is saying. When understood and used in this manner, its overtly educational thrust is suitably harnessed to educative ends.

"Is that all there is?"

To this question I quickly say, "Not necessarily." Once again, the intent is not to be excessively prescriptive for any church's worship. The goal is only to name certain historic acts of worship that have solid reason to have a place in our worship and to illustrate how they may be helpfully ordered in worship that is really about God. Scripture, sermon, and creed do not exhaust all that can be said or done in the Galilee Moment. Other acts of worship might surely find a legitimate home here. But the best criterion to determine this would be their potential to be an educative vessel of God's revelation.

3. THE JERUSALEM MOMENT: THE RECONCILIATION OF GOD

"God . . . reconciled us to himself through Christ, and has given us the ministry of reconciliation."—2 Corinthians 5:18

Presumably, in an ideal world, it would be sufficient for us simply to hear wisdom spoken, and we would have enough good sense to practice this wisdom and all would be well. Hearing alone would be enough. In such an ideal world all that our Lord would need to do for us would be to speak his words of wisdom and each succeeding generation would heed his words and conform its life to this revelation. His words would be enough—but this is not an ideal world. This is a fallen world, a world in which wisdom is regularly trampled underfoot.

Accordingly, for us, Jesus did more than speak divine wisdom. His teachings were crowned by his voluntary death and divine resurrection. We know him and are made wise only by entering into his death, burial, and resurrection. In this "knowing," words surely play a crucial role—but God has not limited himself just to ear and word communication. For us and for our salvation God has also given physical, visceral, tangible, bodily communiqués—avenues through which we may know Christ more than by word of mouth and the hearing of the ear.

Christian worship, therefore, provides the congregation the opportunity not only to listen to the word as an acoustical event, but also to access this word as a bodily event. In the Church's vocabulary *sacraments* are the means for this additional access. Much controversy has swirled about this word, its meaning, and how many sacraments there might possibly be. Here, however, that discussion need not overly deter us, for only one sacramental act will be discussed: the Supper.[33]

Within the progression of this book's suggested order of worship, this means our worship now must move from Galilee's pleasant hills to the stony streets and power plays of Jerusalem, from contemplation to conflict, from revelation to the reconciling work done within David's city of Jerusalem.

Two cross-shadowed scenes

Two Jerusalem scenes claim center stage during this portion of the Church's worship. The first of these transpires in an upper room where the disciples gathered around a table for a meal with Jesus. The second scene is of Jesus alone, in the Garden of Gethsemane, immersed in prayer. Both scenes transpire, of course, within the shadow of the Cross. It is therefore understandable if some might insist that this cross is the only Jerusalem scene of importance. Unquestionably, Golgotha is *the* major Jerusalem scene, the all-important one for our salvation. But as a matter of weekly worship for the Church, Golgotha is so singular and unrepeatable that it defies domestication into any weekly act of worship. How does one "do" crucifixion in worship? If we are reverently wise, we won't even try! Its magnitude and once-for-allness prohibit mimicry. If, however, we consider well the scenes of Jesus at the table and Jesus at prayer, I believe we find accessible ways into the ultimate wonder of Jesus on the Cross. In the cameos of table and garden, we are given actions we can copy in weekly worship. In a surprising manner, through these two acts the Church actually does indeed 'do' crucifixion; it enters into death, burial, and resurrection, and thereby participates in God's reconciliation of the world unto God's own self.

A Table

With regard to the table, can anything be more reconciling than a meal shared with others—especially with others who are very different or who have broken faith or even declared enmity? Yet, this is the scene that is captured dynamically in the upper room. The guests at this table are so different from their host and so inferior in every measure that their presence alongside him at the table remains an amazement. Their mental and spiritual thick-headedness, their egocentricity, even their duplicity (personified in Judas, who also sits at this table!) is a tragicomedy. At the same time, their bumbling devotion to this Man is also deep and palpable, and his devotion to them is breathtaking. He calls them "friends" (John 15:12f)—and by this juncture in his ministry there were so very few who still desired or deserved that designation. So he sits at table with them, shares food and drink, small talk and laughter, memories and hope. He gives them, cryptically, signs through which to remember him. He receives them deeply as equals, though they are not worthy to touch the hem of his garment. And before the setting of another sun, he consents to be strung up on a cross for them—a final demonstration and sealing act, verifying that the great gulf between God and humankind has been breached by a holy God's reconciling embrace of the unholy, the fallen.

Christian faith affirms, of course, that all this was done not for the twelve alone, but for all humankind. Church historian Martin Marty illumines this truth when he reminds us that the Apostle Paul's account of this meal (1 Corinthians 11) was penned earlier than the Synoptic Gospels' reports of it and that Paul almost never "quotes" Jesus, but he does "quote" his words at the table. Therefore, the first words of Jesus to be transmitted in writing are his words at this meal. As Marty says, "Before we hear anything else from Jesus' lips, we hear him saying, 'This is my body which is for you.' The initial act of Jesus is to overcome the distance between Jerusalem and our town, to cut across the years from his own time to ours. He cuts away all the debris and clutter of secondary themes and says, 'for you.'"[34]

Thus, two words from the upper room reveal to us that we are the objects of concern at this table. Through these words a heavenly mindfulness arches across millennia and penetrates every intervening moment to include all souls everywhere. What is visible here, is valid everywhere, always. This is being done "for you," regardless of your birth year, your merit, even apart from your knowledge—it is "for you." This is divine graciousness, God's inclusion of "you" within the gathering; it is reconciliation from above. The magnanimity of it is knee-buckling.

Now pair this stunning statement with another coming from the same scene: "Do this." These words are most often interpreted as referring only to the meal—and it would be erroneous to deny this meaning—but another interpretation of these words is also possible. It's not just a meal that's being commanded in these words, but also a manner of life—the "for you" manner of life displayed by Jesus throughout his ministry and now brought to high intensity at this table. In other words, "Do this" means "*Do* what you've seen and now see me doing. Treat one another as I am treating you. Forgive one another. Accept one another. Live in generosity with one another. Do life like this!" Thus, it was an imitative largeness of spirit, a reconciling lifestyle that Jesus commanded—as well as a meal that would exemplify it "in remembrance" of him. And through his immediately-following death for us and our salvation, he freed us sufficiently from our "self"—our pride and our sloth—that we *can* do this, if we will.

This way of interpreting the Table's significance—as an occasion to remember God's all-inclusive reconciliation of us and to practice such reconciliation with one another—is just one of the many facets of meaning visible within this sacred meal. Others will be identified in a moment. But this reconciliation facet is a dominant one, one we dare not sleepwalk through if we want to learn of formative Christian worship that is really about God.

For reconciliation continues to be the deepest need of humanity. Our alienations in race, nationality, gender, economics, family, political perspectives, personal integrity, and religious practices lie at the heart of every trouble of the world—and of the Church. And deeper than all these is our suicidal alienation from God—but this is an alienation God long ago overcame through Christ in forgiving mercy. Most appropriately, therefore, the Church has historically placed this Supper act as a centerpiece—indeed, the climax!—of its weekly worship, mandating that a reconciliatory meal be re-enacted every Sunday as reminder ("for you") and as challenge ("do this"). This is the Word coming to us not as a verbal message, but as a high voltage act.

So, to come to the table is to enter the threat as well as the wonder of being reconciled to God and to one another. On an interpersonal level we know such reuniting never comes cheaply or easily; it arrives through much overlooking of injury and taking courageous risks—akin to what God in Christ suffered and suffers to reconcile us.

Therefore, when we come to the table we, in a measure, actually "do" crucifixion—and we await resurrection. We do this ritually with bread and wine on the Lord's Day that we might do it interpersonally every day. Paul's counsel to the Corinthian church to "discern the body" (1 Corinthians 11:29) may today be understood as a plea for us to see Jesus' body in a new way, "not as a miracle of physics occurring in the elements, but as a miracle of community in which atoms of solitude are re-created into new families and friends."[35] Whatever more may be said about the Table, we can begin by asserting that this holy meal "says" reconciliation and it forms a people for whom worship is impossible without reconciliation from God and with one another.[36]

A Garden

The other essential Jerusalem scene for this moment of worship is our Lord in the Garden of Gethsemane. By means of this scene our worship enters into the work of reconciliation on another frequency, for it is in Gethsemane that we are summoned to our ancient calling to be a kingdom of priests for the world's sake.

Gethsemane is most frequently understood as being about Jesus' prayers of shuddering, bloody sweat as he faced the enormity of Golgotha. Such an understanding of the story has obvious grounding in the texts. But if our imaginations go no further than to see Jesus at prayer for himself in this hour, we have unwittingly re-crafted the person of our Lord. Is it really possible that he who lived so selflessly, who was so oriented to the needs of others, would in these last moments become self-absorbed? A richer understanding of this moment is needed. These prayers were not so much for himself as for the world he was to die for. His agony in the garden was to discern for a final, confirming time that the world's salvation was inescapably linked to the gift of his life. His prayers were of a piece with the so-called high priestly prayer recorded in John 17; they are a searching for what is needful for the world, not just what is avoidable by the Son. In this way, Jesus in Gethsemane provides for his Church the model par excellence of a priest concerned for what is best and needful for others, interceding as much for their well-being as for his own needs, asking for "thy kingdom come, thy will be done on earth as it is in heaven." And it is the Church's high calling to follow her Lord in this practice, to take up her cross of intercession for the world and its need. Seen in this light, Gethsemane also portrays the theological theme of reconciliation, albeit in a different appearance than at the table.

Before pursuing this idea further, remember what was said earlier about the primary worship word *leitourgia*, liturgy, the work of the people. Originally, the word had no specific religious connotations; it indicated any kind of labor done on behalf of the public. It could be used of state officials building a roadway or of a legislative body conducting its work. Its one distinctive was the idea that the work was always being done for the benefit of the wider community. A "liturgist" was someone who took care of the people's business. When the Old Testament was translated out of its original Hebrew into the Greek language, the translators used this word *leitourgia* to describe the worship services of the Jerusalem temple,[37] extending the idea of public service to include the conduct of worship. There are instances within the New Testament of the word being used in both senses.

Thus, inherent within the biblical vocabulary of worship is the idea that worship is an activity that is entered into for the sake of others, as an act done on behalf of a wider public—not just for oneself or the worshiping community. It is, at least in part, an engagement in priestly activity for those who cannot or will not offer worship to God. Those who worship become the surrogates for non-worshipers, a cadre who stand-in-for those for whom revelation has not yet brought grateful, believing response. Through our praise we sing not only for ourselves but for those who don't yet know the song and in our prayers we groan for the final reconciliation of all things, soon or late, in all places and times.

Jesus in the Garden of Gethsemane thus becomes the dramatic incarnation of this aspect of the Church's calling. To worship rightly is to pray rightly, and to pray rightly is to take one's place alongside Jesus, interceding for the world of God's making and yearning. It is to escape from the suffocating coffin of the self and to enter into the wideness of God's compassion. It is to lose oneself, at least for a moment, in caring remembrance of those persons and situations that God cherishes in all moments. It is to be a co-laborer with God, sharing in God's patient work of reconciling all things unto himself. Consequently, a worship service that minimizes such Godly work, that deletes the bloody sweat of Gethsemane, is hardly worth the name of worship. For in sad fact it only reveals worshipers who care little about the world God cares about profoundly.

To repeat, at the table and through prayer, the Church in its worship "does" crucifixion and awaits resurrection. In these worship practices the kinship of the present Church with the earliest Church is visible—for table and garden have as much if not more apostolic age attestation than any other act of worship. And, in these worship actions so underdeveloped in present evangelical worship, the Church draws nearer to the heart of God than in any others. For in these she identifies herself most closely with the anguish of God. Through these she is formed into a people who are joyful recipients and also caring agents of God's costly reconciliation.

A second look at a table rich with nutrients

Nonetheless, the feast prepared for us at the table is too splendid to be reduced to the "dish" of reconciliation alone, as nourishing as that may be. There is more, indeed a multi-flavored and many-textured banquet here. Unfortunately, even our divisive theological viewpoints concerning this meal indict us, revealing the deep need of internal reconciliation within the Church itself.[38] Those who are children of the Swiss reformer Ulrich Zwingli (1484-1531), for example, are most familiar with a "memorialist" understanding of the supper in which the bread and wine are said to be aids for our memorial recall of Jesus' death for our salvation. But those who are children of John Calvin (1509-1564) and the Presbyterian/Reformed tradition are more prone to view the supper as an occasion to experience an inexplicable sacramental nearness of Christ as the bread and wine are shared; they prefer to speak of this meal as a visible sign of an invisible grace. Those whose faith lineage stems from Thomas Cranmer (1489-1556) and the Anglican tradition have also come to appreciate the meal as a sacrament through which, in the words of the Catechism of the Episcopal Church in the USA, "the sacrifice of Christ is made present, and in which he unites us to his one offering of himself."[39]

Given these subtle—yet sometimes apparently conflicting— ideas about the essence of the elements and their precise meaning, perhaps we are better served today to restrict ourselves to some of the dynamic meanings latent within the Supper. One well-respected theologian of the mid-twentieth century, John Macquarrie, stated exciting potentials here when he wrote that "the Eucharist sums up in itself Christian worship, experience and theology in an amazing richness," adding that "it seems to include everything."

> It combines Word and Sacrament; its appeal is to spirit and to sense; it brings together the sacrifice of Calvary and the presence of the risen Christ; it is communion with God and communion with men; it covers the whole gamut of religious moods and emotions. Again, it teaches the doctrine of creation, as the bread, the wine and ourselves are brought to God; the doctrine of atonement, for these gifts have to be broken in order that they may be perfected; the doctrine of salvation, for the Eucharist has to do with incorporation into Christ and the sanctification of human life; above all, the doctrine of incarnation, for it is no distant God whom Christians worship but one who has made himself accessible in the world. The Eucharist also gathers up in itself the meaning of the Church; its whole action implies and sets forth our mutual interdependence in the body of Christ; it unites us with the Church of the past and even, through its paschal overtones, with the first people

of God, Israel; and it points to the eschatological consummation of the kingdom of God, as an anticipation
of the heavenly banquet. Comprehensive though this
description is, it is likely that I have missed something
out, for the Eucharist seems to be inexhaustible.[40]

I daresay that when many evangelicals hear such a rhapsody
being sung about the riches to be found at the Table, it is an introduction
to previously-unheard melodies. Whatever our church backgrounds may
have been, the meal wasn't understood there as being so rich in meanings
nor valued so highly. However, when Macquarrie hymns it so fully, the
significance of the ancient term Eucharist ("thanks") becomes more com-
prehensible. For we begin to see why this worship act has been prized, at
least by some Christians, as the joy-filled, power-packed summit of the
time of worship. Perhaps we also can begin to wonder what others of us
might have forfeited by demoting it to an every-now-and-then worship
addendum for tradition's sake or to a funky thing to toss in occasionally
or as a ceremony requiring creative innovations.[41]

Gordon Smith offers additional avenues for a widened appreciation for the Supper by using seven words to elucidate its meanings. His
words and their sketched meanings, are:

1. Remembrance: The Lord's Supper as a Memorial

2. Communion: The Lord's Supper as Fellowship
   (This is the nuance earlier presented in this chapter, as enacted
   reconciliation.)

3. Forgiveness: The Lord's Supper as a Table of Mercy

4. Covenant: The Lord's Supper as a Renewal of Baptismal Vows

5. Nourishment: The Lord's Supper as Bread from Heaven

6. Anticipation: The Lord's Supper as a Declaration of Hope
    (This joyful facet—"until he comes" [1 Corinthians 11:26]—of the
    supper as a foretaste and rehearsal for the final Marriage Supper of the
    Lamb, keeps "second-coming" hopes anchored in "cross-based" wor-
    ship rather than surrendering them to fanciful apocalyptic schemes.)

7. Eucharist: The Lord's Supper as a Joyous Thanksgiving Celebration[42]

Old Testament scholar Walter Brueggemann would likely wish
to add an eighth "word" to these. With his `always-alert eye for the socio-
political significance of biblical texts, Brueggemann reminds us the origin
of the Eucharist is within the Exodus story of manna from heaven (16:1-
36). Manna—given each day and sufficient for every person for that day
alone, but never to be hoarded by anyone—serves as "a model for the
right distribution of food and a paradigm for a covenant community
that is trustfully organized around God's unfailing generosity." So, for
Brueggeman, "the Eucharist reenacts and keeps visioning what the world
will be like when the bread from heaven is not hoarded . . . Thus the
Eucharist is not some otherworldly act of spirituality, but a glad affirmation"[43] of an alternate way of life that is not lived in competition and
hoarding but in generosity and equity.

Anglican writer Dom Gregory Dix offers still another vantage
for appropriating the meal's profound nature. Dix demonstrated this
through what he termed the "shape of the liturgy" found in the four primary verbs of Jesus' action at the Table: he took, blessed, broke, and gave
the bread (of himself). These verbs tell us more than just what Jesus did
with the bread, they also proclaim the open secret of his fruitful life and
of our own. Life is to be received ("take") as a gift and thanks ("bless") are
to be offered for it; then it is to be broken ("break") unselfishly in order
that it might be given ("give") for the needs of others and the glory of
God.[44] Consequently, each observance of the Supper reenacts this pattern even as it involves us in a symbolic replication of it (and therefore
formative and educative worship are very much at work in this act).

Every observance of the Supper engages us in spiritual muscle memory, training us in the disciple-way of gaining life by losing it.

When all these many themes and nuances begin to be processed one can no longer wonder why the early Church exulted in this Eucharist—even if some of these meanings are the discoveries of subsequent generations of the Church. One can, however, wonder why so many evangelicals have so easily discarded or discounted the significance of this holy meal.

An act too boring for frequent observance?

It is, for instance, not uncommon to encounter the opinion that granting the Supper a frequent and central place in worship would spawn boredom among today's more active worshipers. Regrettably, there may be validity in this concern, but if so it is a validity grounded in the realization that too many are so addicted to desserts that they cannot digest meat. The many meaty meanings just named do indeed require "chewing," but for that very reason they also offer us a grand opportunity to deepen the theological wonder and conviction of all believers, be they active or lethargic. Indeed, observance of the meal can be done, as we shall see, in a much more participatory manner than typically practiced among evangelicals. Surely the most action-oriented of today's worshipers can be led to a deep appreciation for this meal when they learn of its significance to Christians throughout the ages, beginning with Jesus' disciples. This does not mean every observance of the Supper ought to develop one of these concepts thematically. Nor does it mean that every communion service ought to have an accompanying sermon that interprets one of these multiple meanings. Those options are available, of course, but what is most needed are other, non-worship occasions when the treasures within the Eucharist can be explained. Then, when the meal itself is eaten, the anticipation can be real and the meal experienced rather than analyzed.

An act too special for weekly observance?

There are still others who object to frequent observance of the Lord's Supper on the grounds that it is too special to be made a frequent act. Such frequency will diminish its impact, it is said, and therefore only quarterly observances, or perhaps even less frequently, is the practice that will most truly preserve the sublimity of this meal. At its best this objection may be akin to the wisdom that realizes there can be too much of a good thing—that, for example, Christmas retains its magic in no small part because it comes only once a year. And who can argue successfully against that? Indeed, one must applaud the impulse that wants to reverence the Supper by not making it a commonplace. But one must also challenge its assumptions.

The foundational assumption is that the meal is a "special treat." However, from the vantage point of the Church's two millennia history, this meal is less like a "special treat" than it is like needed nourishment—it is meant to be the Church's "daily bread," not its holiday feast. Just as the human body would suffer if it were fed only on special occasions, one may rightly infer that the Body of Christ also suffers if this nutrient is infrequent. A balanced diet for the Church consists of gathering, listening, communing, and going in mission. To delete any portion of this diet is to risk spiritual malnutrition. The Word seeks entrance not just through our ears (i.e. via scripture and preaching), but also through our smell, our taste, our touch, our sight (i.e. via communion, but through other means as well, such as baptism, art, etc.).

It is curious that one never hears it said that we ought to hear scripture or sermons only occasionally because they are just too special, too holy, too important to be engaged in frequently. No, what we say is that we must hear the scriptures read and preached regularly precisely because they *are* so special, so important, so essential to our spiritual wellbeing. To the degree, then, that we are guilty of damning the supper by faint praise ("It's too special to be a frequent act"), we would do well to recall that Jesus' "do this" command for our assembling times had to do with the Supper—not the sermon.

If all this is even partly true, if the Supper is in any way a staple of the regular worship diet Jesus intends for his people, change needs to be sought. Even if achieved incrementally and requiring decades in its accomplishment, a retrieval of the wonder and value of this meal is well worth the effort. 1) We can, as suggested earlier, begin by providing frequent educational opportunities that teach worshipers the rich history and multiple layers of meaning within this meal. 2) We can give more attention to the ceremonial/demonstrative enactment of the meal—the pouring of the wine, the cup held aloft, the use of one loaf, the bread torn apart before the eyes of all, the tenor of the prayers offered, etc.—all without succumbing to showy ceremonialism. 3) We can inject more congregational participation within it—short interjections of spoken or sung praise as a part of the spoken portion of the service prior to the actual partaking of the elements. 4) We can vary the means by which worshipers partake, sometimes asking them to stand and go to the table to receive the elements and sometimes having them remain seated while the elements are brought and served to them (mirroring the evangelical experience of grace coming to us as well as our need of responding or going to it). 5) We can vary our postures as we partake, sometimes being invited to kneel and sometimes asked to stand or remain seated. 6) Above all, we can engage in a more celebrative observance of it, refusing to let this joyful feast continue to be experienced only as a grief-saturated wake, the identity it bears in most evangelicals' minds.[45] Recall the jubilant, victory-oriented Eucharist prayer of "Hippolytus;" recall the very meaning of the word Eucharist! This celebrative understanding must be re-appropriated if we are ever to anticipate and delight in the Supper of our Lord.

A second look at a garden and its care

Prayer has always received far more praise than practice, its virtues always more lauded than its promises experienced. No doubt this is because prayer, like a garden, is the object of labor before it becomes the source of delight. Perhaps this is also why prayer, especially public prayer, seems currently to be the neglected step child in much evangelical worship. It is usually included as an obligatory guest at the family's table, but is seated near the foot so as not to detract from the more valued guests at the head: song and sermon. Moreover, when it does speak up, what it has to say has shrunk to the depressing radius of the immediate concerns of those in the room, their aches and pains. If something is happening on the global scene, if nations are erupting in violence, if hunger is decimating the populace of an African nation, if a peace accord has been reached between combatants, if the county school board is bitterly divided—that is, if anything of extra-church or global significance is transpiring, it's too seldom heard within the Sunday prayers of God's people. The world and its groaning have no audience; that cry is muzzled. The educative significance of this is huge. Such microscopic prayer reduces the apparent circle of God's concern to "me and my wife, my son John and his wife, us four and no more." Whenever this pattern prevails, God has become the patron saint of our little flock and our priestly vocation has been traded for the role of local lobbyists. This is a far cry from Justin Martyr's record of his church's practice of standing together and offering prayers "both for ourselves and for those who have received illumination and for people everywhere, doing so with all our hearts."

Thankfully, there are exceptions to the bleak picture just painted. A prayer experience in one open-country church both stunned and elated me by its breadth and intercessory depth. The pastor concluded his solicitation of members' prayer concerns by saying that in addition to the names and needs mentioned, their prayers that morning would also be offered for those suffering from mental illness. Then, in tender manner the pastor's prayer included not only the appropriate intercessions for the needs of this church family, but also the needs of the mentally ill and their families and care teams—and petition for wise societal response to their needs. My impression was that most Sundays this pastor includes at least one specified group or issue within the pastoral prayer, and thereby the congregation's sensitivity to neighbors' needs is sensitized every week in their times of prayer—and the divinely-promised benefits of intercessory prayer are also being released.

One might also note that this pastor's prayer was almost as impressive by its presence as its contents. The phenomenon of a pastor leading a congregation in such prayer is surely not a given today. Perhaps this is in reaction to the interminably long "pastoral prayers" of the past, when the children in attendance counted the number of panes in the windows and all but the most saintly adults dozed until the Reverend had finished his soliloquy.

There are no doubt many reasons for the absence of the "pastoral prayer," but its loss is to be lamented. A flock without a visible-audible shepherd interceding for it and for the world is an under-served flock. Pastors are to be many things for their people, but surely one of the principal responsibilities is to show the people how they are to pray. Praying is, after all, something we learn to do by listening to the prayers of others. This was in no small part the basis for the early Church's concern about worship leadership—that the prayers that were offered would be of such merit to be affirmed and copied. How we approach and converse with God is at the heart of this faith! There is, therefore, a great need for worship leaders to understand the extreme importance of their prayers—and there is a great gain when pastors understand themselves to be priests who are charged to lead their flocks often and rightly to the throne of grace and through such praying teach their flock how to pray.

To be sure, they must not pray so tediously or lengthily that the congregation "checks out." In a well-designed worship service, there would be several occasions where shorter and more specific prayers might be offered—an invocation, an offertory, a benediction, etc. This dispersion of prayers throughout the service does away with the need to have one needlessly long, omnibus prayer covering all points of the globe and each intermediate stop.

The mandatory requirement is that the pastor *lead the people* in praying, not ask them to eavesdrop on hers! Even if the historic name given to such prayers is "the pastoral prayer," that is, the long prayer spoken by the pastor, the better name would be "the prayers of the people" which the pastor is charged to voice on their behalf. The pastor-priest's assignment in these moments is to help the people say to God what they want and need to say; she is to voice for and with them the regrets, the yearnings, and the joys that constitute this life. Of course, he ought also to disturb them occasionally by taking them into petitions and intercessions they need to say, but perhaps are reluctant or too insensitive to do. And, surely, it is fitting for a pastor to ask from God good things for his or her flock. The task of prayer leadership, by whatever name this prayer moment is called, is always to pray sincerely and rightly and thus to form the congregation, week by week, into a community of priests.

Accordingly, prayers cannot always be left to impromptu utterances. There is no requirement that the pastor manuscript such prayers (though the discipline of doing so is itself an act of prayer), but surely there is a requirement for the pastor to pray about what is to be prayed come Sunday. Throughout the week, the wise pastor will note the news of the week as well as the life of the parish, its members and ministry. This awareness becomes the stuff of the pastor's daily prayers, and those prayers in turn become the basis for Sunday's prayers with the people. The pronouns are changed, of course, so that while leading the prayer, the pastor now speaks of "us" and "we" rather than of him or herself; thus the pastor compassionately voices "our" prayers. When such spiritually prepared, "prayed-over" prayers are spoken—and even if written out, they must read as expressions of the heart rather than droned as literary documents—the congregation has been blessed with caring pastoral leadership. All this is devoted to the high goal that when a congregation is called to prayer it ought to feel itself being called up to a lofty mountain, to an audience with God, and that the words they are being asked to say Amen to will be words that ring with truth, sincerity, and world awareness. It becomes a time when heaven and earth meet, an experience of reconciliation.

Sometimes this can be done by the use of bidding prayers. In this form of prayer the pastor will describe a prayer concern such as those who are hospitalized or ill—but rather than always read off a list of names, the pastor then bids the worshipers to pray silently for those who are hospitalized or ill. After moments of silence, the prayer leader then may offer a one-sentence, summarizing petition for all who've been prayed for silently, and then move on to name or describe another area of prayer concern. In such bidding prayers, the responsibility of praying is released more fully to the congregation, and the resultant moments of silence are honored as acts of worship.

Another model for congregational prayer can be found in the use of well-prepared litanies. In litanies a series of intercessions is offered by the prayer leader with frequent pauses for worshipers to add additional concerns or to utter an Amen to what has been prayed. When this form is used the leader must prepare well in advance, prayerfully reviewing the public events of the week as well as the concerns of the community and local church. These can then be grouped by themes or issues, and spoken by the leader on Sunday, leading the congregation through them, group by group. An example of this is the following, excerpted and modified from the *Book of Common Prayer*:

> For all who fear God and believe in you, Lord Christ,
> that our divisions may cease, and that all may be
> one as you and the Father are one,
> **We pray to you, O Lord.**
> For the mission of the Church, that in faithful witness
> it may preach the Gospel to the ends of the earth,
> **We pray to you, O Lord.**
> For those who do not yet believe, and for those who
> have lost their faith, that they may receive the light
> of the Gospel,
> **We pray to you, O Lord.**
> For the peace of the world, that a spirit of respect and
> forbearance may grow among nations and peoples,
> **We pray to you, O Lord.**

For those in positions of public trust [especially
_____], that they may serve justice,
and promote the dignity and freedom of every
person,
We pray to you, O Lord.
For a blessing upon all human labor, and for the right
use of the riches of creation, that the world may be
freed from poverty, famine, and disaster,
We pray to you, O Lord.

                  (*Prayers of the People, Form V*)

The danger in this particular example is that it, like any other
worship aid, can become rote and ritualistic rather than honest prayer
uttered with faith and longing. However, when sincerely "prayed," such
litanies can be invaluable. When litanies are prepared freshly each week
by a caring pastor or worship leader, a congregation can be greatly helped
in fulfilling its mission as a priestly community. In their worship they
can join their spirits with God's Spirit in concern for county commis-
sioners, artists, bullied children, soldiers in harm's way, scientists seeking
understanding, the dying, the unemployed, overwhelmed parents, police
persons, entertainers, journalists, the imprisoned, social activists, teachers, etc. The peoples' common, shared life is brought before God in faith
and hope and love. Thus they practice the wisdom of carrying *everything*
to God in prayer.

    There is of course another prayer that is the Church's treasure: the
Lord's Prayer. We know this prayer was commended for Christian's use
three times daily from as early as the first century's *Didache*. Throughout
Christian history it has also been a component of the Church's worship,
although offered at various points within individual worship traditions.
Often it has found its place as a preparation for or as a conclusion to the
Eucharist, sometimes even as a first prayer of worship. Like litanies and
countless other worship acts, its use can become formulaic and meaningless, but that danger ought not keep us from praying with the historic

Church what Jesus taught us to pray. Once again, educational programs that teach us the meaning of the acts of worship—in this case, the riches within this brief prayer—are needed.

"I'll be somewhere a'listening . . . "

If prayer is anything more than a gush of words spewed heavenward, that is, if it truly is a conversation with God, then we must also consider the challenge of listening. No conversation worthy of the name is one-sided. It is both rude and wrong to imagine that prayer is disposed of once we have said our piece. Stilled hearts and listening souls are the courteous as well as the believing accompaniments for our voiced prayers. Said differently, silence is as important for worship as is speech. Gethsemane was nothing if it was not a place of quietness, an arena for listening and attentiveness. Worship should provide the same.

It has previously been advanced that God speaks in many ways during the course of worship. Indeed, the more disciplined one becomes in worship, the more overwhelming the messages can be—on some occasions one can actually get the impression that John Donne's prayer ("batter my heart, three person'd God") is being answered, for even the most routine of gestures or phrases strike home with fresh radiance and power. Nonetheless, the age-long story of mankind's interaction with God points repeatedly to the immense power of silence in the maturation of faith. When the "noise" stops, God begins (1 Kings 19:1-13).

Ironically, worship planners often forget this surety. Some seem to believe that a worship service must click with the speed of an express train, allowing no quiet moments or transitions where minds might, God forbid, dangerously wander off into Holy Spirit-led paths! Other worship planners seem to have ears that hear only the admonition to "make a joyful noise to the Lord" (Psalm 100:1) and assume the noisier it gets the more praise has been offered. Perhaps this fascination with decibel levels shouldn't surprise us participants in a society that invented "muzak" for two-story elevator trips, thumping iPod earbuds for use when exercising, and even "white noise" machines to help us go to sleep! Quietness has become the great satan of our age.

The record of the ages, on the other hand, declares that attentive quietness is the soil in which deep souls grow. "Be still and know that I am God!" (Psalm 46:10) is a command, not a limp suggestion. More specifically, it's a command that appears in a psalm filled with ecological threat (trembling mountains and foaming seas) and political terror (nations in uproar, tottering kingdoms, wars to the end of the earth). Yet in the midst of this chaos, the psalmist exults that there is God, "our refuge and strength, a very present help in trouble"—"the LORD of hosts, the God of Jacob" who is "with us." And therefore the command is to "Be still and know that I am God!" The command is to drop one's defenses and excuses, one's participation in frenetic scurrying about, one's distracted mental busyness—and quiet oneself in the presence and knowledge of the One who abides. The pertinence of this psalm and its command for our destabilized, frantically-fearful society is apparent. Why then should Christian worship not provide weekly sanctuary and retreat from the blaring belligerence of such a world? Why should worship not teach us to wait patiently on the Lord and to listen as well as to speak? Why should worship not be conducted at a measured pace and with a faith-filled calmness that encourages worshipers to be reconciled with God, and to all that is unreconciled within themselves? Given today's culture, Psalm 46:10 may well be a better worship mantra than Psalm 100:1 ("Make a joyful noise unto the LORD . . . ").

One pastor gave beautiful expression to this through the sixty seconds he called the Fellowship of Silence at the end of each Sunday's worship service. Earlier moments of quietness had been offered during the service, but always a final opportunity for reflection and prayer was provided. Initially, and for some visitors in subsequent years, this sixty seconds of silence was unnerving. But for those who worshiped there week after week, this became a cherished moment within their worship. It helped them become and be a different kind of people as they went out to serve the Lord in a world indifferent to that Lordship.

Is that all there is?

As is the case for each "moment," the suggestions given here are just that, suggestions. They point only to the major and most helpful actions that will facilitate the meaningful flow of the drama of Sunday's worship. Other actions may well be useful. If, in fact, a worship planner wished to train the spotlight on the theological theme of reconciliation, various other rituals of reconciliation might be included here. If your tradition would countenance it, the foot-washing ritual earlier described has a powerful contribution to make precisely at this juncture. If one's gathering is relatively small, the practice of offering "the right hand of Christian fellowship" to all present can be meaningful. As I have seen this practiced, those in attendance formed a circle and each person was obliged to go around the circle and extend to each person a handshake or hug of Christian inclusion. Forced fellowship? Perhaps. Probably. But nonetheless effective in "saying" reconciliation within Christian worship.

And, most surely, there is not one thing inappropriate in a hymn of invitation or some other such opportunity for persons to actualize reconciliation with God. Probably in the vast majority of evangelical churches the discontinuance of such a hymn would be perceived as a repudiation of our heritage. That is not at all what is sought in this book. By all means, then, let no one interpret the earlier critique of worship as evangelism or the plea for the elevation of the table and the garden as a denigration of an invitation hymn or moment. Worship does and should have its evangelistic impact and we are wise to anticipate and plan for ways this might be harvested. In some contexts this might be the inclusion of an invitation hymn, in other contexts it might be the availability of a pastor/soul-friend in an adjoining area or at the conclusion of the service. Perhaps in other places it could the opportunity to come forward and kneel in prayer.

Whatever acts of worship are planned for or encouraged during this segment of the worship service, they need only to keep the worshiper's attention focused upon the reconciling work of God. If this once-for-all givenness of God's mercy is clear, the Jerusalem moment will have been helpfully engaged—for the health of the people and to the glory of God.

4. THE OLIVET MOMENT: GOD'S MISSION

"You will receive power when the Holy Spirit has come upon you; and you will be my witnesses . . . " (Acts 1:8)

Once upon a time, and even within my lifetime, worship was actually a scorned word among many evangelicals—at least in the part of the United States I called home. The thinking was that worship was the ritualistic ceremonialism engaged in by some churches that never did much except watch priests shuffle around in fancy paraphernalia and mumble prayers printed in a book. It was thought that worship was a pompous "playing church" substitute for getting one's hands dirty and winning souls to Jesus. To put it more pointedly, there were the Catholics and the Episcopalians who "worshiped," and then there were the rest of us who actually "got it" and were doing what Jesus wanted us to do.

In retrospect it's obvious that so very much of this was driven by ignorance of what those worshiping churches were actually doing, both in their worship and as a consequence of their worship. And much more of it was fed by prejudice and fear. In any event, worship was very much a secondary if not suspect activity among "my people."

But there was and is within this unfortunate mindset of "my people" an understandable concern. It's a concern that church services that aren't geared to some productive outcome are actually an exercise in self-culture and pietistic grooming. It's a fear that those who advocate worship as I have throughout this book, are, in spite of all our denials, really advocating a religiosity that's actually "all about us" rather than all about doing God's work on earth. This suspicion, even if unfounded, comes from a right place. It fears that if worship is elevated, mission will be a casualty.

Worship indeed can become an unfortunate in-house game for those who like to play church. It can recreate the very situation so vehemently and frequently denounced by God with regard to Israel's worship. Her Sabbath ministrations of elegantly-robed priests circle-dancing their way around the altar with their smoke and incense, texts, prayers, shouts, and trumpet blasts—they were all waste if they didn't lead to care for the poor, justice in the courts, and uprightness of life. When this occurred it was a primal case of "holding to the outward form of godliness but denying its power" (2 Timothy 3:5). This possibility is certainly an ever-present, easy-to-take path that, if taken, permits us to congratulate ourselves for having conducted "right" worship, even if the life-consequences are negligible. This is an admitted unending danger.[46]

But the same possibility is present for worshipers of whatever stripe or style. Though we evangelicals no longer scorn the word worship—now we fuss over it—even on this new ground all of us face the legitimate question of what difference our Sunday gatherings make in us or the world when Sunday's last "Amen" has been said. The crux at this juncture is not the purpose of our worship but its fruit; worship cannot be approached as "useful" for any purpose other than honoring God, but if it fails to yield fruit that does honor God, we must ask if that worship has been rightly conceived or practiced. Whether our worship is conducted in shirttails or clerical collars, to the accompaniment of conga drums or pipe organs—at the end of the day, does our worship amount to anything other than a weekend callisthenic for the religiously inclined?

Mission disconnects

Whenever worship fails to issue into mission it can be attributed to one if not two worship errors. The first of these is an understanding of worship that is restricted to just the Sunday event. In the opening paragraphs of this book I said that when worship is seen holistically, Sunday's event is just one of the three facets of worship, daily lifestyle (ethics) and personal prayer (piety) being the other two. All three of these must be held in union. When they are not, the door is open to the shallow idea that once

Sunday's worship concludes, there will be no further worship until next weekend. In point of fact, when Sunday's worship concludes, Monday's worship begins—although expressed in a different form. Our weekday attitudes and actions are as vital a component of our holistic worship of God as are our Sunday prayers.

A second error contributing to a disconnection between worship and mission stems from a failure to understand the character of God. If worship truly is about God, then it is impossible for a sincere worshiper not to give weekday evidence that she or he is concerned about the concerns of Sunday's God: justice, mercy, integrity, relationships, love, salvation. The validity of Sunday's hosannas is determined by Monday's life. Hence, it's usually premature to say "We had a good worship service today" immediately following the benediction. Only the following days will reveal the value of the hour. If the God of Christian faith was truly the focus of the hour, all who participated will know that the proof will be in the living, not in the meeting.

It might be most beneficial to think of the missional consequences of true worship not as things we do but as who we are and are becoming. To evangelize, to teach, to welcome and serve others—these are best thought of as expressions not of our work but of our character. If we are submitting ourselves in true worship to the God who really is God, then something of the character of that God becomes our character. Worshipers always become like the gods they worship; as we "seek God's face" we are "changed into the same image from glory to glory, even as by the Spirit of the Lord" (2 Corinthians 3:18 KJV). Thus, a last minute "useful" purpose for worship is not being sneaked in, a hidden agenda now confessed. To the contrary, this simply reiterates a marvelous fact of true worship: it fashions us into a people who continually re-present the God and Father of our Lord Jesus Christ to the eyes of the world.

Therefore, worship that is patterned in the shape of the Gospels that reveal this God reaches its culmination only with an ascent to Olivet, to the place of sending, to the heights where God is near and duty clear.

Mission expressed liturgically

Sadly this fourth "moment" of worship, the Olivet Moment of Commissioning, has historically received the least attention of the four focus-points of worship.[47] But its great significance can be traced to at least the fourth century when we know worship leaders were concluding the worship service with a Latin instruction: "*Ite missa est.*" Roughly translated, that meant, "Go, you are sent (out)." The word *missa* eventually became anglicized to the word Mass, and became the name for the entire service. But some have seen in this original dis-missal statement an early evidence of the Church's understanding that the laity's weekday mission was intrinsic to the full meaning of worship. Others, of course, see this interpretation as revisionist history. (Still others, less reverently, say that the only reason "*Ite missa est*" was ever remembered was because it signaled to the non-Latin-speaking laity that the service was finally concluded.) Whatever may be the truth about this matter, it is now clear that the service of worship needs to conclude not with a whimper but with a clear "sending." And it is also clear that worship leaders have sadly neglected this culminating act of worship.

In some strains of the Church, this "moment" is accomplished with a simple closing prayer. In others, a more focused prayer of blessing or benediction is said to be sufficient. However, upon inspection, it is apparent that there are inadequacies in both practices. Those who are content with a prayer culmination, in whatever form, overlook the fact that prayer is speech that is directed to God, not the worshipers. Moreover, benedictions by definition are meant to remind and reassure the congregation that they are beloved and cared for by our gracious God. This is a necessary word, but if this is the last word that is heard, mission is minimalized and comfort without challenge becomes the takeaway message.

A commission on the other hand, is speech directed to disciples. And a commissioning ought to have "Go ye" force within it rather than simply a reassurance that "God will be with you." When Jesus spoke last words to his disciples, he spoke clearly of comfort and of challenge.

The comfort [*com* (with) + *forte* (strength) = "with strength"] was within his statement: "All authority in heaven and on earth has been given to me" and the reassurance of "I am with you always, till the end of the age." But this comfort was matched with his central challenging words of commission: "Go . . . make disciples . . . baptizing . . . teaching them to observe all things . . . (Matthew 28:19-20).

Once again, Jesus provides our model even in "sending." In departing from worship, congregants need to be 1) reminded who and whose we are and in what strength we live and move and have our being and to be 2) charged to be the people-on-mission all our moments with God have made us. The final moments of worship are not an occasion— and indeed must not be—for a follow-up re-preaching of the sermon or an additional sermonette. The actual "sending" ought not be lengthy at all. One sentence—maybe two will do. But it ought to be spoken to the congregation, eyeball to eyeball, not to their bowed heads. And it ought to send the congregation back into the world with a loving mandate to continue to be Christ's people, living their worship of God throughout the week in lives that declare the goodness and the healing of God for all that is broken.

If this can be followed by a hymn or song of "sending," a recessional act that actually puts our feet moving in the direction of mission, all the better. The weakest thing that can happen is for the worship leader to have given no thought to these closing words or gestures, so that the best that can be muttered is: "See you next week." That is the speech of a weekend performer, not a worship leader. Worshipers, from the gathering to the sending, deserve better. They deserve to be welcomed into the Bethlehem-born family of praise; they deserve to be told of the Galilee-given revelation of an everlasting King and Kingdom; they deserve to be fed from Jerusalem-offered wine and bread and prayer; and they deserve to be sent out as children and emissaries of the triune God.

One well-known commissioning statement that can be used in its beloved original form, or used as a model for prayerful adaptation, is:

Go forth into the world in peace; be of good courage; hold fast that which is good; render to no one evil for evil; strengthen the fainthearted; support the weak; help the afflicted; honor everyone; love and serve the Lord, rejoicing in the power of the Holy Spirit; and the blessing of God almighty, the Father, the Son, and the Holy Spirit, be among you and remain with you now and always. Amen.

The day's "sender" may actually desire to be more specific, and to build upon the sermon or scriptures for the day so that the day's "sending" recalls challenges heard in the Galilee Moment. But, as said, this should never become a reprise of the sermon; its purpose is to be an aid and encouragement in applying the revelation recalled or received in the day's worship.

As indicated, oftentimes a hymn or sending song can be effectively used. Delores Dufner's text[48] is an excellent example:

The Spirit sends us forth to serve, we go in Jesus' name
to bring glad tidings to the poor, God's favor to proclaim.
We go to comfort those who mourn and set the burdened free;
where hope is dim, to share a dream and help the blind to see.
We go to be the hands of Christ, to scatter joy like seed;
and, all our days, to cherish life, to do the loving deed.
Then let us go to serve in peace, the gospel to proclaim,
God's Spirit has empowered us; we go in Jesus' name.

The possibilities and variations for this final act are many. The planners of worship need only to remember that these worshiping souls really are the salt of the earth and the light of the world. With one step outside the walls of this place of meeting they become the gospel the world sees and hears, for good or for ill. Therefore those who plan and lead their worship must take this identity and the potential within it most seriously and send worshipers from the time of worship with the promising, empowering word of the Kingdom come—and coming.

There is more to be said about this Olivet Moment than simply the concluding words that speak its ending, however. There are several other worship acts that might precede this final word, acts that comfortably find a place within this Moment and underline the mission mandate of any worship that is truly about God.

Now concerning the collection . . . (1 Corinthians 16:1)

Prime among those acts is the offering, the giving of tithes and offerings. For far too long this act of worship has been treated as a necessary evil. In some churches it's even treated as a negligible act of worship; baskets are placed at the exits, and those who are so motivated may leave their gifts there as they leave. With few exceptions, however, the worship of God needs to include opportunity to give one's monies. But not just because this is a tangible way of "sending" the gospel or because the financial needs of the church require it. As valid as those purposes may be, the better purpose is that our spiritual formation needs to include training in generosity and therefore the discipline of giving is an essential ingredient in worshiping God. For all we do not know about God, surely we are not in thick darkness about this: God is amazingly generous, indeed even prodigal in provisions plus. And therefore giving in imitation of God's self-giving is itself a participation in the mission of God.

Any left-footed, apologetic embarrassment that "we have to pass the hat now" to pay the bills is actually an affront to the gospel. No, we need to give because giving is the rule of life! And we need to give as an act of worship because there is no characteristic of God more evident than God's giving to us. Nor should we be ashamed that a portion of our gifts will be used to pay the church's bills. If this church is indeed an expression of the Church of Jesus Christ, it deserves our glad support. And, in most instances, another portion of our gifts will be used for missional purposes around the globe. In "the passing of the hat"— or however it's done locally—we come to as important a moment in our worship as in any other moment.

One of the many gratifying moments in my classroom teaching came when a student told how he "takes the offering" in his church, attended as it is with folks who are barely subsisting. Rather than embarrass them with monetary expectations every time they come to worship he developed a pattern of having them indicate on a slip of paper what they are giving to God each Sunday. Sometimes the slip might indicate that a mother working sixty hours a week is going to give her children ten more minutes of listening time; at other times the slip might declare that a troubled teenager is going to give greater effort to understand his warring parents, or an elderly couple might "give" the pledge of more prayer for this little church. Those who have monies, of course, are urged to honor the Lord with their financial offerings, but when the plate is passed each Sunday, every worshiper has something in hand with which to say, "Here, Lord, I give myself away." This represents grand worship planning!

It is also a right instinct and habit, after collecting the peoples' gifts, to dedicate them in the presence of the congregation to the Lord's service. This is an additional way of affirming mission. It is a cardinal means of expressing that these gifts are not simply the payment of dues but are a gift offered in gratitude to God. The missional implications of this moment can be even further enhanced if planners include some agency or community service—including those that are outside the ministry-management of the congregation—and include a tangible symbol of that ministry as the gifts of the congregation are presented. These symbols can be anything from a badge (to symbolize the service of police persons) to a pair of shoes (to symbolize a local clothing ministry) or a clipboard (to symbolize the petitioning work of community organizers). Of course, the congregation must be informed of the day's symbol and the community ministry it represents, but in this symbolic presentation of the gifts of the people and the ministries of the community, worshipers are helped to see the gratifying, larger work of God in the world—and to give thanks for others as well as for their own role in God's caring mission for the world's healing.

If it is practicable, when these gifts are presented, let a worship leader lift up the plate(s) to God as a visualizing of this offering-up of the people. Simply placing the plate(s) and symbol wordlessly on a table forfeits a fine ritual opportunity. With or without verbal statement by the leader, worshipers "see" that their gifts are truly offered up to God. Again, this is educative, not wordily educational.

For this same educative reason a cautionary note might be entered about the practice of "giving" by means of authorized drafts on checking accounts. Admittedly, the practice makes good sense from a financial management perspective but it does so by divorcing the worshiper from the actual moment of congregational worship through giving. If the efficiency of the draft process is chosen, perhaps a representative gift can still be given during worship. Given as an act of congregational solidarity within worship, the act then has a formative power we are foolish to forfeit in the name of fiscal efficiency alone.

"Children are an heritage from the Lord"

Another worship act that has an appropriate place during the Olivet Moment is the dedication of newborn infants and their parents. Those traditions that practice infant baptism have their own time and ritual of baptism, but for those traditions that practice believer's baptism, these (non-baptismal) dedicatory moments with young families and the greater congregation can be high missional moments. These parents can present their infant while the other gifts are being brought forward, as an additional response and witness to the goodness of God.

For the congregation this is an occasion to acknowledge that they value children and family life as also being gifts from God and want to dedicate them to God's service. This act says that these worshipers understand each home to be a mission outpost of God's reign and that they covenant with these parents to help bring up these children in such fashion that they will soon understand themselves to be loved and called into God's mission. Through this act the people of God declare that what happens to the people living in Apartment 12B at 3269 Elmhurst Street (the young parents' address), and in all other apartments and homes in this city, matters to this congregation. They and their wellbeing are our mission!

"Did they have announcements in Jerusalem?"

Even the announcements, that loathsome necessity of every worship service, find a fitting home in the Olivet Moment of worship. Many congregations choose to assign them a place at the very first, perhaps even preceding the actual beginning of worship, judging them to be largely promotional in nature. Those who do this want worshipers to depart on a spiritual high rather than heading out the doors with mundane reminders of life-cluttering meetings. The intent in this approach is laudable, but more can be said about their spiritual nature and when they can be rightly spoken.

Properly presented, announcements can be understood as naming ways for members to live out their character and mission in serving, teaching, evangelizing, and caring for others. In short, they can be spoken so as to show worshipers where they can join in the *missio dei* (mission of God) in the coming week.

This means the worship leader will first have to determine which announcements are best left in printed form (be it in worship folders or projected on a screen or some other manner) and which merit verbalization. Then, a clustering of the chosen announcements into missional categories is essential. (E.g.: "This coming week we have the opportunity to *serve* in Christ's name by staffing Tuesday's lunch meal for the homeless at Good Shepherd Church; see Jim Brown or call the number you see listed there for more information. Also, the ladies of the Missionary Society are providing us an opportunity next Thursday evening to *learn* about Interfaith Dialogues; it's a grand way to launch fruitful conversations with persons of other faiths . . . ") Done in this manner, the announcements become more than announcements; they become a naming of missional opportunities; they indicate ways in which Sunday's adoration can be implemented in weekday action.

Until he comes . . .

Latent within all these acts of worship there is a tomorrow-ness or, in theological terms, an eschatological flavor. By this I mean that these acts of worship reveal a forward look, an anticipation of God's presence and victory today and tomorrow just as surely as in days past. In the two previous moments of worship (Galilee and Jerusalem), yesterday—remembering—plays a leading role. In this final moment the focus turns fully upon tomorrow. In the seemingly mundane actions of offering of our gifts, of the dedication of ourselves and our children, and even the week's announcements, tomorrow-ness takes tangible shape. Not one of these acts is sensible without Christian hope. One does not give money to a dead enterprise or a dead Lord, nor enter parenthood or engage in service if there is no future worth striving for. So these humble acts point to a most important dynamic, even a mood that ought be evident throughout any worship service that is truly about the God who is and who was and who *is to come*. That mood is one of a people with a future focus, of people gathered in anticipation of a great day coming—in biblical terms, the mood of a messianic feast.

In such a messianic feast there is both painful realism and joyful anticipation. The Messiah has come and was murdered as a victim of the world's inhumanity—a cruelty that persists to this day. This is the painful realism worshipers cannot ignore, but joyful anticipation is just as essential because we are assured this Messiah will not permit sorrowing to be history's only script. The Messiah has another chapter and, sentence-by-sentence, this chapter can be glimpsed even amid cruel times. Thus, worship should have about it a remembrance of things past and present—but surely worship should also have about it an expectation of things to come, of the final messianic feast. Each Sunday's "messianic feast is not an ecstasy that transports us into another world," writes Jurgen Moltmann, but it does give voice to that event and to its hope in certain though muted tones:

> The service of worship reveals the heights of life, but also the poverty of the depths of our own lives. These dissonances are part of its harmony. They make it at once realistic and hopeful. "How shall we sing the Lord's song in a strange land?" asks Psalm 137. The messianic feast is the Lord's song in a foreign land. Its melodies mingle thoughts of home with the sighs of exiles. For it is the feast of the lordship of God under the cross of Christ, and at the point where Christ's discipleship in the world belongs . . . The liberating feast "in the foreign land" is the fragmentary anticipation of God's free and festal world.[49]

So, even the pedestrian acts of receiving an offering and giving the announcements are "world-defying" moments of worship; they are signboards contradicting the world's alliances with the status quo; they point to the Church's unwavering conviction that history is God's to write. These simple acts of generosity and of service say our faith in and hope for God's future; they bear witness to our yearning for the "marriage supper of the Lamb."

Let there, then, be no slouching through the final Mt. Olivet moment of worship. Here, if anywhere, the connections between liturgy and life should come together powerfully. It has been said that Paul's epistles "begin in the heavenlies but always wind up in the kitchen." So does worship. The offerings of money, of daily energy and time, the dedication of ourselves and our children —all are signs of hope-filled missional engagement. They are to be shared in joy and gladness, not dispensed with in embarrassed rapidity. They are signs of tomorrow's world today.

QUESTIONS FOR DISCUSSION

1. How is the worship you participate in structured? What rationale stands behind that particular ordering?

2. In what ways does your present worship seek to be formative and or educative?

3. What acts of worship were discussed in this chapter that your congregation already practices? Which would they resist? Why?

4. Can you explain the vertical-dialogical function of the various practices within your worship service?

Conclusion

The Worship Journey Before Us

~

This book began with a repeated observation that among evangelicals the word worship has become so garbled and confusing as to make it an almost non-useful word. However, as you've likely noticed long ago, nowhere have I offered a clear definition of the word worship. Now, only after all the centuries, continents, and convictions surveyed, does it seem fitting to risk such. Here then, in light of all we've reviewed and considered, is the best definition I have: *Christian worship is the Church's Spirit-led, joyful work of responding in love to the continuing revelation of the triune God through historic corporate acts offered in the belief that they are pleasing to God and with the hope that through them, God will transform the Church into a people reflecting God's glory in this world.*

Note some of the details of this definition. First, this definition really is about God—and more specifically, the triune God. God is the one who initiates worship through self-revelation, God is the one who receives it as a loving response to that self-revelation, God is the one to whom it is offered, and God is the one whose glorification is being sought in it. If repetition is of value, the word God appears four times as an indication that the vertical-dialogical priority of seeking God's face is foremost. Second, this definition asserts the churchly base of worship and, by saying that worship is the Church's deed (rather than the clergy's task), the whole Church's participation is affirmed. Third, the statement that worship is the Church's "work" implicitly rejects all ideas that it is an entertaining program one attends, but the adjective "joyful" signifies that the work of worship is not onerous labor. Fourth, this work is not ours alone for it is affirmed that worship is "Spirit-led"—God enables what God seeks. Fifth, this definition alludes to unpredictability in worship by speaking of a "continuing revelation"—not in the sense of a changing revelation, but in the sense of a revelation that is never static or without potential to amaze afresh. Thus we worship in watchfulness and in wonder. But, this serendipitous factor is anchored in a sixth detail, the specification of "historic corporate acts." Through these acts we not only honor the "rules," but also drink from ancient wells of grace rather than ignore or pave them over. (This certainly does not criminalize innovation or creativity, but it does require continuity with the Great Tradition.) Finally, the definition ends with a statement of objectives which, though two in expression are actually one in desire: to glorify God by rendering the homage that is rightfully God's by "playing" before him and doing so in the hope that eventually we will reflect God's radiance (in character and conduct) before the world. Corporate Christian worship therefore is a labor of responsive *love*, offered by *faith* and in *hope*—in God.

The limits and gains of definition

The trouble with this definition, as with all definitions of worship, is its inadequacy. The reality our definitions seek to express is so much greater than any definition.[50] Hence, they tend either to expand to a full paragraph (and thereby overwhelm us in detail),[51] or to compress into a detail-deficient phrase (lacking enough specificity to be practically useful).[52] In either case, the definition is less or other than what one seeks.[53] Embarrassingly, though the definition offered above includes the "right" words, it doesn't dance, it doesn't sing—the beauty, the grandeur of the thing itself slips my little verbal lariat. Yet this is the limitation of language (specifically this author's vocabulary) and also clear evidence of the magnitude of the subject. Nonetheless, we proceed with the best we can cobble up. So be it.

The service a definition such as this one may perform, however, is still helpful. It points to essentials that may be ignored; it distills central themes; it suggests boundaries. But it certainly doesn't perform the service of propounding a final answer to all our worship questions. For instance, this definition doesn't say anything about one of the most crucial issues of our time, the style in which this worship is offered. But it does offer implications.

Implications for Style

For instance, when this definition states that worship is the *Church's* work, the implication is that all forms of "performance" worship are suspect. When a performance mentality shapes either the leader's thought world or that of those in attendance, worship as "the Church's joyful work" is short-circuited. The ambience of the meeting is changed from a corporate endeavor calling "us" to give our best efforts, to an audience-oriented program offered by "them" for our approval or benefit. The congregation becomes an audience—and this terminological shift from congregation to audience is huge, denoting that the worship of God has morphed into a "show" for those in attendance. The earlier comment about worship leaders being more akin to personal trainers than to performers may be recalled here.

One might add that this performance mentality stricture applies as appropriately to the preacher whose over-sized ego or over-long sermons take the lion's share of a congregation's worship time, just as it does to the dramatic soloist or the choir and orchestra or virtuoso organist or praise band. All such performances eventually draw attention to the performers. Even if the performers harbor a sincere desire to "give God all the glory," the danger is always present of stepping into a spotlight reserved for God alone—and that is a most dangerous stage-location! Consequently, those who lead worship always and inevitably bear a dual responsibility—to offer their best without parading their giftedness. It is a responsibility that is both glorious and perilous. But a first indication that the glorious has been abandoned in favor of the perilous is when either leaders or worshipers allow a performance mentality to enter. An evidence of this might be found in the not-uncommon act of congregational applause. If this is practiced, one might well ask if the applause is being offered *as* an act of worship or *for* an act of worship. If it is the latter, the danger zone has been entered.

Naturally, the issue of performance also has implications for our use of technology in worship. The stunning effects which can be created electronically increase exponential with each new generation of gadgets. With the proper equipment the drabbest of worship spaces or occasions can be transformed into its polar opposite. Virtual reality is possible! Worship leaders must therefore consider where the line is to be drawn concerning simulated reality, between staging things that are "cool" and "state of the art" or deleting some in consideration of their performance nature. One rule of thumb which might be considered is: Whenever worship is in any way imagined as "wowing" the crowd—or worse, given over to manipulating them—the performance mentality is present. (My students currently seem to be most "turned off" by the use of fog machines!) The show may be impressive, but the integrity of the worship loses in this trade-off.

So, issues of style are involved within this definition, though not as an endorsement or condemnation of specific styles of worship. Rather this definition asks those who worship in whatever style to give thought to the congruity of that style with the definition itself. As stated earlier, content is always the most important factor; it provides the "meat" of and for the assembly. If the content is there and the order is thoughtful, then the style in which it's offered must be determined by the context and culture of the worshipers. When this is sensitively done, worship among evangelicals will present a more credible Christian message and unity.

Instructions in how to worship

Whatever style is chosen, it is imperative for congregations to be taught how to worship. This, of course, should always have been the case. We have provided all manner of classes designed to teach people how to pray, engage in personal evangelism, study the Bible, minister in crisis situations, etc., but seldom offered instruction in how to worship. Seldom have we even understood the importance of worship instruction. What is sure, however, is that the inertia from generations of performance-oriented worship can't be overturned without clear and persistent instruction in the "joyful work" of congregational worship.

Wandering attention has always been a problem in worship. Such wandering is a form of the wandering attention that bedevils all our times of prayer—for worship at its best is simply prayer in corporate expression. So, worshipers must taught how to do this work, must be helped to understand the significance of each moment and act of worship, and be given repeated encouragement to stay at this work—until it becomes a sacred "game" of delight and the laborious becomes joyful and rewarding as well.

The future prospects

I hope the definition of worship given above—as well as the historical and theological background informing it and the Gospel-shaped order of worship implementing it—can be utilized in a wide range of evangelical churches. Perhaps this is an extravagant hope because the "rules" this conception embodies will be more easily integrated within the traditions of some than with others. Nonetheless, my hope isn't childishly naïve. Reggae worship in a store-front church in Boston, children's worship in an East St. Louis neighborhood mission, or a county-seat Disciples of Christ church in east Tennessee can use this template. Admittedly, some churches will have to undergo significant alterations in their philosophy of ministry if they seek to appropriate this book's suggestions.

To further the problematic nature of the situation, it must also be admitted that if they braved such a change, some churches might suffer a numeric decline—while others might grow. Constance Cherry offers an encouraging word when she says "there is no study that shows that the use of any certain worship style guarantees church growth"[54] Even so, this is a book about the integrity of worship, not church growth. And it has been written with the conviction that if the worship of God is offered as rightly as we know to offer it, then we have honored God majestically—regardless of our numbers.

As a pastor for most all my adult years I fully appreciate the anguish of seeing parish life fail to flourish—and all the infrastructure and morale issues that follow. But I also have found a counter-cultural joy in leading people to do what we believed to be right even if it did not produce numerical growth. As surprising as it may seem, one of the most valorous acts a pastor can do in many churches is to lead the church to engage in worship that is really about God.

When the issue before a congregation centers on the matter of its corporate worship, one fundamental question—and its answer—determines all else: For whom is Sunday's service of worship conducted? For God or for man? If our weight comes down decidedly on the "for man" side of this question, I believe we err. Unquestionably, worship is "for" man in that we must always give concern to offer worship that is accessible to real persons in their specific context and time. Far too often, unfortunately, this necessity has led us to offer services that are so much "for man" that what is offered simply "gives them what they want,"[55] while too little attention is given to what they need. God, and seeking God's face, is what is needed in the hour of worship. And the deepest need, in which all our deepest longings are met, is to give God what is God's due. Indisputably, worship attendance may improve when "for man" becomes a priority, but as Australian poet Peter Kocan reminds us, numbers aren't the final test.

Hear his full counsel, for it expresses the matter provocatively, even if from an outsider's point of view.

Cathedral Service

I'm only here because I wandered in
Not knowing that a service would begin
And had to slide into the nearest pew
Pretending it was what I'd meant to do.

The tall candles cast their frail light
Upon the priest, the choir clad in white,
The carved and polished and embroidered scene
The congregation numbers seventeen.

And awkwardly I follow as I'm led
To kneel or stand or sing or bow my head.
Though these specific rites are strange to me
I know their meaning perfectly—

The heritage of twenty centuries
Is symbolized in rituals like these,
In special modes of beauty and of grace
Enacted in a certain kind of place.

This faith, although I lack it, is my own,
Inherent to the marrow of the bone.
To this even the unbelieving mind
Submits its unbelief to be defined.

Perhaps the meager congregation shows
How all of that is drawing to a close,
And remnants only come here to entreat
These dying embers of the obsolete.

Yet when did this religion ever rest
On weight of numbers as the final test?
Its founder said it was all the same
When two or three are gathered in his name.[56]

I am sure one reason I'm drawn to this poem is Kocan's apparent recognition that believers do some things as a matter of theological conviction rather than to cater to popular opinion. Though the poem identifies a particular style of worship as representing the "dying embers of the obsolete," I believe history shows that all styles of worship have their fifteen minutes of fame and greatest success. The paramount concern, therefore, is never style but substance. Whatever style, idiom, or "sound" a congregation chooses for their worship is secondary—so long as, to use Kocan's words, "the heritage of twenty centuries is symbolized in rituals" and words that declare the greatness of God and link us to God's ongoing story of redemption through the ages. Those congregations which wrestle through to clarity about this priority have every reason and right to claim the Founder's promise that the weight of numbers is not the final test.

My powers of prophecy are nil, so I cannot predict if worship as I have urged it in this book "is drawing to a close" or undergoing a miraculous rebirth.[57] Lacking prophetic powers, however, I confess that the unwanted burden of anxious concern is mine. My concern is that searching, postmodern humankind might turn once again to the Church for the centering and restoration of life, but find her worship so gutted of content and depth as to be a disappointment, as something "not worth stopping for."[58]

One who wrestled with that specter in a previous generation, Samuel Miller gave a wise response still worth pondering. In Miller's accounting of it, all worship of God is ultimately a desperate act, an act to which we are driven by what he called "the embarrassment of life." Eventually, he said, our inward contradictions, our finitude, our helplessness before life's ultimate realities—eventually this cumulative "embarrassment of life" either drives us "to the false magic of drug or drink for relief," or to the house of God. Then he adds:

> Now if when we get here, all this is covered up, hidden
> in art or rhetoric or conviviality, hushed up or smoothed

over, then worship becomes a devilish deceit and is
no better than getting drunk or being soothed by an
ecclesiastical entertainment. It becomes a blind alley,
pompously decorated with liturgical rites and reverent
phrases, but for all that a blind alley of escape, and only
an escape. It is a treacherous falsehood, a hypocritical
farce, a veritable den of thieves.

Miller's sledgehammer indictment applies to all styles, be they
characterized by "conviviality" or "ecclesiastical entertainment" or "liturgical rites." But if our gathering "puts the whole garbled picture of our
lives in the presence of the Eternal Holy God—for this is worship"[59]
and seeks the judgment and mercy of God to recreate it week after week,
afresh in his image, then this is worship worthy of the name.

The number of those in attendance is ultimately beyond our
control. Our proper task is much more humble. Ours is to maintain
something deep and rich and unimaginably true within this house of
God. Ours is to offer worship that really is about God.

QUESTIONS FOR DISCUSSION

1. Assess the strengths and weaknesses of the offered definition of
   worship. Compose your own definition and ask others to assess its
   adequacy.

2. What programs of education concerning corporate worship might
   be needed in your church?

3. What alterations in your personal worship behavior will be needed if
   you accept this book's understanding of worship?

4. What objections can you anticipate being raised in your church to
   the concept of worship proposed in this book? What responses might
   you make to those objections?

Notes

[1] I must reiterate at this point that the subject of this book is evangelical Christian worship. I leave it to other writers to wrestle with the good question of the validity of the worship offered to God by those with other understandings of God. Without entering into that discussion, one may surely assert that for the Christian worship of God, Christ's person and work is absolutely essential.

[2] Similarly, the best teachers of preaching urge their students to let the literary form of their text be reflected in a sermon built upon that text. Thus, a sermon based upon a parable will display something of the feel of a parable, not of a commandment or a psalm. The sermon, even in its arrangement and feel, will honor the literary form through which the Spirit of God gave us the text. See Thomas Long, *Preaching and the Literary Forms of the Bible* (Philadelphia: Fortress Press, 1989) and Mike Graves, *The Sermon as Symphony: Preaching the Literary Forms of the New Testament* (Valley Forge: Judson Press, 1997).

[3] This characteristic sidelines the often-followed practice of building a worship service around a selected theme, often a theme suggested by or complementary to the theme of the pastor's sermon for the Sunday.

[4] J-J von Allmen, *Worship: Its Theology and Practice* (New York: Oxford University Press, 1965), 22-26, 288ff.

[5] Robert Webber's prescription for the future of evangelical worship called for a recovery of a biblical theology of worship and the historic fourfold order of worship while repudiating all forms of program/performance worship. His first and last named ingredients (content, style) have been addressed in preceding chapters; the need and meaning of his middle ingredient—order—is now taken up. See Webber, "The Crisis of Evangelical Worship: Authentic Worship in a Changing World," reprinted in Dearborn and Coil (eds), *Worship at the Next Level*, 86-101.

[6] von Allmen, *Worship: Its Theology and Practice*, 184ff.

[7] Peter Brunner sees this moment as an eschatological or "last times" moment. In Jesus, the old order has been defeated and through the Spirit the first fruits of the new order are here. In worship therefore "we stand at the farthest edge of history," as pilgrims who almost can see the New Jerusalem ahead. See his "Divine Service in the Church," in Dwight Vogel, ed. *Primary Sources of Liturgical Theology* (Collegeville, MN: Liturgical Press, 2000), 204.

[8]When he went to chapel, the founder of the Cistercian Order had the habit of standing at the door in silence before he entered. The members of the Order began to do the same although he never told them to do so nor did he ever explain what he did during those moments at the chapel door. But the souls of sensitive worshipers intuitively knew and know that such self-collection and preparation is an act of spiritual wisdom.

[9]Some Protestant services begin with a worship leader pouring a stream of water into a basin, followed by a brief encouragement to begin our worship with remembrance of our baptism and the identity thereby given.

[10]William Cowper, "Sometimes a Light Surprises." Before overloading a service with song, however, worship planners might do well to remember there will always be some in the congregation for whom music is not the only bona fide way to offer praise. No less a believer than William Inge (1860-1954), Dean of St. Paul's Cathedral in London, filled his diary with moanings about the abundance of music in worship: "I can and do pray when I 'enter my chamber and shut the door,' but in the midst of howling and caterwauling I cannot;" he wrote; and again: "Music hath charms to soothe the savage beast—but it has the opposite effect on me who am not a savage." Three other entries are worthy of note. First, "If I believed that I shall listen through all eternity to the seraphim blowing their loud uplifted trumpets, it would almost deter me from the practice of virtue;" and then: "They turned the Nicene Creed into an anthem—before the end I had ceased to believe anything;" Finally, a pointed question: "Are we quite sure the Deity enjoys being serenaded?" [A. N. Wilson, ed. *The Faber Book of Church and Clergy* (London: Faber and Faber, 1992), 140-141.]

[11]This "New Creed" in full, says: "We are not alone, we live in God's world. We believe in God: who has created and is creating, who has come in Jesus, the Word made flesh, to reconcile and make new, who works in us and others by the Spirit. We trust in God. We are called to be the Church: to celebrate God's presence, to live with respect in Creation, to love and serve others, to seek justice and resist evil, to proclaim Jesus crucified and risen, our judge and our hope. In life, in death, in life beyond death, we are not alone. God is with us. Thanks be to God."

[12]Marva Dawn, *Reaching Out without Dumbing Down: A Theology of Worship for the Turn-of-the-Century Culture* (Grand Rapids, MI: Eerdmans Publishing, 1995), 87.

[13]It may be noted that temple prophets were charged to interrupt Israel's praise processions to the temple with confronting liturgies of "confession" (e.g. Psalm 15, 24).

Through such acts joyful worshipers were called to sobering account in order to squelch the "cheap grace" kind of worship condemned by prophets (Isaiah 58, Amos, etc.).

[14] *Book of Common Worship* (Louisville, KY: Westminster/John Knox Press, 1993), 88. Other prayers are provided in this book as well as in many denominational worship guides such as *The United Methodist Book of Worship* (Nashville, TN: The United Methodist Publishing House, 1992), 474ff, and *A New Zealand Prayer Book* (London: Collins Liturgical Publications, 1989).

[15] *Book of Common Worship*, 794-795.

[16] Baptism, understood so differently in our theological traditions, has long been rightly considered a key component of corporate worship. I regret it receives little attention in these pages, but urge worship planners to observe it as a powerful component within worship, rather than as a private ceremony. The practice of some churches, already noted, of beginning worship with a symbolic pouring/dipping of water as a reminder of our common baptism is most appropriate and commendable.

[17] While educators may wince at this stark distinction, I hope they will perceive my nuanced meaning here rather than wrongly infer that I believe all teaching is simply the transmission of information

[18] See Wilken, *The Spirit of Early Christian Thought*, chapter 3, "The Face of God for Now."

[19] In some worship traditions the public reading of the Gospel text for the day is introduced by the congregation standing to sing or to say, "Glory to you, O Lord," and is followed by the response: "Praise to you, O Christ." Such actions awaken and perpetuate an awareness that the hearing of this word is a high moment of worship, first a declaration of glory that we should be recipients of this word, and then an acclimation of praise that we have once again be privileged to hear words and deeds through which the world has been redeemed. In some manner all reading of Scripture ought be accompanied by a recognition of its wonder and power; worshipers need to be brought to grateful attention.

[20] An encouraging revival of the use of psalmody within worship is evident in recent works such as John Witvliet, *The Biblical Psalms in Christian Worship: A Brief Introduction and Guide to Resources* (Grand Rapids, MI: Eerdmans, 2012) and a companion psalter: John Witvliet and Martin Tel, *Psalms for All Seasons: A Complete Psalter for Worship* (Grand Rapids, MI: Faith Alive Publishers, 2012).

[21]Guidance in oral interpretation of scripture may be found in G. Robert Jacks, *Getting the Word Across: Speech Communication for Pastors and Lay Leaders* (Grand Rapids, MI: Eerdmans, 1995) and Jeffrey D. Arthurs, *Devote Yourself to the Public Reading of Scripture: The Transforming Power of the Well-Spoken Word* (Grand Rapids, MI: Kregel Academic, 2012).

[22]This is not to say that sermons in a worship setting should not evangelize or inspire or generate experience. It is to ask if, within a worship context, these valid sermon outcomes must be reconceived.

[23]Geoffrey Wainwright's answer comes by means of four well-known words from within worship's historic vocabulary: doxology (preaching should be offered to God's glory); *anamesis* (it should recall and interpret the scripture-reported story); *epiclesis* (it should in every way call upon the Spirit's presence); and, eschatology (it should point to the not-yet). See his "Preaching as Worship" in Richard Lischer, ed. *Theories of Preaching* (Labyrinth Press, 1987), 350-363.

[24]Ironically, the super-preacher of British evangelicalism, Charles Spurgeon, warned his preaching students against discounting of the cumulative effect of the entire worship service by allowing the sermon to unduly dominate it. Charles H. Spurgeon, *Lectures to my Students: A Selection of Addresses delivered to the Students of the Pastors' College, Metropolitan Tabernacle* (London: Passmore & Alabaster, 1906), 52-71.

[25]I assume the preacher's sermon is a faithful contemporizing of the written Word rather than a personal riff on the week's hot topic. Sermons arising from prayerful interpretation of the record of revelation given in scripture are the only appropriate speech within the revelation-response dynamic of worship.

[26]Fred Craddock, *Preaching* (Nashville: Abingdon Press, 1985), 51.

[27]Again, it is mandatory to state that those who "impart information" are seldom satisfied with that goal alone. They, too, wish for information to be received and used in transformative ways. Thus, my distinctions are to be interpreted rhetorically, not literally.

[28]LaRue, *I Believe I'll Testify: The Art of African-American Preaching* (Louisville: John Knox Press, 2011), 96.

[29]Anna Carter Florence, *Preaching as Testimony* (Louisville: Westminster John Knox Press, 2007), xiii. Italics in the original.

³⁰To stand and to speak contested truth will invariably occasion a fresh Calvary, but when done lovingly and persistently it transforms the pulpit from a place of windy banalities to a scene of deep appreciation.

³¹The expression is Walter Burghardt's who, though he was an internationally recognized pulpiteer, wrote that his audience seldom "drooled" so. See his *Preaching: The Art and the Craft* (New York: Paulist Press, 1987), 45.

³²Not to be forgotten is that this same creed has been on the lips of Joan of Arc, Dietrich Bonhoeffer, Thomas Cranmer, Martin Luther, Kagawa of Japan, Francis of Assisi, Susannah Wesley, Savonarola, Mother Teresa, and a multitude of "plain saints" for centuries. When the creed is spoken from our lips we join a mighty "Amen" chorus.

³³Baptism, universally accepted as a second sacrament, is referred to in the Bethlehem Moment section, but it does not here receive the attention given to the Supper because of the historic centrality of the table in weekly worship. Baptism, though it is the initiatory rite of the Church, is an occasional service.

³⁴Martin E. Marty, *The Lord's Supper* (Minneapolis: Fortress Press, 1980), 11.

³⁵Richard Lischer, *Open Secrets: A Spiritual Journey Through a Country Church* (New York: Doubleday, 2001), 71.

³⁶There is reconciliatory significance even in the word sometimes used to refer to the act of eating the bread and drinking the wine: communicating.

³⁷New Testament uses include the report that Zechariah returned home "when his time of service (liturgy) was ended" (Luke 1:23) and the Hebrews 8:6 statement that Jesus "has now obtained a more excellent ministry" (liturgy), i.e., a better kind of public religious service than that of the Temple.

³⁸A very accessible comparison of the Roman Catholic, Lutheran, Reformed, Baptist, and Pentecostal views of the Supper is available in Gordon T. Smith, ed. *The Lord's Supper: Five Views* (Downers Grove: Intervarsity Press, 2008).

³⁹ *The Book of Common Prayer* (1977), 859.

⁴⁰John Macquarrie, *Paths in Spirituality* (London: SCM Press, 1972), 73.

⁴¹A not-untypical example of much evangelical Eucharistic practice is found in the pastor who, professing great interest in making the Supper "more central in our worship," discontinued his church's practice of observing it during the morning service on the first Sunday of each month, and replaced it with an evening observance every third

month, which "allowed for some innovation." Alton H. McEachern, *Here at Thy Table, Lord* (Nashville: Broadman Press, 1977), 7.

[42]Gordon T. Smith, *A Holy Meal: The Lord's Supper in the Life of the Church* (Grand Rapids, MI: Baker Academic, 2005). A similar approach is taken by Fisher Humphreys, "A Baptist Theology of the Lord's Supper," in *Proclaiming the Baptist Vision: Baptism and the Lord's Supper*, Walter B. Shurden, ed. (Macon, GA: Smyth & Helwys, 1999), 117-128.

[43]Walter Brueggemann, "Exodus," in *The New Interpreter's Bible*, Vol. 1, Leander Keck, ed. (Nashville: Abingdon Press, 1994), 813, 817. Also see his "The Liturgy of Abundance and the Myth of Scarcity," in Brueggemann, *Deep Memory, Exuberant Hope: Contested Truth in a Post-Christian World* (Minneapolis: Augsburg Press, 2000), 69-75.

[44]See Dix, *The Shape of the Liturgy.*

[45]Considering the funereal manner in which many Lord's Supper observances are conducted, it is understandable why the observances are few. Most surely, there are occasions when the passion of Christ must be the dominant tone of the observance (e.g., Maundy Thursday). A multi-layered understanding of the Supper, however, permits us to see the supper as Eucharist, as thanksgiving, as a feast hosted by the One who was dead but is now living--and among us! Andrae Crouch's rollicking "Soon and Very Soon" is therefore as fitting for singing at the table as is "O Sacred Head Now Wounded."

[46]William Law, in his most influential 1729 book, *A Serious Call to a Devout and Holy Life*, questioned his British friends' emphasis upon Sunday worship rather than daily obedience: "Is it not . . . exceedingly strange, that People should place so much piety in the attendance upon public worship, concerning which there is not one precept of our Lord's to be found, and yet neglect these common duties of our ordinary life, which are commanded in every Page of the Gospel?" Cited by Gordon Mursell, *English Spirituality From 1700 to the Present Day* (Louisville: Westminster John Knox, 2001), 81.

[47]A welcomed, recent contrast to this pattern is Clayton J. Schmit, *Sent and Gathered: A Worship Manual for the Missional Church* (Grand Rapids, MI: Baker Academic, 2009).

[48]Delores Dufner, "The Spirit Sends Us Forth to Serve," in *Celebrating Grace Hymnal* (Macon, GA: Celebrating Grace, Inc., 2010), 520.

[49]Jurgen Moltmann, *The Church in the Power of the Spirit* (New York: Harper & Row Publishers, 1977), 261, 262.

[50]This definition, for example, restricts itself to the human aspect of worship. One could also speak of worship from God's perspective, affirming that *Christian worship is God's coming afresh within the fellowship of those who gather gratefully to acknowledge God's definitive coming among us in Jesus the Christ.* In such a definition worship is perceived more as gift than as task, and our utter dependence upon God to effect worship—rather than any confection of human artistry or piety—is clearer. But this additional definition only demonstrates the difficulty of defining the indefinable.

[51]The careful, nuanced, five-plus-sentence definition given by Geoffrey Wainwright in *The New Westminster Dictionary of Liturgy and Worship*, is one example of this option.

[52]David E. Aune's definition ("reverent homage paid to God and Christ in the context of a Christian assembly") is an example of this option. See his "Worship, Early Christian," in *Anchor Bible Dictionary*, vol. 6, 974. Gerard Sloyan's pithy definition is nonetheless provocative: "To worship is to be in the presence of God in the posture of awe." See Sloyan, *Worshipful Preaching* (Philadelphia: Fortress Press, 1984), 7.

[53]I would, however, commend two other "short" definitions for comparison purposes. From William Dyrness: "Worship is a set of culturally embedded and corporate practices through which God forms [Christians] into the likeness of Christ, in and through the story of Jesus Christ, by the power of the Holy Spirit, in order that they might live their lives to the glory of God" (*A Primer on Christian Worship: Where We've Been, Where We Are; Where We Can Go* [Grand Rapids, MI: Eerdmans, 2009], 45); and from Robert Schaper: "Worship is the expression of a relationship in which God the Father reveals himself and his love in Christ, and by his Holy Spirit administers grace, to which we respond in faith, gratitude, and obedience" (*In His Presence: Appreciating Your Worship Tradition* [Nashville, TN: Thomas Nelson, 1984], 15-16).

[54]Cherry, *The Worship Architect*, 226. See Marva Dawn's discussion of the interplay between worship integrity and church growth in *Reaching Out without Dumbing Down* and her follow-up volume: *A Royal "Waste" of Time: The Splendor of Worshiping God and Being Church for the World* (Grand Rapids, MI: Eerdmans, 1999). A fascinating testimony of the loss and gain experienced by a church when it moved from a numbers focus to a discipleship focus is given by Kent Carlson and Mike Lueken in their *Renovation of*

the *Church: What Happens When a Seeker Church Discovers Spiritual Formation* (Downers Grove, IL: IVP Books, 2011). Abraham Joshua Heschel in 1965 expressed a similar concern regarding the "spiritual distress" of Judaism. He proposed striking the word "survival" from Judaism's vocabulary because: "'To be or not to be' is not the question . . . How to be and how not to be is the question . . . What is important" he said, "is attaining certainty of being worthy of survival." See Heschel, "Existence and Celebration," in *Moral Grandeur and Spiritual Audacity: Essays, ed. Susannah Heschel* (New York: Farrar, Straus and Giroux, 1996), 30.

[55]This kind of capitulation can occur within congregations using any style. The necessity for leaders is to be sensitive to the appropriate style for their congregation without becoming servants of the status quo regardless of style. The pastoral concern to offer to the members of one congregation varied styles of worship is a valid response so long as the substance and structure of the services "seek God's face," and so long as the varied services are augmented by increased pastoral initiatives fostering the unity of the now-segmented congregation.

[56]Cited in Ben Witherington III and Christopher Mead Armitage, *The Poetry of Piety: An Annotated Anthology of Christian Poetry* (Grand Rapids, MI: Baker Academic, 2002), 169-170.

[57]Much of the Emerging Church emphases may be interpreted as an attempted re-appropriation of the wisdom within abandoned patterns. The work of several writers of Contemporary Christian songs, such as Keith Getty cited earlier, certainly indicates a desire to supplement the corpus of praise songs with songs of greater instructional value. See Paul Baloche, "Mind the Gaps," *Worship Leader* 22, no. 1 (January/February, 2013): 20, for another indication of the same desire. Another encouraging sign of serious thought about worship is the collection of essays in *Gathering Together: Baptists at Work in Worship*, Rodney W. Kennedy and Derek Hatch, eds. (Pickwick Publications, 2013).

[58]The phrase is from Philip Larkin's poem "Church Going," in Larkia, *The Less Deceived: Poems by Philip Larkia* (New York: St. Martin's Press, 1955), 28.

[59]Samuel H. Miller, *The Life of the Church* (New York: Harper & Row, Publishers, 1953), 36.

CPSIA information can be obtained at www.ICGtesting.com
Printed in the USA
BVOW04s1314210813

329211BV00006B/38/P